Faulkner and Postmodernism
FAULKNER AND YOKNAPATAWPHA
1999

Faulkner and Postmodernism

FAULKNER AND YOKNAPATAWPHA, 1999

EDITED BY
JOHN N. DUVALL
AND
ANN J. ABADIE

UNIVERSITY PRESS OF MISSISSIPPI
JACKSON

www.upress.state.ms.us

Copyright © 2002 by University Press of Mississippi
All rights reserved
Manufactured in the United States of America
Print-on-Demand Edition

Library of Congress Cataloging-in-Publication Data

Faulkner and Yoknapatawpha Conference (26th : 1999 : University of Mississippi)
    Faulkner and postmodernism : Faulkner and Yoknapatawpha, 1999 / edited by
John N. Duvall and Ann J. Abadie.
    p. cm.
    Eleven essays from the 1999 Faulkner and Yoknapatawpha Conference, held at the
University of Mississippi.
    ISBN 1-57806-459-7 (cloth : alk. paper)—ISBN 1-57806-460-0 (pbk. : alk. paper)
    1. Faulkner, William, 1897–1962—Criticism and interpretation—Congresses.
2. Postmodernism (Literature)—United States—Congresses. 3. Postmodernism
(Literature)—Mississippi—Congresses. 4. Yoknapatawpha County (Imaginary
place)—Congresses. 5. Mississippi—In literature—Congresses. I. Duvall, John N.
(John Noel), 1956– II. Abadie, Ann J. III. Title.

PS3511.A86 Z7832113   1999
813'.52—dc21   2002000638

British Library Cataloging-in-Publication Data available

Contents

Introduction

1

Relating William Faulkner to postmodernism is a task complicated by the plethora of ways that postmodernism has been defined and periodized. There effectively are in play three distinct versions of postmodernism—the philosophical, the cultural, and the aesthetic. And while the time frame of the latter two can be reconciled to some extent, it does not square with that of philosophical postmodernism. Jürgen Habermas's philosophical modernity, for example, begins with Descartes's belief in the self-sufficiency of reason and continues through Kant and the Enlightenment; Habermas's postmodernism begins with Nietzsche's attack on reason. There is, therefore, at least a three-hundred-year gap between Habermas's modernity and aesthetic modernism, a situation rendered all the more complex inasmuch as certain versions of modernist aesthetics—surrealism, Dadaism, mythic intuitionism—would fall necessarily within Habermas's postmodernism. (That Jean François Lyotard locates the beginning of modernity with Nietzsche shows additionally how easily the terms of the philosophical debate can create confusion.)

When I moved to Purdue University in 1998, I discovered a different issue of definition and periodization—an overlap in the division of the graduate American literature curriculum in the break between what we call America II and America III. America II is defined as the period from the Civil War to 1940. America III, though, runs from 1930 to the present. As a colleague explained it to me, this odd configuration reflected a compromise in a dispute between the modernist and postmodern scholars over who would get William Faulkner.[1] Despite Faulkner's usual identification as a high modernist, our period compromise at Purdue is not completely idiosyncratic, as I hope to make clear in this introduction.

The very term "postmodernism," however, still seems to many undergraduates an odd term, one that strains common sense. After all, we live in the modern world, don't we, so how can anything be designated as after the modern? But of course the "modern" in modernism does not refer to the popular sense but to an aesthetic and a period of literary history. (That "modernism" is contained in the word "postmodernism" should signal that the two terms are not unrelated.) If modernism can be defined as the art's response to the alienating effects of modernization and mass culture, then two questions emerge: is there a point at which alienation ceases to be the dominant affect or emotional felt response that people have to their contemporary existence, and, if yes, is there an aesthetic that addresses this new affect?

The time marking the period break between modernism and postmodernism noticeably varies depending on which literary historian one believes. Some have seen the end of World War II and the advent of the nuclear age as the dividing line. Others point to the canonization of high modernism in the late 1950s and early '60s as the key period break. Here the thinking is that once the modernists can be found between the covers of the various standard literary anthologies, whatever radical agendas (whether formal or political) that the modernists may have had have been co-opted by the order of things. Still others who wish to link contemporary art to the growth of multinational capitalism have fixed postmodernism's beginning as 1973 and the Arab oil embargo. Whichever date one prefers, it may be possible to chart a progressive complication of the felt alienation of the early part of the twentieth century. Following World War II, the continuous threat of nuclear annihilation causes alienation to transform into the paranoia of the Cold War. More recently still, the whirling blitz of information and images in the age of computers and the electronic media has made it much more difficult to sort the significant information from the white noise of culture, so much so that perhaps the paranoia of the second half of the twentieth century has segued into a kind of millennial schizophrenia.

If paranoia and schizophrenia are metaphors describing what it feels like to live in the contemporary world, the postmodern writer thematizes such matters around the representation of identity and identity formation. The modernist still held out hope for authentic identity. Paris may have been a wasteland for the wounded Jake Barnes in Ernest Hemingway's *The Sun Also Rises*, but at least Pamplona, Spain, represented a site of authentic masculinity. The postmodernists, however, tracking in the paths of the poststructuralist critique of unified subjectivity, represent identity as an ideological mirage, much more a social construct or a performance than an authenticity.

Having said this about the postmodern difference, I could immediately turn to Quentin Compson's sense of identity in *The Sound and the Fury* to raise an objection to the distinction. Sitting next to an African American man on a streetcar, Quentin reflects on how living in the North has reshaped his sense of race and realizes "that a nigger is not a person so much as a form of behavior; a sort of obverse reflection of the white people he lives among."[2] Quentin's momentary reflection—in which blackness and "nigger" become unhinged—envisions identity not as an essence or an authenticity but as the performance of social scripts. Yet despite instances in Faulkner's fiction in which his characters seemingly embrace as an intellectual proposition this more contemporary perspective on identity, they generally do not experience themselves and their own subjectivities as so radically contingent and decentered.

One should anticipate, therefore, the response of certain readers for whom any linking of William Faulkner to postmodernism (much less an entire conference on the subject) will strike them as perverse. "Surely," they might object, "Faulkner is unmistakably a high modernist whose writing ought to be spoken of in relation to James Joyce's, not Thomas Pynchon's." But even if one grants this objection, then Faulkner's texts should allow us a point of reference from which to begin to define the postmodern difference and perhaps allow us, if not exactly to mark the moment when postmodernism begins, at least to say what a postmodern text does.

Thinking about these matters had begun well before I proposed this conference on "Faulkner and Postmodernism." In 1987, Brian McHale turned to *Absalom, Absalom!* as a liminal text, one standing on the border between modernism and postmodernism. For McHale, a particular moment in chapter 8 of *Absalom* suggests that "modernist poetics threatens to break down, or more than threatens, actually *does* break down"; this rupture "dramatizes the shift of dominant from problems of *knowing* to problems of *modes of being*—from and epistemological dominant to an *ontological one*."[3] In other words, the novel in one vertiginous moment moves us away from modernism's obsessive questioning ("How do we really know Thomas Sutpen or Addie Bundren or, for that matter, Orson Welles's Charles Foster Kane?") and toward an eerie uncertainty about exactly what kind of world it is that is being imagined:

> In Ch. 8, Quentin and Shreve reach the limit of their knowledge of the Sutpen murder-mystery; nevertheless they go on, beyond reconstruction into pure speculation. The signs of the narrative act fall away, and with them all questions of authority and reliability. The text passes from mimesis of the various characters' narrations to unmediated diegesis, from characters "telling" to the author directly "showing" us what happened between Sutpen, Henry, and Bon. The murder-mystery is "solved," however, not through epistemological processes of weighting evidence and making deductions, but through the imaginative projection of what *could*—and, the text insists, *must*—have happened.[4]

Turning to Linda Hutcheon's *Poetics of Postmodernism*, one may again wonder about Faulkner and postmodernism. For Hutcheon, postmodern fiction is defined as "historiographic metafiction." By this she means fiction written in the 1970s and 1980s that blends the reflexivity of metafiction with an alternative historiography; thus novels such as E. L. Doctorow's *The Book of Daniel* and Robert Coover's *The Public Burning* "juxtapose what we think we know of the past (from official archival sources and memory) with an alternate representation that foregrounds the postmodern epistemological question of the nature of historical knowledge. Which 'facts' make it into history? And *whose* facts?"[5] Like Hutcheon's postmodern fiction, *Absalom* takes the reader where memory and the official archive of history either will not or cannot go. In the self-conscious narration of *Absalom*, it is precisely the filling of such historical gaps that occurs. Once again, if in different terms, *Absalom* seems postmodern *avant la lettre*. Still, for Hutcheon, Faulkner is a modernist and for McHale, Faulkner's crossing into postmodernism in *Absalom* "is an isolated event in his *oeuvre*," and subsequently the novelist "quickly returned to the practice of modernism."[6]

Patrick O'Donnell, however, in an essay he published in 1995, sees things differently. Less concerned with marking a period break than McHale or with defining a poetics than Hutcheon, O'Donnell takes postmodernism as a way of reading Faulkner so that "what makes his fiction powerful and timely is its capacity to resist, disrupt, or exceed both Modernism (with a capital "M") and Faulkner's own modernism—his intended response to the perceived literary, cultural, and historical contexts of his writing."[7] Such a perspective assumes the poststructuralist critique of the unified subject, a move that dismantles authority; the result is that Faulkner's writing "is to be known not by its self-authored intentions but by his procession through shifting contexts."[8] For O'Donnell, the text that most clearly enacts this contradiction is *Go Down, Moses*, which serves as Faulkner's postmodern revision of his more modernist impulses of *Absalom, Absalom!* Figured most clearly in the unwritten and unwriteable life of Samuel Worsham Beauchamp, *Go Down, Moses* resists (in ways Faulkner's other fiction often cannot) the urge to mythologize the "other."

2

While McHale's and O'Donnell's work certainly served as a point of departure for "Faulkner and Postmodernism," the conference became an occasion to develop, challenge, and amend their thinking. The papers presented at the 1999 Faulkner and Yoknapatawpha Conference engage postmodernism in a variety of ways, both as an aesthetic and cultural phenomenon and as a philosophical skepticism about the nature of identity and the possibility of determinate meaning. The essays fall into three broad rubrics: (1) those that use Faulkner's modernism as a way to measure the postmodern difference, (2) those that, much as McHale and O'Donnell, see postmodern tendencies in Faulknerian textuality, and (3) those that read Faulkner through the lens of postmodern theory's contemporary legacy, cultural studies.

Within this first group, I have arranged the essays to suggest a continuum that runs from a greater to a lesser certainty about the period difference and distinctions between modernism and postmodernism. The collection begins with Ihab Hassan's meditation in ten parts, "The Privations of Postmodernism: Faulkner as Exemplar." Hassan, longer than any other critic in this volume, has concerned himself with defining postmodernism. Reflecting on more than thirty years of his thinking about postmodernism, he raises an objection to those who would read Faulkner through a postmodern lens. For Hassan, Faulkner is the consummate modernist and to read Faulkner as a crypto-postmodernist is a dehistoricizing error. Hassan is less concerned with aesthetic postmodernism than in understanding the malaise of cultural postmodernism, which he identifies as the sterility of media culture and our loss of the ability to think spiritually, a loss that undercuts the liberating possibilities of decolonization and that generates instead the genocidal postmodernism of ethnic cleansing. This is why, for Hassan, reading Faulkner's fiction has an important place in the contemporary moment: Faulkner's modernist universalism allows for a recovery of the possibilities of loyalty, courage, truth, and justice from the radical skepticism of the present.

In "Postmodern Intimations: Musings on Invisibility: William Faulkner, Richard Wright, and Ralph Ellison," Philip Weinstein questions the utility of identifying particular texts as modern or postmodern and wonders if some theorists of postmodernism have created a straw-man modernism in order to celebrate contemporary cultural production. Weinstein's essay proceeds intertextually by examining the complex space constituted by Dostoevsky's *Crime and Punishment*, Faulkner's *Light in August*, Richard Wright's *Native Son* (as well as "The Man Who Lived Underground"), and Ralph Ellison's *Invisible Man*. Drawing on John Barth's notion of identity as a series of masks, Weinstein marks this overtly postmodern articulation of identity to measure "borderline postmodern practices" in the modernists Faulkner, Wright, and Ellison, practices that include a representation of subjectivity as "the performance of roles rather than genuine identity, an insistence on parody, [and] a conviction that texts cannot access the real but derive from and rewrite other texts."

My essay, "Postmodern Yoknapatawpha: William Faulkner as Usable Past," continues Weinstein's questioning of how we identify the postmodern difference. Starting with John Barth's essay, "The Literature of Exhaustion," I consider several contemporary fictional appropriations of Faulknerian plots, themes, and language. In particular I use two novels that have been identified as postmodern, Kathy Acker's *In Memoriam to Identity* and Toni Morrison's *Beloved,* to raise questions about Linda Hutcheon's emphasis on parody and Fredric Jameson's insistence on pastiche as the defining tropes of postmodernism. I argue that Acker's appropriation of Faulkner, her parody of Faulkner's language, performs in a fashion more akin to what Jameson sees as the role of pastiche, while Morrison's pastiche of Faulknerian discourse performs the cultural work that Hutcheon ascribes to parody. In light of this inversion, it becomes more difficult to identify a novel's postmodernism on the basis of particular representational or intertextual practices.

In "Modernist Design, Postmodern Paranoia: Reading *Absalom, Absalom!* and *Gravity's Rainbow,*" Molly Hite perhaps most thoroughly confuses the attempt to demarcate a line between modernism and postmodernism. Beginning with the way Faulkner's novel thematizes design and Pynchon's represents paranoia, Hite considers the two authors' content as a way to distinguish the concerns of the modernist and the postmodern novel; however, she sees this distinction collapse in the way that *Absalom, Absalom!* already takes the reader beyond Sutpen's individual design and toward larger systems or agencies (God, Fate, alternative emplotments) that insinuate that storytelling (both novelistic and literary critical) may unavoidably be a form of paranoia. After illustrating the limitations of a content-based period distinction, Hite draws upon McHale's differentiation of modernist and postmodern text-processing strategies in order to suggest a reader-response model of sorting the modern/postmodern divide. If modernist reading strategies sought coherence, totality, and unity, then such strategies are paranoid (inasmuch as they create readings that see connections everywhere within the text), a situation that perversely means that modernist reading is akin to postmodern thematics. Hite's essay enacts both modernist and postmodern text-processing strategies. In terms of the opposition that motivates her essay, her reading is paranoid because it seeks out parallels that reduce *Absalom, Absalom!* and *Gravity's Rainbow* to mirror images of each other; alternately, her reading is anti-paranoid to the extent that it resists seeking the unity of either novel.

Hite's essay, which began seeking the difference between modernism and postmodernism, only to then blur the boundary, effectively leads us to the second section, those essays that discover postmodern traces in Faulkner's fiction. Each of these three essays deploys psychoanalytic concepts as a way to think about Faulkner's relation to postmodernism. In

" 'I'm the Man Here': *Go Down, Moses* and Masculine Identity," Terrell Tibbets considers various representations of patriarchal masculinity in Faulkner's fiction. Starting with the sense of Faulkner as a modernist with an essentialist notion of personal identity, Tibbets confronts several moments from "Barn Burning," *The Unvanquished*, and *Go Down, Moses* in which a more postmodern sense of identity as a social and relational construct emerges; as a result, Faulkner appears to synthesize modernist and postmodern identity. And in Tibbets's Jungian approach, the true hero of *Go Down, Moses* is Lucas Beauchamp because, unlike the other male McCaslins, Lucas successfully incorporates a female anima into his sense of masculine identity. But postmodern identity, for Tibbets, is still a pathology to be overcome by an act of will fashioned by a core self or personal essence. In this slippery space between essence and construction, however, one may wonder whether such self-fashioning actually recovers a core identity that is prior to the particular enactment of masculinity or whether masculine identity is constituted by its specific enactments.

Casting the issues of identity and Faulkner's postmodernism differently than Tibbets, the final two essays of the second section map the way *Absalom, Absalom!* engages other parts of Yoknapatawpha. The first of these, Doreen Fowler's "Revising *The Sound and the Fury: Absalom, Absalom!* and Faulkner's Postmodern Turn," argues that in Quentin Compson's fall into indeterminacy, one observes the demise of an older linguistic conception that sees words as the transparent medium of meanings existing prior to language. For Fowler, Faulkner's postmodern turn emerges intertextually, as *Absalom, Absalom!* investigates the metaphysics of Southern patriarchy in ways that *The Sound and the Fury* does not. Drawing on Jacques Lacan's rendering of the emergence of subjectivity (as well as his theory of the gaze), Fowler emphases what she sees as *Absalom*'s subversive subtext—the way the novel "investigates and demystifies the cultural structuring of subjectivity and meaning." If *The Sound and the Fury* still laments the disappearance of patriarchal origin and authority, *Absalom, Absalom!* reveals that such imagined male mastery and plentitude are the effect of (and not prior to) language. The second essay of the pair, Martin Kreiswirth's "Intertextuality, Transference, and Postmodernism in *Absalom, Absalom!*: The Production and Reception of Faulkner's Fictional World," positions Faulkner in a continuum that continually fluctuates between modernism and postmodernism. Starting from the numerous instances in Faulkner's fiction where details of names and dates differ from text to text, Kreiswirth suggests that Faulkner's texts approximate the conventions of postmodern historiography. Turning to the Freudian concept of transference, Kreiswirth charts the reader's relation to those instances in *Absalom* that resonate with a postmodern apprehension of reference and representation. In reading such moments, Kreiswirth sees Faulkner's novel fluctuate on the matter of how to interpret contradictory information: at times Faulkner seems to insist in modernist fashion on an "either/or" stance (in which only one position can be correct), while elsewhere there is a postmodern embrace of the logically contradictory "both/and" (in which mutually contradictory positions appear to be if not true, then true enough).

The third and final section of essays illustrates that another way in which Faulkner may be related to postmodernism is through contemporary readings of his work that invoke the insights of poststructuralism. One of the legacies of the poststructuralist critique of hierarchies and authority has been cultural studies, which questions the privileging of the literary or high cultural text.

In "Postvomiting: *Pylon* and the Faulknerian Spew," Joseph Urgo's meditation on the emetic moment both in Faulkner and in culture more generally leads to a way to conceive of postmodernism as "postvomit." Despite its visceral shock, Urgo's trope directly addresses the way postmodernism is simultaneously the inside and the outside of modernism. Working in the space between theoretical figurations of postmodernism as illness and Faulkner's representations of vomiting, Urgo turns to the vexing intertextual relationship between two novels—*Absalom, Absalom!* and *Pylon*—that occupy almost diametrically opposed places in the Faulkner canon. In this reading, however, *Pylon*, a novel obsessed with the contemporary (rather than the High Modernist and historicizing *Absalom*), becomes the index for understanding Faulkner's relation to postmodernism. Standing as a specific instance of postmodernism's relation to modernism, *Pylon* (the novel Faulkner turned to when he became blocked drafting *Absalom*) represents all that Faulkner's modernism could not assimilate. Like literal vomit, *Pylon* consists of the visible chunks that simultaneously were once inside *Absalom* but that, when expelled in partially "digested" form, are decidedly the not-*Absalom*. In a sense, the radically decentered and fragmented *Pylon* serves as Faulkner's vomitorium, a cite that allows the author a crucially necessary moment of purging that allowed him to return, as it were, to the feast of modernist confidence in the possibilities of narrative transcendence that *Absalom, Absalom!* embodies. Yet whatever modernist confidence that *Absalom* represents, it is always shadowed by the nihilism of its emetic twin.

Cheryl Lester's paper, "Make Room for Elvis," takes as its point of departure the Elvis Presley Conference that for two years in the mid-1990s occurred at the University of Mississippi the week immediately following the Faulkner and Yoknapatawpha Conference. Lester uses this apparently random academic confluence of high and popular culture as a warrant for a biographical and sociological interpretive strategy for reading the cultural significance of both Faulkner's and Presley's texts. In her broad-ranging, speculative linking of Count 'No Count and the King, Lester turns to both Faulkner's and Presley's genealogy to discover surprising resonances between these two sons of the South, whose lives overlapped for twenty-seven years in the twentieth century. In such things as their appropriations of black rural and Afro-urban culture and their attempts to recover a lost legacy of Southern white privilege, Faulkner and Elvis create an intercultural space of race and class that Lester uses to reconstruct Southern culture.

The penultimate essay in this volume concludes the academic portion, so it is only fitting that Philip Cohen's contribution should turn to academic culture and fashion to perform a metacritical analysis of current Faulkner scholarship, one calling for renewed relation to textual scholarship. Postmodern critique and textual scholarship might initially seem to be worlds apart. After all, for a number of years textual scholars saw their work (the investigation of an author's manuscripts, typescripts, and editorial correspondence) as supplanting the first edition of a novel with a scholarly edition, a final and fixed text that represented more accurately an author's intentions for his or her work. But Cohen is a part of the new breed of textual scholars who are keenly aware that the notion of an author's final intention is a highly freighted one. In "Faulkner by the Light of a Pale Fire: Postmodern Textual Scholarship and Faulkner Studies at the End of the Twentieth Century," Cohen argues for a postmodern criticism of Faulkner that more fully engages the insights of textual scholarship and warns that any Faulkner criticism that ignores textual scholarship does so at its own peril, since contemporary textual studies recognizes that the literary text is always plural and indeed decentered in its very genesis. Thus for postmodern Faulknerians to rely on a unitary notion of the text seems at odds with the very theoretical models they deploy.

The academics having had their say, the final word belongs to a novelist, the preeminent metafictionist, John Barth. In "My Faulkner," Barth recalls his own early reading of Faulkner and the less-than-fortunate effect this dense modernist prose had on Barth's master's thesis. Although casting Faulkner as an influence that had to be left behind, Barth nevertheless marks his encounter with Yoknapatawpha County as important to his education as a writer.

John N. Duvall
Purdue University
West Lafayette, Indiana

NOTES

1. However, when the subsequent university catalogue was published, a copy editor "corrected" our division so that American III became "1940 to Present."

2. William Faulkner, *The Sound and the Fury* (New York: Vintage International, 1990), 86.

3. Brian McHale, *Postmodernist Fiction* (London: Routledge, 1991), 10.

4. Ibid., 10.

5. Linda Hutcheon, *The Poetics of Postmodernism* (London: Routledge, 1988), 71.

6. McHale, 11.

7. Patrick O'Donnell, "Faulkner and Postmodernism" in *The Cambridge Companion to William Faulkner*, ed. Philip M.Weinstein (Cambridge: Cambridge University Press, 1995), 31.

8. O'Donnell, 32.

A Note on the Conference

The Twenty-sixth Annual Faulkner and Yoknapatawpha Conference sponsored by the University of Mississippi in Oxford took place July 25–30, 1999, with nearly two hundred of the author's admirers from around the world in attendance. Eleven presentations at the conference are collected in this volume. Brief mention is made here of other activities that took place during the week and a special group of conference registrants.

Supported by Saks Incorporated Foundation, on behalf of McRae's, Proffitt's, and Parisian Department Stores, thirty high school teachers from five Southern states received full fellowships to attend the conference. Emphasizing the deep connection of the company to Southern culture, Brad Martin, chairman of the board and chief executive office of Saks, endowed the fellowships "to provide high school teachers in our communities with an opportunity to broaden their awareness and understanding of the importance and relevance" of the great works of Southern literature. In addition to the conference program, Saks Fellows attended special workshops led by members of the Department of English at the University.

The conference opened with a University Museums exhibition, *Phil Mullen, Oxford Photographer, 1949–1951*, followed by a welcome by University Chancellor Robert C. Khayat. Charles Reagan Wilson, director of the Center for the Study of Southern Culture, presented the thirteenth annual Eudora Welty Awards in Creative Writing. Molly Davis of Greenville, Mississippi, won first prize, $500, for her short story, entered by her English teacher, Emma Richardson, from the Mississippi School for Math and Science in Columbus. Heather Christian won second prize, $250, for four poems nominated by her teacher, Jean Biglane, of Cathedral High School in Natchez. Frances Patterson of Tupelo, a member of the Center Advisory Committee, established and endowed the awards, which are selected through a competition held in high schools throughout Mississippi. After these presentations, Samuel M. Tumey read his prize-winning entry in the tenth annual Faux Faulkner contest, sponsored by the Jack Daniel Distillery, the University of Mississippi, and Yoknapatawpha Press and its *Faulkner Newsletter*. The University of Mississippi Gospel Choir offered a selection of songs, followed by *Voices from Yoknapatawpha*, readings from Faulkner's fiction selected and arranged by actor George Kehoe and Betty Harrington, wife of former conference director Evans Harrington. Following a buffet supper, at the home of Dr. and Mrs. M. B. Howorth Jr., author John Barth read selections from his work and commented on Faulkner's.

Monday's program included four lectures and the presentation of "Knowing William Faulkner," slides and commentary by the writer's nephew, J. M. Faulkner, and Meg Faulkner DuChaine. "Faulkner in Oxford" assembled local residents Will Lewis Jr. and Patricia Young as panelists for a discussion moderated by M. C. "Chooky" Falkner, another of the writer's nephews. Other highlights of the conference included "Teaching Faulkner" sessions conducted by visiting scholars Arlie Herron, James B. Carothers, Robert W. Hamblin, and Charles A. Peek and bus tours of North Mississippi and the Delta, followed by a party at Tyler Place hosted by Charles Noyes, Sarah and Allie Smith, and Colby Kullman. Conference goers also enjoyed exhibitions at the John Davis Williams Library, a walk through Bailey's Woods before the annual picnic at Faulkner's home, Rowan Oak, and a party at Square Books. The week ended with a reception at Ammadelle, the antebellum home of Dorothy Lee Tatum.

The conference planners are grateful to all the individuals and organizations who support the Faulkner and Yoknapatawpha Conference annually. In addition to those mentioned above, we wish to thank Mr. Richard Howorth of Square Books, St. Peter's Episcopal Church, the City of Oxford, and the Oxford Tourism Council.

Faulkner and Postmodernism
FAULKNER AND YOKNAPATAWPHA
1999

The Privations of Postmodernism: Faulkner as Exemplar (A Meditation in Ten Parts)

IHAB HASSAN

By lonely gift and hindered Words
The human heart is told
Of Nothing—
'Nothing' is the force
That renovates the World—
EMILY DICKINSON

1

Let us enter through the stately portals, the titular conceit of this confer-ence, for that is our mandate. Let us commence with a quick commentary on its three key words.

The name "Faulkner" offers a reasonably stable reference, though his works are continually read, reread, and misread. "Postmodernism" is an-other matter: it is not only read or misread, it also unreads itself before our very eyes. (More of this later.) Then there is that slippery conjunction "and," that teasing connective, promising us untold conceptual miseries. How, then, proceed?

I imagine that I have been invited to this conference on the premise that I know something about postmodernism. This is a terrible misappre-hension: after writing about postmodernism for thirty years, I know less about it now than I did then. Still, I must proceed by asking once again: what is postmodernism?

2

To proponents and opponents alike, postmodernism seems a contested signifier floating in a field of hype. But the sign is contested not only because it floats in hype. It is further contested because postmodernism, more than modernism or romanticism, is a combative category. That is, it not only describes a particular phenomenon but also interprets it as a way of self-empowerment; it draws it into the cultural politics of the moment. And like an explosion in a word factory, it scatters neologisms of itself—such as late-, early-, high-, low-, ultra-, proto-, hyper-, restructive-, prostructive-, classic-, radical-, and even post-postmodernism—which become missiles in our cultural wars.

I am not exempt. But if everything is ideology—jejune tautology—"ideologies" still differ crucially in degree and kind. Therefore, without claiming innocence for myself, I can strive for some equity and dispassion in these meditations.

So, then, what is postmodernism again? I think, first, of postmodernism as the equivocal autobiography of an age, a mode of collective, sometimes chaotic, sometimes mocking, self-reflection.

We recall that Immanuel Kant, in a famous essay of 1784 entitled "Was ist Aufklärung?," explicitly asked the question about the meaning of his moment, the content of his contemporaneity. Poststructuralists, Michel Foucault in particular, made much of Kant's philosophical query as it applies to our own epoch. But Foucault, addicted as ever to hyperbolic opacities, ignored that Kant could speak with an epistemological confidence we lack, and that his sense of history permitted him to posit the Enlightenment as a crux that we, children of a more ambiguous chronos, can hardly assume. Versed in aporia, suspicion, incredulity, votaries of decenterment and apostles of multiplicity, pluralist, parodic, pragmatic, polychronic all, we can hardly privilege postmodernism, not even as crisis, as Kant, in the very act of posing his question, privileged his time. Instead, we betray an abandon of belatedness, a seemingly limitless anxiety of self-nomination.

Postmodernism, then, is equivocal autobiography on several grounds: titular (its name prevaricates), epistemic (its knowledge unravels), historical (its moment slips and slides). It accommodates several kinds of temporality: linear, mythic, cybernetic, visionary, sidereal, and kitsch time. Thus, more than equivocal autobiography, postmodernism defines itself, if at all, as a continual exercise in self-definition.

3

Three decades ago, my sense of postmodernism was perhaps more ingenuous. Regarding it mainly as a cultural and artistic phenomenon, I thought the neologism—I too am culpable—"Indetermanence" subsumed its mercurial character. Here I do best to quote at some length from my original statement.

> The time has come . . . to explain a little that neologism: 'indetermanence.' I have used that term to designate two central, constitutive tendencies in post-

modernism: one of indeterminacy, the other of immanence. The two tendencies are not dialectical; for they are not exactly antithetical; nor do they lead
to a synthesis. Each contains its own contradictions, and alludes to elements
of the other. . . .

By indeterminacy, or better still, *indeterminacies*, I mean a complex referent which these diverse concepts help to delineate: ambiguity, discontinuity,
heterodoxy, pluralism, randomness, revolt, perversion, deformation. The latter
alone subsumes a dozen current terms of unmaking: decreation, disintegration,
deconstruction, decenterment, displacement, difference, discontinuity, dis-
junction, disappearance, decomposition, dedefinition, demystification, detotal-
ization, delegitimation—let alone more technical terms referring to the
rhetoric of irony, rupture, silence. Through all these signs moves a vast will to
unmaking, affecting the body politic, the body cognitive, the erotic body, the
individual psyche—the entire realm of discourse in the West. In literature
alone, our ideas of author, audience, reading, writing, book, genre, critical
theory, and of literature itself, have all suddenly become questionable. . . .

Such uncertain diffractions make for vast dispersals. Thus I call the second
major tendency of postmodernism *immanences*, a term that I employ without
religious echo to designate the capacity of mind to generalize itself in symbols,
intervene more and more into nature, act upon itself through its own abstractions and so become, increasingly, immediately, its own environment. This
noetic tendency may be evoked further by such sundry concepts as diffusion,
dissemination, pulsion, interplay, communication, interdependence, which all
derive from the emergence of human beings as language animals, *homo pictor*
or *homo significans*, gnostic creatures constituting themselves, and deter-
minedly their universe, by symbols of their own making. . . . Meanwhile, the
public world dissolves as fact and fiction blend, history becomes derealized by
media into a happening, science takes its own models as the only accessible
reality, cybernetics confronts us with the enigma of artificial intelligence, and
technologies project our perceptions to the edge of matter. Everywhere . . . we
encounter that immanence called Language, with all its literary ambiguities,
epistemic conundrums, and political distractions.

No doubt, these tendencies may seem less rife in England, say, than in
America or France where the term postmodernism, reversing the recent direction of poststructuralist flow, has now come into use. But the fact in most
developed societies remains: as an artistic, philosophical, and social phenomenon, postmodernism veers toward open (open in time as well as in structure
or space), playful, optative, provisional, disjunctive, or indeterminate forms, a
discourse of ironies and fragments, a "white ideology" of absences and frac-
tures, a desire of diffractions, an invocation of complex, articulate silences.
Postmodernism veers towards all these yet implies a different, if not antithetical, movement toward pervasive procedures, ubiquitous interactions, immanent codes, media, languages. Thus our earth seems caught in the process of
planetization, transhumanization, even as it breaks up into sects, tribes, fac-
tions of every kind. Thus, too, terrorism and totalitarianism, schism and ecu-

menism, heresy and dogma, summon one another, and authorities decreate themselves even as societies search for new grounds of authority.[1]

This was published in 1982. Since then, the double process of "localization" and "globalization," as every CEO now glibly says, has become more emphatic. What I had hinted at has become the daily grist of our news: I mean the fluent imperium of high-tech, consumer capitalism, on the one hand, and the sundry movements of secession, decolonization, ethnic and religious and gendered and linguistic and political separatism, on the other hand—satellites here, cargo cults there, Madonna on one side, the Great Satan on the other. In sum, cultural postmodernism has mutated into genocidal postmodernity (Bosnia, Kosovo, Ulster, Rwanda, Chechnya, Kurdistan, Sudan, Afghanistan, Tibet . . . so goes the baleful litany of our time). But cultural postmodernism itself has metastasized into sterile, campy, kitschy, jokey, dead-end games or sheer media hype.

By 1987, when I published *The Postmodern Turn*, I had begun to wonder how to recover the creative impulse of postmodernism without frivolity or reversion, without recourse to etiolated forms or truculent dogmas. Sophistication lacked all conviction, ideology was full of passionate mendacity. What was the way out?

4

Mystics—I am not one—know that the way out is down and out. Can the postmodern turn take a spiritual turn? Can the materialist ideologies of the moment open or crack to let a fresh spiritual gust through? And what would spirit mean in our intellectual culture of disbelief? Certainly, it would not mean atavism, fundamentalism, or occultism; it may not even mean adherence to orthodox religions—Christianity, Judaism, Hinduism, Islam—though it would not exclude them.

I can not answer these questions here in full; nor, I suspect, will I ever answer them. I did, however, make a tentative start in a recent essay on spirit in postmodern times.[2] There, with some encouragement from figures as diverse as William James, John Cage, and Charles Jencks, I envisaged a postmodern, spiritual attitude compatible with emergent technologies; with geopolitical realities (population, pollution, the growing obsolescence of the nation state); with the needs of the wretched of the earth; with the interests of feminists and minorities and multicultural societies; with an ecological, planetary humanism; and perhaps even with millennial hopes. I could so envisage the prospects of a postmodern spiritual attitude, without occult bombinations or New Age platitudes, because spirit pervades a variety of secular experiences, from dreams, creative intuitions in art or science, and a sense of the sublime, to extraordinary, visionary states, including the gift of seeing the eternal in the temporal, an apprehension of primal relations in the universe.

Dictionaries offer many senses of "spirit," which differs from morality. These senses usually center on something fundamental to human existence yet intangible, an activating principle, a cosmic curiosity, a deeper meaning, often religious or metaphysical in character. This bedrock meaning is not obsolete; for as Saul Bellow noted in his Nobel Lecture of 1976, when distraction increases, so does the desire for essentials. Can that desire be alien to our spiritual impulses?

Yet spirit does not offer invariable solace. As mystics and saints know, spirit is exigent; it has its harshness, its clouds of unknowing, its dark nights of the soul. It may begin in agnosticism and end in despair. This is particularly true in postmodern times, times of irony, suspicion, nihilism. Yet even nihilism, at its best, can serve as a penultimate form of lucidity. Thus a postmodern spiritual attitude may become deeply acquainted with kenosis—self-emptying, yes, but also the self-undoing of our knowledge. Witness Søren Kierkegaard, Franz Kafka, Jacques Derrida, Samuel Beckett, to name but a few, outrageously diverse authors.

And William Faulkner? What spiritual attitude does he project?

5

I consider Faulkner a consummate modernist, an author of universal import, as writers from Jean-Paul Sartre and André Malraux to Kenzaburo Oe and Mario Vargas Llosa can testify. What is he to postmodernism, then, or postmodernism to him? That is the inaugural question of the conference—is it not?—which I am prepared now to engage. I engage it, however, from a particular perspective. For me, the question becomes: how can Faulkner help us to redress, redeem even, our spiritual privations?

Whatever the answer, it cannot be that Faulkner is really a crypto-postmodernist, a sort of pre-postmodernist. That were to cannibalize history. The answer, rather, must adduce modernism itself. From Klee and Kandinsky, Mahler and Stravinsky, from Proust, Woolf, and Lawrence, from Rilke, Yeats and Eliot, to the last modernist whoever he or she may be (Pollock? Auden? Bellow? Virgil Thomson?), a powerful spiritual impulse has run through modernist arts. Powerful as it was, though, the impulse *displaced* spirit, which found expression in myth, primitivism, abstraction, surrealism, theosophy, the grotesque, found expression even in negation more often than in orthodox Christianity (say the Catholicism of Claudel or the Anglicanism of Eliot).

The familiar paradox of declining religious belief and heightened spiritual awareness in modernism is really no paradox at all: spirit displaces itself as it can, as it must. It can veer toward the plenitude of mysticism in art, which Kenneth Burke considered a type of rhetoric, an aesthetic solution to certain problems that modern artists confronted. Or it can veer toward negation, acedia, emptiness, or drought, a kind of *via negativa* that invites us in the destructive element to immerse—hence Stephen Spender's signal work on modernism by that name.

Still, from the mutations of the Judeo-Christian tradition, something endured (a Faulknerian verb). It is pointless to remand that spiritual element, as Hans Blumenberg does, to a Gnostic legacy, "not overcome . . . but only transcended."[3] For the spiritual force in modernism remained too versatile, textured by skepticism, tinctured by experimentalism, too alive to its moment for us to dismiss as a Gnostic trace or taint. Indeed, modernism, by transforming and subverting the Judeo-Christian tradition at the same time, has created distinctive spiritual adaptations.

Of these adaptations, one bears particularly on our concern. "The problem of the modern literary artist . . . ," David Daiches acutely remarks, "is not to find usable myths so much, as to find ways of handling knowledge in a context of value."[4] Such contexts of value can be religious or mythical, but they need be neither; they need only make sense of the human condition in some artistic form. Call it Yoknapatawpha County. Not myth exactly, not a religion either, nor simply a verbal fiction, that Faulknerian County emerges as a context of value because it emerges from the mists of rhetoric as a coherent, moral, historical, psychological, and artistic terrain—and, yes, a spiritual terrain too.

6

But it is time to draw closer to Faulkner. I do so, let me say at once, with keen admiration, if not hushed reverence. I confess that his personal posturing and gesturing alternately irk and amuse me. And I admit that in Faulkner some archaic qualities—more of this later—nearly repel me. Yet my admiration stands. Why? The answer must lead us through selected works of Faulkner, and back to the burden of this paper: what example Faulkner offers to our postmodern privations?

The simplest works of an author often prove his most revealing: unmediated, they lack the consummate cunning of great art. I want to begin with Faulkner's nonfiction, his occasional prose. And I want first to remark on the vocabulary of works like *Essays, Speeches, and Public Letters* and *Faulkner at Nagano*. The vocabulary might shock an unregenerate postmodernist, among whom I do *not* count myself.

The famous words that ring in his Nobel Speech are easy to recall: "courage and honor and hope and pride and compassion and pity and sacrifice which have been the glory of his [the writer's] past."[5] "Love" is there too, in another sentence, as well as "the old verities and truths of the heart, the old universal truths lacking which any story is ephemeral and doomed." And of course "spirit" and "soul" sound plangently in the speech. But if you flip—I almost said scroll—through the other pages, you will encounter more words, kin and cousin in the same moral and spiritual clan: humility, courtesy, endurance, purity, truth, sincerity, justice, tolerance, discipline, dignity, loyalty, liberty, decency, grace, patience, charity, conscience . . . all within the span of barely two hundred pages of easy prose.

It is a stigma of our postmodern privations that I find this vocabulary striking. But let me push on. Another vocabulary bristles on these same pages, fierce, ungiving words, often prefixed with "in." They are what I call the "in-words," not because they exhibit snobbery, a trite exclusiveness. Quite the contrary; they express negations of an altogether different kind; they stonewall depravity. Here they are: invincible, indomitable, inexorable, invulnerable, incorrigible, intractable, inviolable, inflexible, inalienable, incontrovertible, also immitagble, implacable, immutable, impregnable, irrevocable, irremediable, unalterable, unvanquished, unsurrendered, undeviable . . . and so it goes. (Can you imagine, Vonnegut next to Faulkner? Who would tower above whom?)

This vocabulary of obduracy and opposition, this language of adamantine resistance and ultimate resolution, draws on Romantic heroism certainly. But it draws more deeply on contexts of value and belief. Its defiance may seem a form of tragic pride or rigid hubris. Yet, more than any statement of personal pride, the language creates meaning, by the very force of its commitment, in a bleak universe. The "tale told by an idiot, full of sound and fury," is *made* to signify something. "Man prevails," as long as he prevails, because in certain human beings the will to meaning outlasts all denials. This, I suspect, is the archimedean point, a point spiritual, not physical, nor simply moral, by which Faulkner means to move the world. "The human spirit does not obey physical laws" (152), he announced to Athenians at their Academy in 1957.

It is no great wonder that Faulkner finds relativism repugnant. Here is what he says about Truth in his fine essay on "Privacy," more agonizingly relevant today than in 1955:

> Truth—that long clean clear simple undeviable unchallengeable straight and shining line, on one side of which black is black and on the other white is white, has now become an angle, a point of view having nothing to do with

truth nor even with fact, but depending solely on where you are standing when
you look at it. Or rather—better—where you can contrive to have him standing whom you are trying to fool or obfuscate when he looks at it (72).

Here Faulkner defines the postmodern view without acceding to it—
defines it rather too simply, since black was never so black nor white so
white as Faulkner pretends, neither in the South nor in the North, neither in America nor in the world, neither then nor now. Still, Faulkner
exposes relativism, less as philosophy than practice, a kind of ideological
manipulation intended to justify what most human beings would find
unjustifiable—for instance, the egregious invasion of privacy.

Dyed-in-hype postmodernists may howl and hoot at Faulkner's univer-
salisms; and the rest of us, unless fundamentalist, may wish to qualify it.
But that Faulknerian universalism is already in some measure self-quali-
fied. For in his work, as in his mind, universalism serves partly as an act
of necessary faith, faith almost by virtue of the absurd. "To believe, to
believe . . . ," Faulkner cries repeatedly, "and to believe more" (9). It
could be a belief in the value of purity or fidelity or integrity; it could be
belief in "more"—whatever it takes in rigor and agony—to "complete"
the world. "Because only man can complete it. Not God, but man" (135).
The "universal," then, is an aspect of the will to believe (William James)
or, a postmodernist might argue, the will to lie in the ultra-moral sense
(Friedrich Nietzsche)—in either case, it remains a radical will to mean
and be in the universe.

But Faulkner's universalism has another, almost contradictory aspect.
It embodies not only the power of enabling fictions in human existence.
It embodies further the presence of things as they are, or, to paraphrase
Joyce, the ineluctable modalities of existence. We should not scoff, then,
when Faulkner considers truth inescapable: "truth was not where you
were standing when you looked at it but was an unalterable quality or
thing which could and would knock your brains out if you did not accept
it or at least respect it" (164). Call it the reality principle; call it death or
the incredible weight—not lightness, weight—of being.

In any case, the two aspects of Faulkner's universalism, and indeed
ours, are reconciled in the complicity of human aspirations and human
limitations. Our desires and deficiencies are in one imagination compact.
We would not wish for justice, freedom, love, or immortality so much,
did we not lack them more. Willy-nilly, we live and die by the equivocal
universals embedded in our languages. And is not language itself such an
equivocal universal? *All* human beings—Kaspar Hauser and the Wild
Boy of Aveyron notwithstanding—possess language, though it may not
be the same language.

Let us then resist the intimidations of postmodernists who like to cant: "there are no universals!" Indeed, there are no absolute universals, neither in nature nor in history, only in mental abstractions. In practice, however, many principles serve as working generalizations or soft universals. I do not mean only biological facts like death, hunger, or sexual reproduction. I also mean, empirically, some transcultural practices like languages, rituals, taboos, spirits, social organizations of marriage, hierarchy, and status. They may vary drastically according to time, place, tribe. Yet as human practices, they pervade the earth.

7

I can not proceed to the major fiction of Faulkner, our very reason for being here, without some comment on that most curious work about, but not of, literature: *Faulkner at Nagano*. As a frequent visitor and lecturer in Japan, I respond to the work with a shock of numbing recognition. Numbing is the word: numbing questions, numbing repetitions, numbing courtesy even, a work of truly stupefying simplicities. Yet I respond to that same work with poignant nostalgia, because of its courtesy, because of its unencumbered verities.

Allowing for its oral, half-improvised occasion, I find its very naiveté—a postmodern shibboleth—and its humility profoundly revealing. Consider again the word "soul." Most readers would concede to Faulkner that indeterminate quality we call soul, and concede it also to his best characters, a quality André Gide fails to recognize in them, perhaps because their intransigence seems so alien to Europeans. Faulkner himself is explicit about his personal beliefs: "Well," he answers a direct question, "I believe in God. Sometimes Christianity gets pretty debased, but I do believe in God, yes. I believe that man has a soul that aspires towards what we call God, what we mean by God."[6] And to him the proof of God lies "in the firmament, the stars"; in the very conception "that there could be a God, that the idea of a God is valuable"; and especially, in the fact that man "writes the books and composes the music and paints the pictures," for these "are the firmament of mankind" (29). Thus belief, aspiration, and art become themselves articles in Faulkner's theodicy.

This is neither a "Southern" nor a conservative theodicy particularly. A Transcendentalist like Emerson noted in his *Journals*: "It is not certain that God exists but that he does not is a most bewildering & improbable chimera."[7] And a Pragmatist like William James declared himself ready to "take a God who lives in the very dirt of private fact [like human suffering]—if that would seem a likely place to find him."[8] I find the statements of Emerson, James, and Faulkner as eminently compatible with one another as they are with a pluralist, postmodern attitude.

And I could say the same about Faulkner's idea of truth, further eluci-dated in this interchange at Nagano:

> Q: You always talk about truth. Could you give us your definition of what you call truth?
>
> F: Yes, truth to me means what you know to be right and just, truth is that thing, the violation of which makes you writhe at night when you try to go to sleep, in shame for something you've done that you know you shouldn't have done. That to me is truth, not fact. Fact is not too important and can be altered by law, by circumstance, by too many qualities, economics, temperature, but truth is the constant thing, it's what man knows is right and that when he violates it, it troubles him. Well, I doubt if he ever does toughen himself, toughen his soul, to where it doesn't trouble him just a little and he'll try to escape from the knowledge of that truth in all sorts of ways, in drink, drugs, various forms of anesthesia, because he simply cannot face himself.
>
> Q: Will you distinguish between truth and ideal?
>
> F: Well, an ideal is a hope, an aspiration, it could be an impossible dream. Truth is not an impossible dream, it's not an ideal or aspiration. Truth is a quality which one must accept or cope with. (101–2)

The colloquialism, the informality, can not conceal from us Faulkner's stand: that for him truth, like God, is neither fact nor dogma but a lived experience, an existential principle, conscience in action, belief at risk—in short, a commitment that reality can neither specify nor thwart because the commitment derives from a lived context of values.

I find the moral and spiritual commitment of Faulkner balm to post-modern privations. More, I find it vital to all, not just postmodern, arts. Could George Steiner, after all, be right—I demurred on this point once—that "where God's presence is no longer a tenable supposition and where His absence is no longer a felt, indeed overwhelming weight, cer-tain dimensions of thought and creativity are no longer attainable"?[9] Or does it suffice to have a commanding, imaginative apprehension of the human condition, a live truth (in Faulkner's sense) or a comprehensive attitude about existence, to produce great art? And is it better to be a hedgehog, knowing one thing deeply, like Dante (and some modernists, including Faulkner), or a fox, knowing brilliantly so many things, like Shakespeare (and some postmodernists, say Pynchon)?

Let us move on to the more subtle articulations of Faulkner's fiction, in search of an answer.

8

No great writer composes in a single key, not even Faulkner, obsessive "provincial" that he was. Some of his stories rollick with frontier humor, roil with gothic and grotesque energies—say, "A Justice" and "Was." And his best work, brief as "Red Leaves" or plenary as *Absalom, Absalom!*, possesses narrative and dramatic extravagance. Some, of course, like *Light in August* and *A Fable*, carry explicit Christian references. Christian or pagan, though, the spiritual dimension of his work remains indubitable, not willed as in his Southern compatriots, Charles Brockden Brown and Edgar Allan Poe, but complicit in his vision, as in his Northern compeer, Nathaniel Hawthorne.

In their knowledge of psychic terrors, all these writers prove to be gnostics of a certain kind: they have fathomed darkness and seen the color of blackness. They have also seen spirit as kenosis, as ultimate dispossession, negation, absence. But in Faulkner's fiction, spirit seem always complicit with a social hierarchy and moral order, resting not on material achievements but on transcendent obligations. Family cycles are also spiritual sagas; the myths of Yoknapatawpha invoke a reality larger than Mississippi, the South, or America can possess. The mystic doctrine of correspondence, between the world and a grain of sand, eternity and a flower, fits Faulkner's rhetoric to a universal fatality. Malcolm Cowley's "bardic poet in prose" can create compelling myths precisely because he sings in a voice both eerily personal and vastly impersonal.[10]

Impersonal destiny, conjunct with the individual will, reveals a spiritual aspect rarely remarked in Faulkner's work. Critics have noted often enough Faulkner's attachment to the past, the "old time, the old days." But this attachment expresses something more than personal nostalgia or historical retrogression. It expresses a particular ontological view of time, memory as the Hebrew *emunah*, recollection as the house of being, endurance as the very principle of existence. For to endure is not simply to be; it is also to honor the past, even preterition, and to guaranty futurity. And this is what stories can do supremely well. Thus, narrative remembrance overreaches preservation or restitution; it may be our only portion of the infinite. In quasi-Christian terms, memory is not only edenic, and so inevitably lapsarian; it is paradisal as well, eschatological. In the humbler terms of this paper, memory may adumbrate the spiritual possibilities of human kind, and hence transfigures time. Surely this is what so many characters of Faulkner intimate to us, characters from old Ikkemotubbe and Sam Fathers, through various Compsons, Sartorises, McCaslins, through Lusters and Dilseys of diverse kind, to the last wretched Snopes of our time.

Let me now blood these critical abstractions with three superb stories, exemplary of my theme.

9

I have in mind "Spotted Horses," from *The Hamlet* (1940), "Old Man," from *The Wild Palms* (1939), and "The Bear," from *Go Down, Moses*

(1942). They are bunched in time, though unrelated, and tidily, gradually, they reveal Faulkner's spiritual concern.

"Spotted Horses" is a glorious (not glorified) yarn of untrammeled exuberance; its droll, narrative manner suits well those wild-eyed Texas ponies. But of course, the yarn is a tacit moral parable of the rapacious Snopeses who corrupt the all-too-corruptible denizens of Frenchman's Bend. Money machines, you say? No, machines lack slyness and wile, which the Snopese possess to a grotesque, hilarious,and indeed malefic degree. There is no whisper of piety, no whiff of righteousness, in the story. Yet such is Faulkner's art that the sheer, unbridled, and natural violence of those horses, whirling through the hamlet, leaves it finally—with some exceptions—in its sad, exhausted moral vacuity. There is no tact in saddling this yarn with spiritual encumbrances; it is enough to feel, between deep guffaws and down-home barters, its moral weight.

"Old Man" is something else, less yarn than sodden saga, drenched odyssey, in a rotten, rickety, oarless argosy, a harrowing testament of pride, endurance, and weird probity. Of course, with a man, woman, and infant in the tossed skiff—throw in a bushel of water moccasins—the story also alludes to Noah's primal Ark as well as the Mississippi's (Old Man's) flood of twenty seven.

I have always considered the tall convict in that story an inscrutable figure. He is never named, of course, and this makes him less Everyman than Noman—or rather, makes him both, at once concrete and enigmatically allegorical. I do not understand the tall convict, and so I endow him with preternatural qualities, almost—I said almost—spiritual. The author tells us that this convict wants nothing for himself; he has been defrauded not of money but of "liberty and honor and pride." But whence his inexhaustible obduracy? Does he act out of overweening pride, or abyssal ignorance, or limitless innocence, or unassailable rectitude? This silent convict seems simple, but his simplicities beggar our explanations. His jailers do not understand him, nor do his fellow convicts, nor do his random companions, nor do his readers, nor certainly does he understand himself. Does his author, William Faulkner?

My point is this: our man touches the secret of rightness, the mystery of responsibility, which elude all rules—the very rules he himself unquestionably obeys. Justice is not the real issue here, neither for him nor for that woman of calm and infinite fortitude; justice is not the issue nor some inchoate sense of honor, his "good name" (on whose lips)? What, then, is at issue? Let us look further.

This convict cannot lie for the oddest of reasons: "his hill-man's sober and jealous respect not for truth but for the power, the strength, of lying—not to be niggard with lying but rather to use it with respect and even care, delicate, quick and strong, like a fine and fatal blade."[11] Well, it was lying, the tawdry illusions of dime novels and pulp fiction, that induced him to attempt armed robbery, a botched and risible attempt, in the first place. Does the convict hold a high ideal of lying, of illusion and high romance, that the Great Gatsby himself might have shared? More, is the "fine and fatal blade" of lying Platonic in its purity, lethal to unworthy users who betray its essence?

Perhaps the answer lies in certain recurrent, almost talismanic, words that unveil a vital region of Faulkner's sensibility. I have already noted some of these words; here I want to remark yet another. The word, a refrain, is "outrage." What is this pervasive outrage all about? What, particularly, does it mean to our convict? Here is a passage describing the woman's delivery, as she cries out for an instrument to sever the umbilical cord:

> When the woman asked him if he had a knife, standing there in the streaming bed-ticking garments which had got him shot at, the second time by a machine gun, on the two occasions when he had seen any human life after leaving the levee four days ago, the convict felt exactly as he had in the fleeing skiff when the woman suggested that they had better hurry. He felt the same outrageous affronting of a condition purely moral, the same raging impotence to find any answer to it; so that, standing above her, spent suffocating and inarticulate, it was a full minute before he comprehended that she was now crying, "The can! The can in the boat!" (130).

I would like to suggest that this "condition purely moral" is not moral but metaphysical—hence the "raging impotence to find an answer to it." It is the condition of human existence, affronting a destiny that declines to answer to man. In short, the outrage, once again, is ontological, like the outrage of Job or Ivan Karamazov; or as Nietzsche would say, "'why' finds no answer."[12]

Why receives no answer, also, from the unspeakable power and fury of Old Man River, an incarnate stream of fatality on which the man, the woman, the infant, in the frail skiff, barely float. The Mississippi—Eliot's brown god in the *Quartets* who teaches flow, that is, dispossession—literally transcends itself, but also invades the inner life of the tall convict: "it was now ineradicably part of his past, his life; it would be part of what he would bequeath" (170). A bequest from what the author calls the "cosmic joker" (160)? Indeed, Faulkner apprehends the lives of his characters not only in personal or social terms but also cosmically, not simply ethically but, as it were, theologically.

Here, as elsewhere, the narrative techniques of Faulkner heighten the sense of fatality. For instance, the jarring flashforwards—later conversations between the tall and plump convicts or the tall convict and his jailers—hint continually at predestination, at least *narrative* predestination. Time and time again, our man tries to surrender in vain—in vain, it almost seems, because the "cosmic joker" has already decided to refuse his surrender. And the compulsive repetitions of certain actions and events in the convict's life suggest not only that character is fate but also—with a touch of "doom," still another key, obsessive Faulknerian word—that fate is fate. Even—yes, "even" is another intensifier, yet another key, obsessive word—even those maddening parentheses and digressions, meandering syntactically, temporally, meandering chronically within a single, endlessly sinuous sentence, even those riffs on time, remind us only how determined the outcome of the sentence is.

I do not mean that Faulkner's world is ruled by Calvinist Predestination. Such a statement would be neither wholly false nor precisely true. I mean, rather, that in Faulkner's fiction, both theme and form create a powerful intuition of fatality; his language repeats itself even as it perpetually teases eternity.[13] Yet even so guarded a statement requires nuance, qualification. Look at the ending of "Old Man." It is neither tragic nor apocalyptic. It is not even unambiguously spiritual: the saga, odyssey, the sodden epic of our hero ends with woman trouble—the man is jilted. We are back, four square, in the lived, ironic, sublunary world.

"The Bear" gives us a glimpse of another world. The novelette is one of the author's most glossed works, glossed smooth by critical interpretations. Yet, in my view, it remains harsh, jagged, a demanding piece of work. The work is demanding, of course, because its structure and style require unremitting attention. But "The Bear" is demanding in another, deeper, more disquieting sense: its spiritual exactions, on both characters and readers, seem endless. Such are the demands of dispossession, relinquishment, abnegation, self-immolation—kenosis again. That is what the story, in all its fierce intricacies, is all about: renunciation, in emulation of the Nazarene.

Everything seems to rest on dispossession: the myth of the wilderness, the hunting code, the guilt of slavery, the extermination of Indians, the miscegenation of races, the dissolution of patrimonies, the exploitation of the land by railroads and logging camps. It is the tragic story of the South, you say. It is the story of America, no, the human condition, I reply. Faulkner, though he both romanticizes and critiques the "lost cause" of the South, as Irving Howe has noted nearly half a century ago, invariably reaches for the largest implications of his statement (as postmodernists rarely do).[14] Here is a cento to remind you of the drive to dispossession, nearly tactile, in "The Bear":

> About a log: "almost completely crumbled now, healing with unbelievable speed, a passionate and almost visible *relinquishment*, back into the earth from which the tree had grown" (199).
>
> Of Ike McCaslin: "He had left the gun; by his own will and *relinquishment* he had accepted not a gambit, not a choice, but a condition in which not only the bear's heretofore inviolable anonymity but all the ancient rules and balances of hunter and hunted had been abrogated" (200).
>
> Of Old Sam, dying shortly after the bear is killed: "He lay there—the copper-brown, *almost hairless body*, the old man's body, the old man, the wild man not even one generation from the woods, *childless, kinless, peopleless*—motionless, his eyes open but no longer looking at any of them" (237).
>
> Ike on his inheritance: "I cant repudiate it. It was never mine to repudiate. It was never Father's and Uncle Buddy to bequeath," never anyone's really, except God's, who gave the earth only to hold it "mutual and intact in the communal anonymity of brotherhood" (246f).
>
> And the final madness, hysteria, the very opposite of dispossession, of plebeian Boon—who was the one to kill the bear with Lion's help—banging at his impotent gun under a treeful of squirrels, and crying to Ike: "Get out of here! Dont touch them! Dont touch a one of them! *They're mine!* " (316).
>
> (All emphases mine.)

These are some aspects of kenosis, the exigencies of spirit, in Faulkner's fiction, threatening extinction of the social, even the historical self. But there are still other aspects to which I need briefly to advert.

Myth, ritual, and totemism in the story have received comment enough. So has the spiral structure of time, recalling certain events, certain scenes, recalling them obsessively even as the plot unravels, even as human time speeds toward eternity. Simply put, in Faulkner's work, eternity seems always imminent, if not quite immanent, and characters, actions, objects continually transcend themselves. Thus the bear, Old Ben, possesses a "furious immortality." Ike's initiation into the Big Woods is a "novitiate." The accidental discovery of Lion, the killer dog, has an immemorial "fatality in it." The annual hunt, like Keats's Grecian urn, embalms actions into a perennial and unitary truth, which "doesn't change." And most notably, this passage of cosmic reconciliation toward the end of the story:

> . . . he had not stopped, he had only paused, quitting the knoll which was no abode of the dead because there was no death, not Lion and not Sam: not held fast in earth but free in earth and not in earth but of earth, myriad yet undiffused of every myriad part, leaf and twig and particle, air and sun and rain and dew and night, acorn oak and leaf and acorn again, dark and dawn and dark

and dawn again in their immutable progression and, being myriad, one: and
Old Ben too, Old Ben too. . . . (314)

Indeed, the signal achievement of Faulkner in "The Bear" is to trans-
figure one kind of time into another. The first is historical time, Southern
time, you might say, with all its convolutions, its legacies and dissolu-
tions, its crimes and atonements, the time of Ariadne's thread, no, Faulkner's thread, of moral responsibility, followed through the foul, dark,
deadly labyrinth of the Minotaur, through slavery and war. This is the
time of the long, tortuous, outrageous sentence of part 4. But Faulkner
frames—I would say transfigures—this kind of time by another, more
cosmic and spiritual. It is the time of the ritual hunt in parts 1, 2, 3,
and 5. Though Ike McCaslin grows from adolescence to manhood in the
intervening years, the time of the hunt is like transparent air, "taint-
less"—another Faulknerian word—without stain of reality. Here, what is
true of Boon is true of all, "waiting for daylight so he could rise and hunt
again, as though time were merely something he walked through as he
did through air, aging him no more than air did" (220). In this transparent
air, time eternal, the self sheds its attachments, the colors of quotidian
reality. And that may be the ultimate demand that the self can make upon
itself.

Hence the importance of courage in Faulkner's work, the aboriginal
virtue from which all others—loyalty, pride, humility, endurance, wisdom—ensue. This is not the crude courage of Boon or Lion, nor of the
aristocrats of the South, nor even of Sam Fathers and old Ben himself; it
is finally the courage of pure selflessness, holy indifference. I would call
it ontological courage, but that is something of a paradox; for in that
courage worldly being is dissolved in the name of a vaster mystery, which
we may name Being or Nothing.

I say Being *or* Nothing consciously: a premonition of the Void stalks
Faulkner's work. In "The Bear," that premonition strikes when Ike speculates on the responsibility of God for both heaven and hell, "shaped
out of the primal Absolute which contained all" (271). Yet, for me, that
speculation admits doubt about cosmic "responsibility"; for me, that
speculation, which ends somewhat piously, invokes the specter of radical
nihilism, the specter of Nothingness or the Abyss.

*And that, indeed, is the specter that haunts both modern and postmod-
ern literature*—haunts the latter often playfully—the specter who must
be challenged to speak the meaning of spirit in our own postmodern
times. But can this challenge take any but a Jamesian (William), pragmatic turn? Oddly, with a touch of irony perhaps, Faulkner may concur
with James. Here is the key passage:

He had heard about an old bear and finally got big enough to hunt it and he hunted it four years and at last met it with a gun in his hands and he didn't shoot. Because a little dog—But he could have shot long before the fyce covered the twenty yards to where the bear waited, and Sam Fathers could have shot at any time during the interminable minute while Old Ben stood on his hind legs over them. . . . He ceased. McCaslin watched him, still speaking, the voice, the words as quiet as the twilight itself was: 'Courage and honor and pride, and pity and love of justice and of liberty. They all touch the heart, and what the heart holds to becomes truth, as far as we know truth. Do you see now?' (285)

What "the heart holds to becomes truth, as far as we know truth." Is that where Faulkner touches postmodernism, its covert "will to believe," in a pragmatic intuition of the spiritual? Or is it merely a momentary retreat from Christian belief into the purported wisdom of the heart?

10

The particular question need not engage us; the general issue, regarding Faulkner and Postmodernism, must. And so I move decisively toward my insecure conclusion.

Clearly, my concern with postmodernism in this essay has been secondary. Rightly so, I think: postmodernism is not our fate in full. Some eminent critics, like the Australian Bernard Smith, see postmodernism as "nothing but the mask which twentieth century modernism adopted in its struggle" with the great formal achievement in this century—"the Formalesque," he calls it.[15] As mask, dialogue, or critique of one version of modernism, postmodernism may be already history, a belated period or phase still in search of its name.

But my concern, I repeat, is less with the fate of postmodernism than ours. For I experience a large aspect of postmodern culture as privation, an arid land we all need to traverse. Here Faulkner may prove our guide. He inhabits a different, a richer, moral universe—and not moral only, but also richly spiritual. The crux of this spirituality is self-emptying, the terrible courage of renunciation—a "piercing Virtue," as Emily Dickinson put it, known to all great mystics and perhaps great skeptics too. This has been my theme.

It remains for me to stress a point implicit in all these remarks: the quality of Faulkner's renunciation reaches into our postmodern moment. It moves, past rhetoric or theology, toward absence (Derrida); it touches nihilism (Nietzsche); it knows the infinite play of irony as of resignation (Kierkegaard). In short, it invokes the negative conditions of a postmodern spirituality, *without* disclaiming transcendence, *without* repudiating the contexts of values from which Faulkner's language derives its darker, distinctive energies.

The case, then, does not rest on Christian orthodoxy, nor on Biblical allusions scattered throughout his work. It rests, rather, on an intuition of kenosis, an idea of self-dispossession, so thorough as to create, and indeed maintain, that particular spirituality we both desire and lack in our clime. Thus the privations of postmodernism, stemming from its "indetermanences" and the decreations of radical doubt, mirror the same privations that Faulkner transmutes into the perennial possibilities of a spiritual life. And they mirror distractions that later writers decry—for instance Saul Bellow who avers: "The concern of tale-tellers and novelists is with the human essences neglected and forgotten by a distracted world."[16] The "human essences": Faulkner knows them.

In truth, William Faulkner has much to offer us, especially so-called postmodern critics more eager to "reread" him mingily than to confront his difficult, towering, lowering, and lasting achievement.

NOTES

1. Ihab Hassan, *The Dismemberment of Orpheus*, 2nd ed. rev. (Madison: University of Wisconsin Press, 1982), 269–71. But the term first appeared in my "Culture, Indeterminacy, and Immanence," *Humanities in Society* 1, 1 (Winter 1977–78).

2. Ihab Hassan, "The Expense of Spirit in Postmodern Times: Between Nihilism and Belief." *Georgia Review* 51 (1997): 9–26.

3. Hans Blumenberg, *The Legitimacy of the Modern Age*, trans. Robert M. Wallace (Cambridge: Harvard University Press, 1983), 136.

4. David Daiches, "Theodicy, Poetry, and Tradition," in *Spiritual Problems in Contemporary Literature*, ed. Stanley Romaine Hopper (New York: Harper and Brothers, 1952), 92.

5. William Faulkner, *Essays, Speeches, and Public Letters.*, ed. James B. Meriwether (New York: Random House, 1965), 120.

6. William Faulkner, *Faulkner at Nagano*, ed. Robert A. Jelliffe (Tokyo: Kenkyusha Ltd.,1956), 23–4.

7. Ralph Waldo Emerson, *Emerson in His Journals*, ed. Joel Porte (Cambridge: Harvard University Press, 1982), 43.

8. William James, *Pragmatism* (New York: Meridian Books, 1955), 61.

9. George Steiner, *Real Presences* (Chicago: Chicago University Press, 1989), 229.

10. *The Portable Faulkner*, ed. Malcolm Cowley (New York: Viking Press, 1946), 23.

11. William Faulkner, *Three Famous Short Novels: Spotted Horses, Old Man, The Bear* (New York: Random House, 1942), 170.

12. Friedrich Nietzsche, *The Will to Power*, ed. Walter Kaufmann, trans. Walter Kaufmann and R. J. Hollingdale (New York: Random House, 1967), 9.

13. See Donald M. Kartiganer's fine essay, "Faulkner's Art of Repetition," in *Faulkner and the Art of Fiction*, ed. Doreen Fowler and Ann J. Abadie (Jackson:University Press of Mississippi, 1989), 21–47.

14. Irving Howe, "Faulkner and the Southern Tradition," in *Literature in America*, ed. Philip Rhav (New York: Meridian Books, 1957), 412f.

15. Bernard Smith, *Modernism's History* (New Haven: Yale University Press, 1998), 354. See also his "Last Days of the Post Mode," *Thesis Eleven* 54(August 1988): 1–23.

16. Saul Bellow, *It All Adds Up: From the Dim Past to the Uncertain Future* (New York: Viking Penguin, 1994), 169.

Postmodern Intimations: Musing on Invisibility: William Faulkner, Richard Wright, and Ralph Ellison

Philip Weinstein

In the white world the man of color encounters difficulties in the development of his bodily schema.

—FRANTZ FANON

Three modern novelists of race relations: what in their work begins to appear—within our contemporary optic—as implicitly postmodern? How does their representation of the "invisible" racial subject intersect with a later postmodernism's more wholesale deconstruction of the subject? That is my question, and—since I plan to be critical myself—it may be best to begin on a cautionary note. Critics invested in postmodernism can be remarkably simpleminded about modernism. Their most strident remarks often have a déjà-vu quality, indicting modernism with the very naivetes that modernism used (a generation earlier) to indict realism: the centered subject, a foundational project, claims of disinterestedness and universality. Since this lazyminded approach to modernism drives me crazy, I need to be careful not to oversimplify postmodernism in the same ways.[1] For postmodern fiction has evolved in numerous directions, making a unified field theory impossible. How could the same characterizations have a purchase on textual worlds as different as Barthelme's parodic games, Italo Calvino's self-generating narratives, Gabriel García-Márquez's magic realism, and Toni Morrison's brooding reframing of American history?[2]

In what follows, the postmodernist generalizations I shall offer refer mainly to the brilliant, brittle American fictions of the '6os and '7os—typically white-male authored, self-reflexive, terminally playful. Its practitioners include Donald Barthelme, John Hawkes, Robert Coover, and John Barth; its philosophers include Roland Barthes, Jean-François Lyotard, Jean Baudrillard, and Richard Rorty; its commentators include Brian McHale and Linda Hutcheon. (These names, I know, hardly make up a school, but they do suggest some familial contours.) Rather than trying to say that such-and-such is postmodernism (a fruitless endeavor), I am talking about some of its salient tendencies. A penchant for the performance of roles rather than genuine identity, an insistence on parody, a conviction that texts cannot access the real but derive from and rewrite other texts, a suspicion about master narratives and a consequent leaning toward the "local," a Nietzchean preference for play/construction rather than truth/correspondence, a recurrence to pragmatic terms like "conversation," "utility," and "pleasure," a pervasive anxiety that the global spread of technological capitalism has erased the very meaning of "the individual" and that amnesiac/schizophrenic flight represents one of the few options still remaining: these are the stances I have in mind and that operate, in miniature, in Barthelme's minimalist definition of the "sentence": the sentence is "a manmade object, not the one we wanted of course, but still a construction of man, a structure to be treasured for its weakness, as opposed to the strength of stones."[3] Barthelme's postmodern "sentence" rebukes an earlier time's more ambitious sentence: play-artifice rather than truth-correspondence, language's weakness rather than its strength, a tone of wry acceptance of irreducible linguistic conditions rather than a raging desire to overcome them and somehow speak the real itself. These orientations radiate out of that little "sentence" and serve as context for the following argument about Faulkner, Wright, and Ellison.

I want to launch this musing on postmodern Yoknapatawpha, however, by citing a fourth novelist from the that postmodernist group identified above, John Barth. Before moving into the arena of borderline postmodern practices—as glimpsed in Faulkner, Wright, and Ellison—let's start with the real thing (slipping past postmodernism's horror at the notion of any "real thing"). Barth opens his 1958 novel *The End of the Road* with these arresting words, "In a sense, I am Jacob Horner."[4] In a sense only. Here we have a salient version of the postmodern subject: a fictional role I perform, a linguistic phrase that stands in for me (who I would be if my name really identified me). This sentence hooked me when I read it years ago, and even more the funny/terrible moment when putative Jacob Horner talks Rennie Morgan into eavesdropping on her dignified, all-American-type husband Joe. Rennie demurs: "*Real* people aren't any different when they're alone. . . . What you see of them is authentic." To this Horner replies: "Horseshit. Nobody's authentic. Let's look" (67). What they see is Joe Morgan in front of the mirror antically practicing the military moves that support his all-American mask, then rushing back to his writing desk, "his tongue gripped purposefully between his lips at the side of his mouth . . . masturbating and picking his nose at the same

time. I believe he also hummed a sprightly tune in rhythm with his work"
(70–1).

Musing on invisibility: for postmodern Barth identity is pure mask.
The chasm between the role-playing self visibly performed in public and
the incoherent self invisibly enacted in private is breathtaking, scandalous. This chasm between visible and invisible invalidates the very concept of authenticity: a state in which concealed and revealed would both
refer to an essential core. As the sinister "Doctor" in Barth's novel explains to Jacob Horner, identity has nothing to do with essence but is
rather a matter of visibly asserted masks, "Don't think there's anything
behind them: *ego* means *I*,and *I* means *ego*, and the ego by definition is
a mask. . . . If you sometimes have the feeling that your mask is *insin-
cere*—impossible word!—it's only because one of your masks is incompatible with another" (90). Behind the mask, beneath the role, deeper
than the language that proclaims it, there is—nothing: a nothing that
passes itself off as a something. As Baudrillard writes, "To dissimulate is
to feign not to have what one has," whereas "to simulate is to feign to
have what one hasn't."[5] Dissimulation is a staple of Western narratives—
what the Victorians comfortably called hypocrisy, a fullness of motive
seeking to conceal itself but always outed by the end of a Victorian novel:
Uriah Heep in a hundred different incarnations populates reassuringly
the vast stage of Victorian fiction. Simulation, however, is postmodern.
Identity in Barth's *The End of the Road* is a simulation, not a mask hypo-
critically concealing an essence but a mask deceptively standing in for a
void. It's an exhilarating idea.

For Faulkner's Joe Christmas, however, it is an unbearable idea, gen-
erating unassuageable nausea. Being no one—lacking essential identity,
empty at the core—is worse by far than having to be black: " 'I aint a
nigger' [little Joe Christmas says to the black man working at the orphan
yard] and the nigger says 'You are worse than that. You don't know what
you are. And more than that, you wont never know. You'll live and you'll
die and you won't never know.' "[6] It is desperate in Faulkner not to know
who we are—who our parents are, what our culture is, what racial, gender, and classed narratives have been internalized and shaped our identity. These arrangements have fundamentally formed and deformed us,
prior to consent and at a level beneath consciousness. It is not possible
in Faulkner to lack deep identity, although it is recurrent to suffer—often
fatally—from conflicting forms of identity that have been willy-nilly "in-
stalled" within us. "Memory believes before knowing remembers": Joe
Christmas's entire life exhibits a stunning unconscious consistency. The
crisis-moments Faulkner chooses to narrate Joe's becoming accumulate
to produce not a simulated selfhood masking emptiness but an overfilled

identity—intolerably coherent, however decentered—that must in the course of time erupt. His modernist invisibility has little in common with that of John Barth's postmodern characters. Seen or not seen, Christmas is, unfortunately, culturally marked to the core, doomed to be who he is.

To situate Faulknerian invisibility further and then move from it to the different kinds of invisibility operative in Wright and Ellison, I want first to backtrack to Dostoevsky. Whatever else they are doing, all three later writers are engaged in revising Dostoevsky, for *Notes from Underground* gives us Western literature's first invisible man. A low-grade Russian civil servant, Dostoevsky's underground man tortures himself by walking up and down Nevsky Prospect in St. Petersburg: invisible. He spends years seeking revenge for the insult of being, precisely, ignored. (An officer had ignored him by removing him bodily from the edge of a billiards table without noticing him). Ignored by others, he is also incoherent to himself: "And now I am living out my life in my corner, taunting myself with the spiteful . . . consolation that it is even impossible for an intelligent man seriously to become anything . . . only fools become something."[7] The two states seem inseparable yet incompatible: on the one hand, to be coherent for oneself (to be anything) involves being coherent for some others, i.e., recognizable to them. On the other hand, he passionately rejects all the terms for recognizability that his culture offers him: "only fools become something."

It is not so much that he is invisible as that he does not count: the forms of visible identity available to him are in the eyes of others socially demeaning and in his own eyes ideologically repellent. What he looks like is a failed petty bureaucrat, yet one who fiercely opposes that humiliating take upon him. Repudiate as he might St. Petersburg's official codes for self-making, he is alienated from any more traditional resources and is incapable of piecing together a viable identity of his own. He thus remains cravenly dependent for his self-esteem upon the very ones he scorns and who in turn scorn him.[8] "I'll show them" is the motto of the resentful misfit who cannot rise to conceptual rebellion and exit from the game altogether. His "refusal to accept a definition of himself . . . in terms imposed by the alien world of European culture" avails him nothing.[9] Dostoevsky pursues this plight of an overly intelligent man who will not be a disempowered functionary, yet who remains ensnarled within a bureaucratized social system that has dispossessed him of all native resources for self-making. In this text he goes underground, but by the following year Dostoevsky has found his way into the more sinister form of revenge such unharnessed and resentful energy must eventually take: murder, radical repudiation of the social pact that disempowers him.[10] Invisibility translates here as a humiliating impotence within a bureau-

cratized culture's identity norms, and Dostoevsky's next hero, Raskolnikov, even more pinched and beleaguered, launches with his murderous
act the novel that the subsequent ones I'm exploring could be named:
Crime and Punishment.

Dostoevsky's philosophic murder enters Faulkner's American canvas
as a race murder. It is race—rather than any set of maverick ideas beyond
traditional good and evil—that *Light in August* knows to be most explo-
sively invisible. Raskolnikov, scorning both the pieties of his orthodox
upbringing and the secular/bureaucratic assumptions of St. Petersburg,
raging at his fate as an insignificant intellectual misfit, aspires to Nietz-
schean revenge, a guiltfree murder.[11] Joe Christmas, by contrast,
wouldn't recognize an iconoclastic idea if it hit him over the head: what
he will not, cannot, make sense of—what releases his acts of violence—is
an incoherent racial inheritance. Christmas himself is achingly visible
(his parchment-colored skin is abusively witnessed by all), but his racial
identity is invisible, socially disappeared, biologically unknowable.
Faulkner creates him discontinuously, through a series of violent scenes:
beating Joe Brown in the early chapters, then the toothbrush-vomiting
scene when the dietitian calls him a "little nigger bastard," followed by
his adolescent beating of the black girl in the shed, his being ritually
beaten by McEachern over the catechism, his being beaten by Max and
the stranger at the end of his romance with Bobbie, and finally his beating Joanna Burden during their foredoomed affair. The question of Joe's
invisible racial identity coils within most of these scenes of assault; he
can access his racial identity only *as* a violent question. (When a prostitute fails to be scandalized by his announcement that he "is" black, he
nearly kills her; he requires repudiation to know himself.)

Deep identity in *Light in August* is perversely secured by such acts of
passionate aggression calling themselves "training." In Christmas, Faulkner shows us a man who is Calvinist in his behavior ("*I had to do it*," he
thinks before killing Joanna, "already in the past tense" [280]) though
believing in nothing, as well as a man who is black in the behavior visited
upon him ("nigger murderer" the town delights in labeling him), though
he himself is not culturally black nor is any biological basis for his racial
identity knowable. The social engine producing narratives of normative
identity is thus stripped of legitimacy—its knowledge base shown to be
a patchwork of rumor or assumption—but it does not therefore dismantle
itself, it just becomes more lethally effective. The training imposed by
social code now passes outside the realm of conscious pedagogy altogether, moving automatically into the muscles rather than engaging the
brain, issuing in murderous behavior that requires no foundation in arti-
culable belief or demonstrable fact. Identity in Jefferson is lodged deeper

than thought, producing a community that—at its worst—assumes every-thing and interrogates nothing. As Byron tells Hightower, "[Hines] knew somehow that the fellow [who called himself Mexican] had nigger blood. Maybe the circus folks told him. I don't know. He aint never said how he found out, like that never made any difference. And I reckon it didn't, after the next night" (374). That is, by the next night, the fellow (Milly's lover, also invisibly black) is as dead as Joe will be by the end of the novel. In the oppressively racist world of *Light in August*, no under-ground space exists in which the subject might be free of a culture's lethally polar predications; everyone must simply *be* white or black.[12] Racial invisibility emerges as worse than useless, enraging white folks in search of their tag and bringing down violence upon the putative black man, producing in Joe a ceaseless sadomasochism that he would gladly trade in for peaceful self-acceptance.

All of Faulkner's art is marshaled to give us the pathos of this undoing, for if we (like everyone else) never learn *who* he racially "is," we do learn—we alone learn—what it is like to *be* Joe Christmas: Faulkner posi-tions us overwhelmingly inside his sentient mind and nerves during the first half of the novel. Reversing expected sequences, giving us effects before we can fathom their causes, the form of *Light in August* patiently reveals the constructedness—the ungivenness—of all forms of racial, gender, and religious conviction, even as it shows the murderous insis-tence of a culture that cannot afford to interrogate its convictions.[13] Mod-ernist constructedness is thus a far cry from postmodern randomness.[14] The convictions represented in *Light in August* may be startlingly arbi-trary in the sense of ungrounded, but they are anything but arbitrary in the consequences they unleash. Put otherwise, he is not Joe Christmas in a sense, but Joe Christmas all the way. Though everyone inside the novel (including Joe) gets his identity wrong, though there is no way in Faulkner's 1930s South for anyone to get his identity "right," Joe Christ-mas has identity in surplus. "Horseshit. Nobody's authentic," Jacob Horner proclaimed. Christmas, however—not that it does him any good—is authentic. Mangled and mangling, abused and abusive, wound-ing others and finally crucified himself, Christmas's viciously acquired racial, gendered, and religious identity reveals the contradictory insis-tences of an entire culture: this is exactly why he matters. The mounting tension between the peace he inchoately seeks, inside, and the violence he suffers and is doomed in turn to inflict, outside, fuels the entire novel—giving us not the weightlessness of postmodern absurdity but the gravity of modernist tragedy.

A glimpse at the protagonists' names may help to make the same point. Raskolnikov's name carries the word "transgression" within it, but no one in the text finds him therefore fated. (He has a mother and a sister whose lives move along different emotional and ideological axes. There are several ways of being Raskolnikov; it is almost a normal name, lightly predictive for the reader but not compelling for the character.) At the other extreme is Jacob Horner. His name means nothing to him—there is and can be no family of Horners—it merely exists as the arbitrary word that others (including the reader) use to label him; it in no way serves to anchor his being or communalize his options. So far, Dostoevsky's realism and Barth's postmodernism; in between we have Faulkner's modernism. Joe Christmas's misnomer is no less absurd than "in a sense" Jacob Horner: but Faulkner's narrative loads this absurd name with increasing significance. Joe's name carries his entire past—not the family of Christmases who might (like Raskolnikovs) have bestowed it but the drunken workers at the Memphis orphanage who inflict the name as a bad joke on Christmas Eve, the scar of a name that McEachern dislikes and will seek to alter but which Joe secretly maintains, the sign of a set of inerasable memories and the portent of a doomed future. It is as unprivate, unserviceable, unsustaining, as a name can be, one that can neither be lived into normatively (like Raskolnikov) nor jettisoned like a no longer useful mask in a game one is no longer playing (like Horner). The symbolic order in *Light in August* thus all but screams its dysfunction at us in its way of allocating identity-narratives to its subjects. Yet Joe's painful, touching way of making that name his own ends by indissolubly fusing the polarity of "must matter" and "cant matter" that energizes Faulknerian narrative—a time-soaked polarity that, separated out, would give us the simpler coherences of Raskolnikov on the one hand, and Horner on the other. I turn now to Richard Wright.

Native Son appears eight years after *Light in August* as a sustained meditation upon both that book and *Crime and Punishment*. Since I have made this sort of cross-cultural literary claim more than once, I should acknowledge that, in a critical climate suffused with identity politics and committed to materialist cultural studies, my insistence that a black writer's text is deeply affected by the work of two white writers (one of them a nineteenth-century Russian) may seem offensively naive. I do not deny that it took a nightmarish childhood in racist Mississippi to launch Richard Wright's career, but that experience alone could not have produced his voice. As Ralph Ellison said in another context, the "main source of any novel is other *novels*; these constitute the culture of the form, and my loyalty to our group does nothing to change that."[15] Wright, I want to argue, is thinking through Dostoevsky and Faulkner, as well as the aggregate of his own cultural experience and imagination, when he composes *Native Son*.

The reverse of Joe Christmas, however, Bigger Thomas has visible racial identity—it is all people see—but he himself is not: his skin wholly conceals him. Faulkner's text, focused on his white culture's fear of racial contamination, zeroes in on the hysterical effects of a racial code when the visual cues it draws on to sustain its narratives are not forthcoming. Wright's text, however, focused on the deformity his culture has undergone at the hands of virulent white racism, zeroes in on the invisibly deformed subject wearing his all too visible black mask. As in *Light in August*, racial identity in *Native Son* may ultimately reduce to a set of convictions that constrain behavior, but Bigger eventually learns—more interestingly than Joe—how to do things with these convictions.[16] Until then, though, the convictions and practices that constitute the reality of race do things to him, things that seem to well up from his solar plexus through his arms and mind: "Mixed images of violence ran like sand through his mind, dry and fast, vanishing. He could stab Gus with his knife. . . . He could do a lot of things to Gus for making him feel this way."[17] Like Faulkner, Wright positions the reader immovably inside his protagonist's sensorium—virtually in Bigger's gut—and we as readers remain privy to his knotted contortions. The cultural codes that sustain racism have trained Bigger's mind by tyrannically controlling the feel and deployment of his body. At Dalton's house "He stood with his knees slightly bent, his lips partly open, his shoulders stooped; and his eyes held a look that went only to the surface of things. There was an organic conviction in him that this was the way white folks wanted him to be when in their presence" (54). Organic: Joe Christmas, the creation of a white author, is allowed to escape the race dimension of this awful organ-training—in more senses than one Faulkner gives him a "white" body—but Bigger's body is physical inheritor of hundreds of years of fearful servitude. It is an unconsciously trained body, the training begun long before Bigger's birth. Thus when Jan and Mary seek to change his bodily norms overnight (a naively arrogant move that precisely reveals their privilege), Wright conveys Bigger's bodily distress as these two white people cozy up next to him: "they made him feel his black skin by just standing here looking at him, one holding his hand and the other smiling. He felt he had no physical existence at all right then; he was something he hated, the badge of shame which he knew was attached to a black skin" (76). "Organically," like Joe Christmas, Bigger feels his culturally imposed body-borders being transgressed—"the man" is suffocating him—and he realizes, like Joe, that "something is going to happen to me." His race-engineered body is going to explode.

Once it does explode, something unexpected happens, and here is where *Native Son* departs from its parameters of Faulknerian doom. This apparently naturalist novel—the story of a man destroyed by social forces he can neither understand nor resist—suddenly becomes briefly post-modern. That is, it begins not only to foreground the linguistic but to see language as prior to the scenes language launches.[18] *Native Son* starts to play with its culture's differential narratives for licensing identity. Trapped within the very citadel of patriarchal space—the smothered girl's bedroom inside the Dalton mansion—Bigger starts (perhaps for the first time in his life) to reflect:

> And, after all, was not Jan a *Red*? . . . Fingerprints! He had read about them in magazines. . . . But suppose he told them that he had come to get the trunk? That was it! The *trunk*! His fingerprints had a right to be here. . . . But there was still a *better way*! Make them think that Jan did it. Reds'd do anything. Didn't the papers say so? . . . If Mary were missing when they got up, would they not think that she had already gone to Detroit? He. . . . *Yes*! He could, he could put her *in* the trunk! She was small. Yes; put her in the trunk. . . . He stooped to put her in the trunk. Could he get her in? . . . He pushed her head into a corner, but her legs were too long and would not go in. . . . [then after carrying her in the trunk down to the basement] He stared at the furnace. He trembled with another idea. He—he could, he—he could put her, he could put her in the furnace. He would *burn* her! That was the safest thing to do. . . . He had all but her shoulders in . . . her clothes were ablaze and smoke was filling the interior. . . . He gripped her shoulders and pushed hard, but the body would not go any farther. He tried again, but her head still remained out. . . . He got his knife from his pocket and opened it and stood by the furnace, looking at Mary's white throat. Could he do it? . . . Gently, he sawed the blade into the flesh and struck a bone. He gritted his teeth and cut harder. . . . But the bone made it difficult. . . . He whacked harder, but the head would not come off. . . . He *had* to burn this girl. With eyes glazed, with nerves tingling with excitement, he looked about the basement. He saw a hatchet. Yes! . . . He . . . sent the blade of the hatchet into the bone of the throat with all the strength of his body. The head rolled off. (100–6, emphases in original)

Bigger pulls off precisely the murder that *Crime and Punishment* is committed to make fail. Seeking a stance beyond his culture's imprison-ing norms of good and evil, Raskolnikov committed murder—only to find himself sinking into the torments of traditional guilt. His body could not bear the consequences of what his rebellious mind had irresponsibly pro-posed. The cautionary core of Dostoevsky's novel centers on just this lawfulness lodged within the subject at a level beneath thought. Bigger, however, rises into the freedom of amoral crime—a freedom profoundly troubling in its gender configuration yet intoxicating in its liberation from a white scenario of values.[19] Dismembering Mary, once clear of biblical codes of judgment (codes produced by and for "the man"), reduces to a hatchet job, an engineering problem. In a setting suddenly departing from humanism and reduced to pure pragmatics, Mary is so much matter to be disposed of. From this guiltless height Bigger assumes his own invisibility, resurveys the entire scene (its race-saturated biases startlingly visible to him, as though highlighted by ultraviolet), and he recognizes others' systemic blindness: "The very manner in which [his sister Vera] sat showed a fear so deep as to be an organic part of her" (122). "Organic": the word now characterizes behavior *others* take as nature but which Bigger decodes as training. This newfound grasp of the racial narrative being performed serves as a skeleton key that momentarily opens all doors.

He begins to manipulate, undetected, the part he earlier merely enacted. His "yessuh" sounds no different but it has become artful; his culture's repertory of scripts now cues—rather than suffocates—his "dumb nigger" agency. Communism, racism, the Leopold-Loeb case: these once opaque phenomena now become so many miniature narratives he is able to deploy, providing grist for his mill, motives for his gestures. He mixes and matches, making it up as he goes—a Lévi-Straussian bricoleur before Derrida ever glossed the term. Wright shows all the plays and players in this unfolding scenario to be scripted, but Bigger's invisibility consists in alone recognizing—and exploiting—the script he speaks. Not for a moment does he believe a word of it; he has become "in a sense Bigger Thomas." We are in the world of arbitrary language games, and in the presence of a sort of negotiated freedom that Michel de Certeau calls "tactics": "The space of a tactic," de Certeau writes, "is the space of the other. Thus it must play on and with a terrain imposed on it and organized by the law of a foreign power. It does not have the means to keep to itself, at a distance, in a position of withdrawal, foresight, and self-collection: it is a maneuver . . . within enemy territory."[20] Bigger needed a hatchet to take care of Mary, but all he needs is linguistic self-consciousness to handle Dalton and his minions. Like Hawthorne's Wakefield, Bigger thus becomes sublimely present at his own absence, watching others not see him. Wright fiendishly stations him in the very guts of the white master's home—tender of its flame and visible keeper of its domestic viability, secret murderer of its precious offspring. A successful Raskolnikov, a focused Joe Christmas, the invisible Bigger exults in the drama of Mary's corpse being only a few feet away from some of the most powerful men in Chicago speculating on its whereabouts.

I've called these scenes postmodern, by which I mean that they enact an almost manic release in Bigger's performance of roles others take to be natural. All is script and pastiche here; we are beyond the modernist longing for some authentic discourse uninflected by ideology. And Bigger is beyond ideology.[21] If for Dostoevsky the religious law has ceased to compel intellectual assent, it remains precious and—stubbornly encoded in Raskolnikov's body regardless of his mind's presumption—it ensures the transgressor's defeat. If for Faulkner the law has become race-deformed, a license for torture and murder when in the hands of Hines or McEachern or Grimm, we yet continue to register (from an implicitly white perspective) the gravity of social training, the tragic consequences of social training gone wrong. Like *Light in August*, *Native Son* knows that the law is the law, and it will make its protagonist die the death for his transgression, but it lets him briefly exercise his powers (enjoy a tactical success) before doing so.

More, Wright reveals, as perhaps only a black writer could reveal—in the dark comedy of Bigger's violent release—a racial world suddenly emptied of justification and tonically clarified. (Joe Christmas's crime is never revelatory in this way, never anything but an unavoidable mistake; Bigger's crime is no mistake at all, but terrifyingly pedagogic.) As linguistically limited as Joe, Bigger has yet learned to manipulate others' speech, to maneuver on their space, and to behave—nihilistically—as if there were no deeper purposes legitimizing this drama, ordering its unfolding. Indeed, Bigger reads this Foucauldian power scene so effectively that Wright is unable to provide any later justificatory narrative (including Max's) that Bigger will accept as a mirror for his own motives and behavior. Bigger cannot be mirrored; the text can provide no ideological frame that might hold him within its focus. In this protopostmodern novel everyone suddenly speaks only *language*. Awaiting his execution, Bigger remains not only invisible to others (his executioners think him a black beast while even Max sees him as just a black victim), but opaque to himself as well, lacking any conceptual schema that might turn his exalted moments of release into a new self-narrative. "Only through the intersubjectivity of community can consciousness become *self-consciousness*," Houston Baker says of the absence of epiphany here.[22] There are no others on this stage whom Bigger might recognize as potential extensions of himself, in whose company he might verbally reaccess himself. Instead, "he smiled a faint, wry, bitter smile. He heard the ring of steel against steel as a far door clanged shut" (502). On this implacable note *Native Son* ends.

Wright's "The Man Who Lived Underground" serves as the obvious segue between *Native Son* and *Invisible Man*. The postmodern elements glimpsed in *Native Son* are here more fully displayed; once again Dostoevsky gives Wright his cue. On the run from the cops for a murder he didn't commit, Fred Daniels goes literally underground, diving into a sewer. Become invisible himself, Daniels is now permitted to see every-thing. His sewer (no longer malodorous, transformed into a place of promise rather than of excretion) becomes a sort of Deleuzian rhizome, a line of escape underlying (and opening into) all the institutions of the city above ground (church, movie house, morgue, typing office, butcher shop, etc.). It is as though Wright had taken Bigger's furnace scenario of *Native Son* and made it *movable*. The earlier text's concealment trans-forms into the later text's mobility. To use de Certeau's terms, a *tactical* invisibility (confined to the enemy's territory) opens into a *strategic* invis-ibility (command of a new space liberated from the enemy's control).

A limitlessly networked Daniels outdoes not only Bigger Thomas but Robinson Crusoe in his capacity to gather up a culture's entire arsenal of goods. But Wright has Daniels do with those purloined goods what no realist novelist like Defoe could imagine: Daniels undoes their symbolic exchange value and recodes them as material objects of play. Light bulbs, paper money, guns with cartridges, diamonds: all of these are spread out and rearranged in Daniels's underground lair, regaining their original innocence, cleansed of their capitalist function as items men once competed for. This Utopian fantasy of a play-space—this deliberate in-fantilizing of capitalism's motives and objects that hold adults in thrall above—cannot elude the consequences of past time forever, and Daniels eventually chooses to exit from his underground kingdom of invisibility, suicidally confessing to the same cops who originally chased him. In an uncanny echo of both Raskolnikov and Christmas, Daniels thinks: "Why was this sense of guilt so seemingly innate, so easy to come by, to think, to feel, so verily physical? It seemed that when one felt this guilt one was retracing in one's feelings a faint pattern designed long before . . . but which had been forgotten by the conscious mind, creating in one's life a state of eternal anxiety."[23] Ultimately, the white man's guilt-centered law recaptures him, instilling its anxieties, and the black man relinquishes his interlude of invisibility, moves to accept his doom. In both these texts, then, the inevitable execution of a black man (recalling the race logic of *Light in August*) is only interrupted, played with, briefly reconceived out-side the law-supported necessity of racist annihilation. These are the hints that Ellison drew on to compose the jewel in this crown of invisibil-ity I have been analyzing.

Rewriting Fred Daniels's underground sewer, Ellison's *Invisible Man* opens in a Certeauvian play-space, replete with 1369 lights tactically "borrowed" from and operated by Monopolated Light and Power. The fact that "the man" monopolizes all the space above launches Ellison's postmodern revision of Dostoevskian and Faulknerian invisibility. Just as invisibility is mainly a defect in *Notes from Underground* and *Light in*

August (it launches no new models of selfhood, provides no landscape beyond the reach of hegemonic norms), it remains here—at the level of plot and theme—pure liability, the motif of victimization. But Ellison turns invisibility, at the same time, into an extraordinary formal resource. *Invisible Man* is not only unseen by others, his body is unseen by the text, and therefore unseen by the reader. Such furnishing of invisibility subtly turns the abuse that lodges in this novel's plot into the privilege that nourishes its narrative procedure, its way of producing its elusive, anonymous protagonist. Freed (so to speak) of a finite and penetrable body, immune to lasting bodily pain, he is allowed to become for the reader a mobile and inexhaustible repository of "soul."[24] As Ellison wrote in "What America Would Be Like Without Blacks":

> Without the presence of Negro American style, our jokes, our tall tales, even our sports would be lacking in the sudden turns, the shocks, the swift changes of pace (all jazz-shaped) that serve to remind us that the world is ever unexplored, and that while a complete mastery of life is mere illusion, the real secret of the game is to make life swing. It is the ability to articulate this tragic-comic attitude toward life that explains much of the mysterious power and attractiveness of that quality of Negro American style known as "soul."[25]

Invisible Man pulses with the insouciance of such articulated "soul." The memorable scenes in the novel are hallucinatorily written, with the narrator somehow adroitly detached even while technically present—immured yet uncaught. Beginning with the Battle Royal, then going on to the hypnotic Trueblood monologue and the manic scene at the Golden Day, followed by the extraordinary explosions at the Liberty Paints factory and the subsequent hospital scene, this book stages a set of carnivalistic tours de force—birthings and testings—that exceed anyone's sense of statistical reality, of what can happen to any single, embodied player. Few of these scandalous encounters would have their tonic effect, though, without a sort of comic-book bodily immunity on the part of the narrator. Even the Battle Royal and the hospital scenes (the ones where the most physical violence comes his way) are bathed in an unbruised narrational poise that allows supreme lucidity. He is never tired for long; he can't be kept down; his experience never damagingly entangles him. But we don't watch him anyway (we can't see him): we watch instead what he hallucinatorily narrates for us to see. That is, he performs at all times (and not only during the set speeches) as an orator, seducing most tellingly not his plotted audience but his myriad reader. This is seduction shorn of mastery, lucidity without omniscience—mastery and omniscience are "illusions"—but the secret is "to make life swing," and Ellison's narrator swings. All eyes and thought and forward-moving ambition (kept clear by Ellison of love or hate relations that might articulate his bodiness, halt his trajectory, and reveal his personal dimensionality), Invisible Man enacts a journey that stages instead the absurdity of institutional America.

"Play the game but don't believe in it,"[26] the Golden Day vet advises him, and though he may not catch up to this advice until many disillusionments later, its mix of naive investment and ironic detachment continuously enriches the texture of Ellison's narrative voice. Like Bigger momentarily, like Fred Daniels when underground, Invisible Man learns to play the prejudicial language games that play him. "I rapes real good when I'm drunk" (521), he assures Sybil, and this tactical exploitation of the stereotype he knows he embodies for others—this use of his invisibility—is almost wholly outside Joe Christmas's range. (Christmas, lacking any sense for how to manage racial prejudice except through violence, does rape, and not just when drunk.) Invisible Man adroitly talks his way out of almost every dilemma that entraps him. His wit and detachment—subtly abetted by bodily invisibility—grant him a sidestepping resourcefulness outside the range of Faulkner's and Wright's less vocal and more exposed, more finite protagonists. More than just a capacity to manage "the sudden turns, the shocks, the swift changes of pace," such adaptability on the part of his protagonist allows Ellison to reprise earlier fictional dilemmas and make them speak their larger-than-life potential: Bigger's crowded family scene blossoms into Trueblood's domestic scandal, Bigger and Gus's J. P. Morgan riff manically escalates into the Golden Day's General Pershing extravaganza. At its extreme such metamorphic flexibility in this novel takes on the name of Rinehart. An almost mythic figure, Rinehard supremely embodies (but that's not the right verb) the elasticity I've been describing in Invisible Man. You cannot see Rinehart; you only see his racial insignia—his dark glasses, his white hat—and these allow him to function in all the games he undertakes: runner, preacher, gambler, lover. He is the ultimate in unsanctioned performativity, in depthless simulacra: "And sitting there trembling I caught a brief glimpse of the possibilities posed by Rinehart's multiple personalities and turned away" (499).

"Turned away": I want to start to close this talk by suggesting why Ellison's novel turns away from its own postmodern investment in identity as simulacra, feigned and useful/discardable entities. The main reason lodges deep in the novel's political imagination. The ever-mobile Rinehart—lacking any core—carries no political promise, the static Ras the Destroyer—arrested on his single core-idea—promises only violence. In between, however, is the politics of race hauntingly voiced by Invisible Man himself. The Saul-become-Paul moment occurs when he wanders into the Harlem scene of eviction. Contingent wandering here catalyzes essential vocation, as he watches an old black couple being turned out, their lifetime possessions cast into the street: a portrait of them when young, a pair of "knocking bones," pots of plants, a straightening comb, a faded tintype of Abraham Lincoln, some cracked pieces of china, a folded lace fan, an old breast pump. . . . Hearing the old woman sob, registering it like the child who sees "the tears of its parents. . . . I turned away, feeling myself being drawn to the old couple by a warm, dark, rising whirlpool of emotion which I feared" (270). At this point he launches into his song/sermon of dispossession, a self-authenticating speech that takes these "evicted" items and reattaches them to the historical narrative that supplies their human meaning. The political resonance of that time-soaked narrative—its locating of objects within an overwhelmingly coherent racial history—is exactly the reverse of postmodern amnesia and its array of verbal signs emptied of reference, carrying only exchange value. Here is Baudrillard on the postmodern semiotic event: "At the limit of an always increasing elimination of references and finalities, an ever increasing loss of resemblances and designations, we find the digital and programmatic sign, whose 'value' is purely tactical"—a far cry from the sign as "bound, impregnated, and heavy with connotation" (22), the sign as metonymic reminder of a shared racial past.[27]

Ellison's novel achieves its surreal elasticity precisely by bypassing its protagonist's finite and embodied racial past. Apart from his grandfather he is without family connections; almost no experience seems to come earlier (or lodge deeper) than his college years. He has little unconscious life, few memories that believe before knowing remembers. Yet this novel draws decisively on the larger race history in which, all along, he involuntarily participates. (Here is his deepest difference from both Joe Christmas and Bigger Thomas, the one simply lacking in a race history—Faulkner could not supply it—the other seeking to escape a race history he registers as pure deformation.) However Invisible Man may try to soar beyond himself, body and past magically transcended, he remains inextricably race-oriented. His brotherhood speeches succeed only insofar as they sound this bass note of racial inheritance and dispossession.[28] Like a rhythmic undercurrent, this novel intimates the larger history of black bondage and freedom through its deployment of vivid, time-saturated, race-imbued items: Tod Clifton's Sambo doll, Tarp's leg shackle, the resonance of yams and chittelings, the snatches and "echoes of blues-toned laughter" (xvi). The narrator may seem deathless (bodiless, invisible), but his alter-ego, Tod Clifton, is not. Ellison reminds us that Tod's name signals death (in German), and Tod's massive funeral ceremony releases into articulation the long history of blacks cut down in their promise. Here, in in the rise and fall of this intensely described, poignantly finite, black body, Ellison returns to the pain of racial visibility that attaches American blacks to their ongoing history on these shores. In thus joining Faulkner and Wright in acknowledging a racial injustice that concludes in murder rather than hibernation, Ellison concedes the disfiguring power of the gaze, the injustice it has long caused and still causes—all this as necessarily prelude to the liberating politics such shared and testimonial suffering may yet launch.

Jacob Horner may be himself only "in a sense," but that novel too closes on the death of Rennie Morgan. We may not be ourselves for sure, but our bodies do surely become extinguished in time. My first-person plural pronoun is appropriately all-inclusive, yet can it be an accident that the desire to escape such extinction—a desire that underwrites the very trope of invisibility—attaches so readily to male protagonists? That it is especially males who seek to run, fly, and flee the fixing, finite-making, yet also communal gaze of the other: the gaze that makes you *seen*? Rennie Morgan is visible to a fault, so are Joanna Burden in *Light in August* and Bessie Mears in *Native Son*. Not only are all three of these women condemned by their texts to death, two of their deaths suggestively revolve about the phenomenon of pregnancy. Is the fact that each of us traces in our altering body a single, unrepeatable existence on earth a condition males never tire of imaginatively transcending, even as this condition registers so differently in the pregnant woman's body, a site that conjoins—simultaneously and unbearably—the realities of generativity, penetrability, and extinction? Is the fact, likewise, that these are among the loneliest narratives in American literature—hypnotic stories of invisible men who register the otherness of the social as shock and wound rather than awakening and possibility—is this cherishing of privacy better seen as a resource to be tapped or a neurosis to be analyzed?

Indeed, the functioning of social reality itself is premised upon visibility—to others and, reciprocally, to oneself as well. As John McGowan puts it in his study of postmodernism, "Just as the self is recognized by the community as a member of that group who occupies a certain position and possesses certain abilities, so the self must recognize the individual recognized by the group as himself" (246). From underground man to invisible man: here precisely is the cost of invisibility, the cultural price that nonrecognition imposes, the isolation it both suffers from and seeks out. Richard Rorty tends to find such nonreciprocity productively liberating: the postmodern ironist, he writes, "is not in the business of supplying himself and his fellow ironists with a method, a platform, or a rationale. He is just doing the same thing all ironists do—attempting autonomy" (97). Autonomy, yes, but didn't Faulkner's ironical Mr.

Compson seek out the same value, imagining himself as socially invisible and betraying the responsibilities of community in the same way? It may be Levinas rather than Barthes who best points us to the requirement that we *be* visible—recognizable to, answerable for, the array of others who necessarily constitute our scene. As Edith Wyschogrod (a writer deeply influenced by Levinas) claims, "It is the vulnerability of the other that challenges the structure of the self as an egology. When the other appears she does not emerge as an object in the world or even a person . . . but as a proscriptive moral datum. Coordinate with her sheer existence, built into it as it were, is her vulnerability which acts as a solicitation and a proscription: 'Do not injure me.' "[29]

"Do not injure me": to what extent do the invisible men in the texts I've examined exercise an "egology" perilously restricted to the first-personal singular pronoun, and disturbingly liable to the injuring of others—especially women—in their pursuit of autonomy? Such questions go further than I can take them, but I could not relinquish this musing on invisibility without at least suggesting the profound uninnocence of the trope. Be that as it may, I began with one postmodernist, Barth, on the ruse of "not being there," and I conclude with another postmodernist, Rushdie, on the stakes of "being there." As Rushdie beautifully puts it in *The Satanic Verses*, "The world is the place we prove real by dying in it."[30] Faulkner, Wright, and Ellison (good modernists all) would not have worded it that way, but their imagination of race finds the world proved real for kindred reasons. Without the concomitant reality of others irrevocably related to us, vulnerable to pain and ultimately to death—as we are—the individual trajectory would have little resonance, its autonomy be of little value. All three writers compel our attention insofar as they honor the gravity of our group-shared yet unrepeatable passage, the ultimate cost and value of our inhabiting bodies that remain—however misrecognized—visible in space and extensive in time.

NOTES

1. Apart from numerous brilliant articles, the booklength studies of postmodernism from which I have most benefited are those of Andreas Huyssen (*After the Great Divide: Modernism, Mass Culture, Postmodernism* [Bloomington: Indiana University Press, 1986]), John McGowan (*Postmodernism and Its Critics* [Ithaca: Cornell University Press, 1991]), and David Harvey (*The Condition of Postmodernity* [Oxford: Blackwell's, 1989]). Each of these writers refuses to romanticize postmodernism as a heroic repudiation of all that has gone before. Instead, they explore the intricate ways in which postmodern developments both proceed from and call into question a range of modernist assumptions (beginning with the Enlightenment), within a broad spectrum of human endeavors (arts, sciences, philosophy, and architecture, most prominently). They all refuse, that is, the shrill rhetorical amazement that, in Robert Siegel's words, we could "ever have supposed that represen-

tations were anything but words, that consciousness was anything but words, that 'Man' was more than a representation, a life in words punctuated by bursts of the inhuman" ("Postmodernism TM", in *Modern Fiction Studies* 41:1 [Spring 1995]: 178). More persuasive, in my view, is Linda Hutcheon's qualified claim that "It is not that representation now dominates or effaces the referent, but that it now self-consciously acknowledges its existence as representation" (*The Politics of Postmodernism* [London: Routledge, 1989], 34).

2. For the purposes of this argument, Morrison and Calvino are both considered postmodernists. It might be more fruitful, however, to analyze Morrison's work within a postcolonial frame of assumptions, for the reconception of a stable (but not bourgeois-appropriative) subject is as important a task of postcolonial literature as the dismantling of the bourgeois-appropriative subject is critical to much postmodern literature.

3. Donald Barthelme, "Sentence," in Gerhard Hoffmann and Alfred Hornung, ed., *Ethics and Aesthetics: The Moral Turn of Postmodernism* (Heidelberg, 1996), 118.

4. John Barth, *The End of the Road* (1958; New York: Bantam, 1967), 1. Subsequent citation refers to this edition.

5. Jean Baudrillard, "Simulacra and Simulations," in *The Baudrillard Reader*, trans. Mark Poster (Stanford: Stanford University Press, 1988), 167.

6. William Faulkner, *Light in August: The Corrected Text*, ed. Noel Polk (New York: Vintage International, 1990), 384. Subsequent citation refers to this edition.

7. Fyodor Dostoevsky, *Notes from Underground*, trans. Richard Pevear and Larissa Volokhonsky (New York: Vintage, 1994), 5.

8. Dostoevskyan commentary, cushioned by existentialist clichés, typically misses this darker, failed dimension of the Underground Man, preferring instead to speak of his rebellion as an "affirmation of the supreme worth of the individual" (Michael Lynch, *Creative Revolt: A Study of Wright, Ellison, and Dostoevsky* [New York: Peter Lang, 1990], 37).

9. Joseph Frank, "Ralph Ellison and a Literary 'Ancestor': Dostoevsky," in *The New Criterion* 2:1(1983): 12.

10. The "underground" is not only a capacious and fluid concept in Dostoevsky's work—embracing simultaneously geographic, economic, psychological, religious, and philosophic realms—but its usage also alters significantly during his career. The mainly negative resonance of "underground" in the 1865 *Notes* gives way to a range of creative reverberations in Dostoevsky's last novel, *The Brothers Karamazov* (1882). See Monroe Beardsley's essay (in *Notes from Underground*, trans. Serge Shishkoff [New York: Crowell, 1969], 229–60) for further commentary.

11. See Joseph Frank's five-volume biography of Dostoevsky (esp. vols. 2 and 3) for a useful mapping of the ideological climate operative in St. Petersburg during the 1850s and 1860s, when Dostoevsky was coming into his powers as a novelist. For an extraordinary reading of the functioning of ideology within Dostoevsky's work, see Mikhail Bakhtin's *Problems in Dostoevsky's Poetics* (trans. Caryl Emerson [Minneapolis: University of Minnesota Press, 1984]).

12. Such rabid insistence on racial markers may testify to a postwar American South of the 1920s in which these markers were becoming suddenly less reliable. Daniel Singal argues that "[t]owns that had been relatively stable suddenly experienced a sizable influx of strangers whose origins were wholly unknown. Where once it had been highly unlikely for a resident to have 'black blood' without the town knowing of it, the system of community genealogy was now doomed" (*The War Within: From Victorian to Modernist Thought in the South, 1919–1945* [Chapel Hill: University of North Carolina Press, 1982], 182).

13. For further commentary on the creative interplay (in Faulkner's great work) of the forms of modernist doubt with the contents of traditional knowledge, see my *What Else But Love? The Ordeal of Race in Faulkner and Morrison* (New York: Columbia University Press, 1996), 167–72, 185–9.

14. To put it perhaps more succinctly: if *As I Lay Dying's* "just a shape to fill a lack" is Faulkner's most haunting formulation for the arbitrariness of words, then a good deal of postmodern fiction takes this arbitrariness as inalterable. The human drama becomes parody because it is unavoidably told second-hand, in that realm of weakness we call words. But Faulkner seemed to believe that, although we *tell* our lives "in the air," we *live* our

lives, unspeakably, "on the ground." In his most compelling work he invents, as no post-modernist seeks to, an unspeakable ground language. This local distinction is also a larger one between modernist and postmodernist ambitions. As Gianni Vattino puts it in *The End of Modernity* (1985, trans. Jon R. Snyder [Baltimore: Johns Hopkins University Press, 1988]), "From architecture to the novel to poetry to the figurative arts, the postmodern displays, as its most common and imposing trait, an effort to free itself from the logic of overcoming, development, and innovation" (105).

15. Ellison cited in Thomas Whitaker, "Spokesman for Invisibility," in Kimberley W. Benston, ed., *Speaking for You: The Vision of Ralph Ellison* (Washington, D.C.: Howard University Press, 1997), 401.

16. Although I stand by this claim as generally true of Joe Christmas, *Light in August* offers several moments of memorable exception: whenever Joe muses sardonically on his racial "inheritance," and most movingly during the last days of his flight from trial (331–9). The man who returns voluntarily to Mottstown, enters a white barbershop and gets a shave, then waits patiently until he is "recognized" by the white racists—this is someone so abreast of the signs of his own racial constructedness that he all but performs these signs as a sort of Irigarayan mimicry: waiting bemusedly for someone to take his social play for social reality, as prelude to the business of executing him. What Joe is actually thinking and feeling during this mysterious "endgame" is scrupulously kept from us: all Faulkner lets us see are the rabidly inadequate constructions of him made by others.

17. Richard Wright, *Native Son* (1940; New York: HarperPerennial, 1993), 29–30. This edition uses the Library of America restored text of *Native Son*; subsequent citation refers to this edition.

18. Only Ross Pudaloff, to my knowledge, has glimpsed this postmodern dimension of *Native Son*: "Wright himself specifically called for literature to go 'beyond the realism of the novel' in order to create a novel 'bigger, different, freer, more open.' Such a novel . . . is Thomas Pynchon's *Gravity's Rainbow*, especially in its characterization of Tyrone Slothrop. . . . [Slothrop's] discovery [that he has no inherent self] . . . does not, however, allow him to express his true feelings and develop the authentic self that Marxism, Freudianism, the traditional novel, and nineteenth-century culture as a whole promised. Rather, Slothrop disappears; he scatters. He has no self and no identity beyond that which was imposed on him. . . . [*Native Son*] prefigures the writings of Thomas Pynchon and Ishmael Reed more than it extends the literary and philosophical traditions of realism or modernism" ("Celebrity as Identity: *Native Son* and Mass Culture," in Henry Lewis Gates and Anthony Appiah, ed. *Richard Wright: Critical Perspectives Past and Present* [New York: Amistad Press, 1993], 119).

19. Faced with Mary's corpse, most commentary on *Native Son* is (not surprisingly) concerned to downplay Bigger's transformation. John Reilly's remarks are typically corrective: "With false confidence growing out of a failure to comprehend that the exhilaration he feels after murdering Mary is private and ephemeral. . . ." ("Giving Bigger a Voice: The Politics of Narrative in *Native Son*," in Keneth Kinamon, ed., *New Essays on Native Son* [New York: Cambridge University Press, 1990], 54–5). Reilly has reinserted the act of murder within a larger humanist schema that undoes its liberating effect. Wright's text, however, scrupulously follows Bigger's moment by moment consciousness, refusing to harness his movement of mind to greater paradigms of either indictment or approbation.

20. Michel de Certeau, *The Practice of Everyday Life*, trans. Stephen Rendall (Berkeley, University of California Press, 1988), 37.

21. By "beyond" I do not mean that Bigger has found his way into some region untouched by ideology. I mean, rather, that *Native Son* proposes no ideological schema that can contain Bigger's gesture and render it coherent—by proposing a way of life within which that gesture would become replicable and self-orienting.

22. Houston Baker, "Reassessing (W)right: A Meditation on the Black (W)hole," in *Modern Critical Views*, Richard Wright, ed. Harold Bloom (New York: Chelsea House, 1987), 137.

23. Richard Wright, "The Man Who Lived Underground," in *Eight Men* (New York: Thunder's Mouth Press, 1987), 68.

24. Invisible Man's invisibility has been, virtually since the book's appearance in 1952, a debated issue. Noting how a range of critics in the 1960s worried about this dimension of the protagonist, Thomas Whitaker argues that the book's rhetorical power requires this bodily absence and vocal flexibility. Invisible Man's eloquence exceeds any single owner-ship of it; his "form is no 'object' but a nexus of conversations with ancestors, contemporar-ies, and readers" ("Spokesman for Invisibility," in Benston, 401). He registers most deeply as a *linguistic* enterprise. Not all contemporary readers agree with Whitaker, and Claudia Tate makes a compelling counterclaim: "I predict that the Invisible Man's efforts to leave the underground, though valiant, will be aborted time and again, since he has no mother to give him birth. . . . He is knowledge without matter; he is a child unborn, suspended between the fact of his conception and the impossibility of his birth" ("Notes on the Invisi-ble Women in Ralph Ellison's *Invisible Man*," in Benston, 171). Tate's argument allows one to glimpse a disturbingly unintended irony in Invisible Man's rewriting of Stephen Deda-lus's "the uncreated conscience of his race" as "the uncreated features of his face" (354): these facial features remain, precisely, uncreated.

25. Ralph Ellison, "What Would America Be without Blacks?" in *Going to the Territory* (New York: Vintage, 1987), 109–10.

26. Ralph Ellison, *Invisible Man* (1952; New York: Vintage, 1989), 153. Subsequent cita-tion refers to this edition.

27. Baudrillard, "Symbolic Exchange and Death," in *The Baudrillard Reader*, 139–40.

28. Michel Fabre cites a letter from Ellison to Wright—written years before *Invisible Man* was published—that sheds light on the later novel's dynamic of memory and forget-ting: "Back when I first knew you [Ellison writes], remember, I often speculated as to what it was that made the difference between us and the others who shot up from the same region. . . . I think it is because the past which filters through your book [*Native Son*] has always been tender and alive and aching within us. We are the ones who had no comforting amnesia of childhood, and for whom the trauma of passing from the country to the city of destruction brought no anaesthesia of consciousness, but left our nerves peeled and quiver-ing" ("From *Native Son* to *Invisible Man*: Some Notes on Ralph Ellison's Evolution in the 1950s," in Benston, 211). That Ellison could see a tenderness toward the past in *Native Son*—where it seems to me none exists whatsoever—reveals just how important such mem-ories were to him (rather than Wright) as he negotiated his journey northward to the city. Eleven years later *Invisible Man* will makes good on this intricate temporal investment, even as the novel works repeatedly to deprive its protagonist of the specifics of his own past. What emerges, miraculously, is the sense of a *people*'s past.

29. Edith Wyschogrod, "Towards a Postmodern Ethics: Corporeality and Alterity," in *Ethics and Aesthetics*, 66.

30. Salman Rushdie, *The Satanic Verses* (Dover: The Consortium, 1992), 533.

Postmodern Yoknapatawpha: William Faulkner as Usable Past

JOHN N. DUVALL

In his famous essay, originally published in 1967 and titled "The Literature of Exhaustion," John Barth speaks of the way that the modernist thematic of alienation may have played itself out; this did not mean, however, that the novel as a genre was exhausted. Barth uses two writers to illustrate this point—Samuel Beckett and Jorge Luis Borges. Beckett's empty stages and late novels represent, as Barth puts it, the used-upness of modernist alienation; moreover, Beckett's turn to silence may be the last best representation of the failure of language to ever say what one means. Borges, however, takes that "felt ultimacy" of the end of the road of modernist thematics and returns, through his metafiction to "rediscover validly the artifices of language and literature."[1] In this paper, I wish to explore what happens when William Faulkner becomes one of the "felt ultimacies" for contemporary writers. By doing so, I hope to chart a portion of the postmodern by discussing what happens when Faulkner's texts are appropriated as part of a usable aesthetic past. This does not mean that every contemporary narrative that employs Faulkner is necessarily postmodern. For example, Graham Swift's 1996 Booker Prize–winning novel, *Last Orders*, chronicles an automobile trip to scatter the ashes of an English butcher and is narrated in a number of short sections by the dead man's friends and family. Each section is headed by the name of that character. One chapter is only one sentence long, and there is even one section narrated by the dead man himself. Clearly, *Last Orders* pays homage to Faulkner's *As I Lay Dying*. But Swift's use of perspectivism in 1996 does not at all feel like a tour-de-force formal experiment; rather, it seems conventionally mimetic, more like realism even than modernism.

   Closer to what I mean by Faulkner as one of the "felt ultimacies" for contemporary writers can be found in the elegant meditation on Faulknerian poetics by the Caribbean poet, playwright, and critic Edouard Glissant. In the years to come, his *Faulkner, Mississippi*, recently translated into English, may well stand to Faulkner studies as Charles Olsen's *Call Me Ishmael* stands to Melville studies. In his call for a radically other reading of Faulkner, Glissant portrays a Faulkner who is already post-modern, producing a discourse that is characterized by absence and defer-ral. Near the end of his study, Glissant speaks of the legacy of Faulkner's work; even if Faulkner's conclusions cannot serve in the contemporary moment, "The unbounded openness of [his] work is such that anyone can find a suitable path among those Faulkner proposes without betraying or losing oneself. He is not one of those authors that squelch the imagina-tion of those they reach, who from then on pathetically repeat the same old stories, supposedly inspired by masters."[2] Glissant goes on to identify a series of writers whose work responds to Faulknerian poetics, including Flannery O'Connor, Alejo Carpentier, William Styron, Gabriel García Márquez, and Toni Morrison. Where I turn my attention now is to two such radically other readings of Faulkner that have appeared in novel form during the 1990s—Kathy Acker's *In Memoriam to Identity* and Toni Morrison's *Jazz*.

Both Acker and Morrison in specific instances have systematically ap-propriated elements of William Faulkner's representations of masculin-ity. Although very different in their prose style and subject matter, both contemporary novelists have been identified as postmodern. In part their postmodernism can be attributed to how they approach canonical mod-ernist texts; the very fact that Faulkner exists for these two writers as part of the aesthetic past announces their temporal distance from high modernism. One significant frame that allows one to place Acker and Morrison together is Linda Hutcheon's concept, "historiographic meta-fiction," which is her term for postmodern narrative. For Hutcheon, post-modern fiction blends the reflexivity of metafiction with an ironized sense of history and the aesthetic past; this mix foregrounds the distinction "between brute *events* of the past and the historical *facts* we construct out of them."[3] In doing so, such fiction draws one's attention to the prob-lematic status of representation. As a vehicle for cultural critique, histo-riographic metafiction plays a paradoxical role because it "depends upon and draws its power from that which it contests."[4] A form of cultural critique may proceed, but it is always aware of its own implication. Hut-cheon's celebration of the power of postmodern parody to produce his-torical thinking stands in direct opposition to the Marxist critic Fredric Jameson and his despair over postmodernism, which for him is not an oppositional aesthetic but only the cultural logic of multinational capi-talism.

For Jameson, postmodernism merely participates in the erasure of his-tory because it fails to provide a new aesthetic form that could comment critically on contemporary culture. From his perspective, postmodern aesthetics and narrative are characterized by pastiche. Parody, Jameson asserts, still flourished "in the idiosyncrasies of the moderns and their 'inimitable' styles" such as "the Faulknerian long sentence," but the notion of any linguistic norm has disappeared "into a host of distinct private styles," the result of which is that modernist styles have become postmodern codes:

> In this situation parody finds itself without a vocation; it has lived, and that strange new thing pastiche slowly comes to take its place. Pastiche is, like parody, the imitation of a peculiar or unique, idiosyncratic style, the wearing of a linguistic mask, speech in a dead language. But it is a neutral practice of such mimicry, without any of parody's ulterior motives, amputated of the satiric impulse, devoid of laughter and of any conviction that alongside the abnormal tongue you have momentarily borrowed, some healthy linguistic normality still exists. Pastiche is thus blank parody, a statue with blind eyeballs. . . .[5]

The remainder of this paper will look at selected moments from Acker's and Morrison's engagement with Faulkner and his representation of masculinity to see how their fiction goes about producing critique. At the same time, I will use the differences between these two novelists' critical appropriations of Faulkner to raise a question about Jameson's pastiche and Hutcheon's parody as the master tropes for postmodernism. Masculinity in Faulkner, refracted through these postmodern lenses, may help us think about contemporary narrative and its relation to the possibilities of historical thinking. Acker's more openly parodic revision of Faulkner, I believe, may actually participate in the flattening of history, while Morrison's pastiche effectively opens a space for thinking historically.[6]

Much less well known than Nobel Prize–winning author Toni Morrison, Kathy Acker, who died of cancer at age forty-nine in 1997, more immediately seems to fall into the category "postmodern." Acker's novels at times seem to function less as works of fiction than as sustained pieces of performance art that double as acts of literary and social criticism. Her style, identified variously as post-punk feminism and post-punk porn, invokes traditions ranging from the Marquis de Sade to William S. Burroughs. Prior to *In Memoriam to Identity*, Acker had published novels with titles such as *Great Expectations* and *Don Quiote*. But rather than attempt (as Borges' character, Pierre Menard does) to reproduce *Quiote*, Acker plagiarizes in order to destroy the earlier text, fragmenting the intertext, denying it any formal integrity. Denying formal integrity to work from the past is a crucial part of Acker's attempt to develop a deconstructive aesthetic that questions the Cartesian *cogito*, as her very title—*In Memo-*

riam to Identity—suggests. A recurring subject in her work is the effec-
tiveness of masochism as the starting point for a feminist politics.
Masochism becomes the tool that can perform the epistemological destruction of cultural representations of the feminine. Acker positions herself against the separatist feminism of Andrea Dworkin, and yet oddly
seems to grant Dworkin her major premise, namely that male sexuality
is based on power and rape.[7] Acker's thinking depends on an absolutizing
of a now familiar feminist distinction between sex and gender, wherein
sex is the baseline of nature and the body, while gender is the enactment
of cultural roles. For Acker, the exaggerated and self-consciously extreme
enactment of feminine masochism deconstructs that cultural role and
leads to women's empowerment and a less mediated relation to the body.

In *In Memoriam to Identity*, Acker appropriates countless pieces of
Rimbaud and Faulkner. Her borrowings, though, are misrepresented in
the oddly academic note that appears on the final page: "All of the preceding has been taken from the poems of Arthur Rimbaud, the novels of
William Faulkner, and biographical texts on Arthur Rimbaud and William Faulkner."[8] This characterization is inaccurate because Acker does
more than simply cut and paste from earlier texts; rather, she constructs
a new narrative, which she clearly intends as a critique of patriarchal
forms of sexuality and identity. Some of her reworkings of Faulkner
would be recognized by a number of readers, such as her reformulated
quotations from *The Sound and the Fury*, but other moments in her text
minimally revise passages from less well-known Faulkner novels, such as
Sanctuary, *The Wild Palms*, and the seldom-read *Pylon*.[9] The two main
female characters are named Capitol and Airplane, which suggests the
anti-representational element of this fiction.

Acker engages the Faulknerian intertext in order to critique his portrayal of gender—both female masochism and male voyeurism. Her character Airplane is a condensation of Faulkner's Temple Drake and
Laverne Shumann, while Capitol blends elements of Caddy Compson,
her daughter Quentin, and Charlette Rittenmeyer. Both Airplane and
Capitol embrace a potentially liberating masochism as a bodily site for
constructing women's empowerment. But even as Acker attempts an in-
tervention in contemporary gender politics, she may end up participating
in the erasure of history that Jameson identifies as a problematic feature
of postmodernism. Quite simply, her appropriation of the aesthetic past
serves to erase historical difference because Faulkner's own attempt to
represent his culture's gender difference is effaced.

In Memoriam to Identity is structured in four main sections—
"Rimbaud," "Airplane," "Capitol," and "The Wild Palms." The first section is a version of Rimbaud's life and homosexual relation with Verlaine.

The next two sections introduce Airplane's and Capitol's narratives. The final section, structured like Faulkner's *The Wild Palms*, contrapuntally alternates Airplane's and Capitol's stories. In the "Rimbaud" section, one sees Acker establish her thematic concern for dismantling bourgeois identity. Verlaine is the villain because his socially scripted roles of father and husband constantly pull him away from his homosexual relationship with Rimbaud. Rimbaud initially is the good guy because, out of his Romantic idealism, he follows his masochistic homosexual impulses to achieve an identity less implicated in oedipally inflected subjectivity.

But Rimbaud turns out to be another bad guy. As Acker tells Larry McCaffery, her novel began as a life of Rimbaud: "But when I came to the end of the affair with Verlaine I thought, 'This guy became a fucking capitalist! He's like a yuppie, I can't do this. I'm bored out of my mind' "; being in England at the time, Acker claims to have missed the United States and started thinking about the myth of America: "That's where the Faulkner material started coming in. I've always felt Faulkner was *the* American writer, and gradually the book started taking off."[10] (In the latter parts of the novel, Rimbaud does return, only as a version of Faulkner's Jason Compson.)

In order to understand how Acker's novel "takes off" from Faulkner, I will briefly summarize the plot of "Airplane," the second section of the novel. Airplane is a coed at the University of Connecticut. Her father is a judge. One night, she and a date, who are underage, go out driving, looking for alcohol. After the intoxicated boyfriend crashes his car, the couple stumbles onto a house of drunken men and a former prostitute who cooks for them. The ex-prostitute tells Airplane that the latter does not know what it is to be desired by a man and explains that the nature of male-female relations is sadomasochistic. One of the men, known as "the feeb," tries to protect Airplane but still tries to initiate sex with her, inviting her to lie down, telling her "It won't hurt you none" (*IM* 110). The "feeb," however, is shot and killed by another man who then rapes Airplane. Still bleeding between her legs, Airplane is driven by the rapist to the city where he installs her at an establishment known as FUN CITY, a club that features live sex shows. Aiplane makes the decision to survive, to use the rapist because she intuits that "somewhere in sexuality was her strength" (*IM* 114).

Faulknerians, of course, immediately recognize Acker's appropriation of the story of *Sanctuary*. But even at the level of discourse, it is apparent how parodically Acker's creative process works.[11] To see this more clearly, I have placed Faulkner's and Acker's texts against each other, the opening of Chapter 4 of *Sanctuary* on the left and material from the second page of Acker's "Airplane" section on the right (see table).

Townspeople taking after-supper drives through the college grounds or an oblivious and bemused faculty-member or a candidate for a master's degree on his way to the library would see Temple, a snatched coat under her arm and her long legs blonde with running, in speeding silhouette against the lighted windows of the Coop, as the women's dormitory was known,	The "townies," rough boys, all had cars. Driving when the sun had descended into its half-light, serene gold lying over the tennis court like a blanket, or without an auto, snooping around the grounds, he or a professor (who was covertly searching for one of his young female students) would see this girl, snatched jacket under her right arm, long unshaven unstockinged legs wet from running, in speeding silhouette against "The Castle" (an actual castle brought over from England, brick by brick, the college legend had it, do be a dorm). Only girls lived in this place, but some of them sneaked males, if they were steady boyfriends, into their rooms. Then, vanishing into the
vanishing into the shadow beside the library wall, and perhaps a final squatting swirl of knickers or whatnot	shadows in the back of the library, where Harriet had seduced a creep into taking off his dirty underpants, not in order to make love with him, but so all of her girlfriends hiding in the bushes could laugh at him; then emerging, only to spring, with a sudden show, not of underpants . . . but
as she sprang into the car waiting there with engine running on that particular night. The cars belonged to town boys.[12]	of nothing . . . into the particular car that was waiting on that particular night. (*IM* 101–02, ellipses original)

At the micro level of language, one sees Acker's urge to dismantle the Faulknerian intertext. The male voyeurs of *Sanctuary* are rewritten in order to expose their pleasure, literally and metaphorically. Faulkner's bemused and oblivious professor is recast as a sexual predator. Rather than the vague male longing of those who hope to catch a glimpse of Temple's underwear, one of the men in Acker's version is teased into removing his underwear, thus becoming the object of a humiliating female gaze. One might also note that Acker refigures Faulkner's fetishizing of female legs. Temple's legs are "blonde from running," his impressionistic figuration of her legs, while Airplane's unshaved legs are, more logically, wet from running.

Despite the obviousness of the parody at the discursive level, the larger critique of Faulkner might be questioned for what it fails to recognize. In this instance, Acker's representation of Faulknerian male voyeurism does not acknowledge that *Sanctuary* itself works to problematize that male gaze by interrogating the ways that the father as (at least potential) rapist stands ready to emerge from the public persona as the father who protects the daughter. Popeye the rapist at the Old Frenchman place very quickly becomes Popeye the voyeur whom Temple calls "Daddy" in Memphis. Conversely, both Horace Benbow and Judge Drake, good daddies, imaginatively participate in the rapes of their own daughters.[13]

So Acker is surely correct when she disrupts the flow of her narrative to insert the following parenthetical metacommentary:

> (In Faulkner's novels, men who are patriarchs either kill or maim by subverting their daughters. Every daughter has a father; every daughter might need a father. One result, a critic who perhaps does not like women has said, is that women have shifting identities [perhaps it is men who don't recognize the shifting nature of identity], as sluts [is a whore a slut? was the reporter a slut?] have a hankering for evil.) (*IM* 220; brackets original)

In her summary of an unnamed critic's position on Faulkner's women, Acker clearly recognizes a strain of misogyny prevalent until quite recently in Faulkner studies. Yet the passage also indicates the tendency of her fiction to level the past. For Acker, every canonical male text can only be another instance of transhistorical patriarchy. But I would argue that Faulkner's mapping the psychology and metaphysics of paternalism in the American South is not necessarily an endorsement of patriarchy. Acker speaks above of Faulkner's patriarchs, but what does she say about Faulkner's men who are *not* patriarchs?

Acker's appropriation of Quentin Compson serves as a useful site to begin to answer this question because it is in her Quentin that she reduces Faulknerian masculinity to a one-dimensional sameness. In the "Capitol" section of *In Memoriam*, Quentin returns from Harvard and is troubled that his sister, Capitol, is having sex with every man in town. Capitol and Quentin go for a walk together down to a pond. She enters the water and gets her dress wet and muddy. She realizes that the real reason Quentin is concerned about her sex life is that he wants to have sex with her, so she takes charge and they have sex. Afterward, they talk and Capitol explains that she hates the men with whom she has sex, except for Quentin. Quentin then masturbates in her face. She rubs his semen into her face and they return home. On the way, Capitol asks Quentin what he is thinking and he strikes her. He then commands her to stand against the wall and masturbate. While she does so, she assures him that they will "fuck [their] brains out with each other" (*IM* 168). The kind of revision of Faulkner's wounded masculinity that we see in Acker's Quentin typifies her transformations of his other male characters whose masculine identity is fragile. The insecure reporter from *Pylon*, for example, becomes a sadistic German reporter who makes Airplane see herself as sexually available on his demand, often for anal penetration.

After this point in the narrative, Acker's Quentin disappears, not as a suicide, but metafictionally as an artist, since "writing is one method of dealing with being human or wanting to suicide cause in order to write you kill yourself at the same time while remaining alive" (*IM* 174). Acker, whose mother committed suicide, writes fiction in which her female characters often consider but ultimately reject suicide. One may wonder, however, about the degree of self-fashioning that may be present in Acker's decision to make her author figure the sadistic Quentin. Faulkner seemed also to use "Quentin" to serve at least a degree of self-fashioning, as drafts of an introduction to the never-published special edition of *The Sound and the Fury* attest: "I was Quentin and Jason and Benjy and Dilsey and T.P. . . . ."[14] I am particularly interested here in the "Quentin and Jason" portion of this formulation, for it suggests that Faulkner's deployment of the signifier "Quentin" is a more nuanced gesture than Acker's fictional critique admits. Any reader's first encounter with *The Sound and the Fury* will confirm that the very name "Quentin" registers a kind of gender trouble: the pronoun references are both masculine and feminine. Although one discovers that there are two Quentins, the initial confusion metaphorically opens a bisexual space of identity. Both Quentins must struggle with a character named Jason Compson (first the father, then the uncle), who articulates a decidedly misogynistic perspective, even if the more contemporary Jason's version lacks the intellectual patina of his father's. Karl Marx's statement about history first enacting its narrative as tragedy and then repeating itself as farce certainly seems applicable to the intergenerational repetition of Quentin and Jason's passionate dialogues that attempt to fix the coordinates of masculine and feminine behavior. Faulkner's male Quentin cannot reconcile himself to his sense of failing to enact his culture's version of masculinity and commits suicide; Faulkner's female Quentin finds the strength to defeat her uncle's designation of her as a whore by embracing that designation. She leaves, taking the money her mother had sent for her support but which Jason had hoarded for his own use. Acker's Capitol (again, a condensation of Caddy and her daughter, Quentin) repeats exactly Faulkner's female Quentin's narrative: she embraces the designation "whore" and leaves, taking Jason's misappropriated money. In this instance, unlike Acker's revision of *Sanctuary* that I spoke of earlier, it is difficult to see what critical purchase she achieves simply by reproducing what is fairly explicit in Faulkner's text.

But even setting aside Faulkner's female Quentin, his male Quentin is the site of a particularly tortured gender enactment, so much so that one is left with an intriguing possibility, one that questions the impetus of Acker's deconstruction of Faulkner: if masochism is the way to a more authentic enactment of a woman's body (Acker's avowed position), then Faulkner's male Quentin may be a better woman than Acker could ever imagine. That is because Faulkner's novel already explores masochism through Quentin. His stream of consciousness provides startling insights into his unconscious, particularly his meditation on the possibilities of castration. He recalls the story of "a man who mutilated himself. He went into the woods and did it with a razor, sitting in a ditch. A broken razor flinging them backward over his shoulder the same motion complete the jerked skein of blood backward not looping."[15] But even self-castration, which would allow him to bleed where women bleed, is insufficient, and the passage continues: "But that's not it. It's not not having them. It's never to have had them, then I could say O That That's Chinese I dont know Chinese" (*SF* 116). Quentin desires an erasure of his masculine identity so complete that he would not know that he did not know sexual difference.

But a more telling moment that unhinges gendered identity occurs when Quentin imagines fulfilling his role as the Southern gentleman charged with protecting the honor of Southern womanhood. Dalton Ames has "ruined" Caddy, and Quentin knows that he should shoot the scoundrel. But in his actual confrontation with Ames, Quentin refuses to touch the gun that Ames offers and only slaps at his adversary, passing out as Ames holds both Quentin's wrists in one hand.[16] (This scene finds its parallel in the contemporary plot when Jason similarly holds

his niece's wrists, a doubling that underscores the male Quentin's femi-
nization.) The day he commits suicide, Quentin thinks longingly, "Dalton Ames. If I could have been his mother lying with open body lifted
laughing, holding his father with my hand, refraining, seeing, watching
him die before he lived" (*SF* 80). In short, Quentin can only imagine
fulfilling his masculine cultural role embodied as a woman, Dalton
Ames's mother. Failing to hold Ames's gun on the bridge, he now imagines holding Ames's father's phallus as it misfires and misses the mark,
as it were, in this imagined scene of coitus interruptus. Quentin finally
does commit suicide, an act Acker's women characters contemplate but
never actually perform. Quentin's suicide, which (once he jumps into
the water) positions him as the passive victim of his own death, completes one of Faulkner's most searching explorations of masochistic
identity.

There are numerous contradictions in Acker's fictive project that continuously deploys pornographic representations only to proclaim "female
empowerment" in the last instance.[17] One of the resulting ironies, as Arthur Redding has pointed out, is that Acker's avowed feminist project,
which features "almost exclusively heterosexual violence, generally
aimed against women, appeals more to men than women."[18] And these
same male readers who take pleasure in Acker's pornographic representations are, one imagines, oblivious to her appropriation (much less critique) of Faulkner. Even if all reading is misreading, one must still grant
that some misreadings are less supportable than others. What makes Acker's parodic, postmodern prose another co-opted discursive practice enacting what Jameson calls the cultural logic of late captialism is the way
her fiction flattens out the aesthetic past and history. Faulkner becomes
merely a metonymy for every male text ever written, all of which then
monolithically are designated "patriarchy." This is not to say that a historicized feminist criticism cannot tell us much about Faulkner, but for that
perspective one must turn to feminist studies of Faulkner from the last
decade rather than to Acker's fiction.[19]

But not all historicized critiques of Faulkner come from academic writing, as Toni Morrison's engagement with Faulkner suggests. From her
1955 Cornell M.A. thesis to the present, one can trace a history of Morr-
sion's reading and teaching of Faulkner.[20] Like Acker, Morrison finds
Faulkner a central figure of American letters, as her comments in the
Paris Review indicate:

> Faulkner in *Absalom, Absalom!* spends the entire book tracing race, and you
> can't find it. No one can see it, even the character who *is* black can't see it. I

did this lecture for my students that took me forever, which was tracking all the moments of withheld, partial or disinformation, when a racial fact or clue *sort* of comes out but doesn't quite arrive. I just wanted to chart it. I listed its appearance, disguise and disappearance on every page, I mean every phrase! . . . Do you know how hard it is to withhold that kind of information but hinting, pointing all of the time? And then to reveal it in order to say that it is *not* the point anyway? It is technically just astonishing. As a reader you have been forced to hunt for a drop of black blood that means everything and nothing. The insanity of racism. So the structure is the argument. . . . No one has done anything quite like that ever. So, when I critique, what I am saying is, I don't care if Faulkner was a racist or not; I don't personally care, but I am fascinated by what it means to write like this.[21]

I am tempted to say that Morrison takes her fascination with Faulknerian story and discourse to her sixth novel, *Jazz*, performing a tour-de-force reclamation of *Absalom, Absalom!* and its representation of African American masculinity. Unlike Acker's deconstructive parsing of Faulknerian style and plot, which focuses exclusively on gender issues, Morrison's appropriation turns to race to revise *Absalom*'s oedipally infected masculine struggle for the father's recognition. Particularly in the unnumbered sections six and seven of *Jazz*, Morrison produces a pastiche of Faulknerian style, subject matter, and plot through her narrator's at times uncertain history of the racially mixed Golden Gray. In *Absalom*, lines of family relations are obscured by Thomas Sutpen's refusal to acknowledge the children he fathers by black women. Miscegenation in Faulkner's novel happens exclusively when African American women have children by white fathers. Within that frame, however, Faulkner teases at the supreme horror of his Southern white community: what if a black man slept with a white woman? This question is central to Quentin and Shreve's construction of Henry Sutpen's motive for murdering Charles Bon. The seductive, charming Charles Bon serves as the white Southern community's repressed ideological horror: if white men can father black men who appear white, then these same "white" black men can beget black children on white women. These are the issues and questions Morrison directly addresses in her critical mapping of the ideological boundaries of Faulkner's already searching examination of "the insanity of racism."

Morrison's Golden Gray starts out by reproducing the desire of Charles Bon but ends perhaps by revising the choice of Etienne Bon. Like Charles Bon, Golden Gray is the product of miscegenation, yet Morrison reverses Faulknerian genealogy: Golden is the son of a privileged white woman, Vera Louise Gray, and a dark-skinned slave, Henry Les-

Troy (or Lestory). Colonel Gray, like Colonel Sutpen, has fathered mixed-race children. His discovery of his daughter's sexual behavior leaves him devastated, and in an act that recalls Sutpen's repudiation of his Haitian wife, Colonel Gray disavows his relationship with his daughter, giving her a large sum of money to go away.

It is here that one key element of Morrison's rewriting of *Absalom* stands out. Thomas Sutpen, the patriarch who wishes to design a lasting empire, is the obsession of all of those—the sons, the daughters, and wife—he denies; however, unlike Faulkner's Southern colonel, Morrison's is peripheral. Sutpen's first wife may live only for revenge, but Colonel Gray's daughter goes off to Baltimore with her servant, True Belle, to raise her son and never gives her father another thought. Old Gray's money, however, like Sutpen's, allows Vera Louise to raise Golden Gray as a gentleman.

Structurally, then, Golden Gray's upbringing more closely parallels and revises Etienne Bon's than his father's. Both are raised by a white woman and a black woman. Both have their sense of their white identity disrupted by unexpected knowledge of their mixed racial background. Still, in Gray's desire to discover the absent father, he recalls Charles Bon's obsession, though with a difference: Bon seeks Sutpen, the white father for recognition; Gray initially seeks LesTroy to kill him. Raised culturally white in the code of noblesse oblige, Gray is confronted with Henry Sutpen's dilemma. LesTroy, after all, is the black man who slept with his white mother, and his white identity tells him he should kill the scoundrel. Yet when he enters LesTroy's cabin and sits on his father's bed, Golden Gray is faced with Charles Bon's sense of loss. What Bon desires from his father, is "the living touch of that flesh warmed before he was born by the same blood which it had bequeathed him to warm his own flesh with, to be bequeathed by him in turn to run hot and loud in veins and limbs after that first flesh and then his own were dead."[22] In writing her scene, Morrison produces a pastiche of Faulkner's distinctive language:[23]

> Only now, he thought, now that I know I have a father, do I feel his absence: the place where he should have been and was not. Before, I thought everybody was one-armed, like me. Now I feel the surgery. The crunch of bone when it is sundered, the sliced flesh and the tubes of blood cut through, shocking the bloodrun and disturbing the nerves. They dangle and writhe. Singing pain. Waking me with the sound of itself, thrumming when I sleep so deeply it strangles my dreams away. There is nothing for it but to go away from where he is not to where he used to be and might be still. Let the dangle and the writhe see what it is missing; let the pain sing to the dirt where he stepped in

the place where he used to be and might be still. I am not going to be healed, or to find the arm that was removed from me. I am going to freshen the pain, point it, so we both know what it is for.[24]

It is worth underscoring the difference between Acker's approach to Faulkner's language and Morrison's. In Acker's hands, Faulkner's language is something to be parodically dismantled and ridiculed, but in the above passage we see Morrison's ability to play with Faulknerian discourse without denying his voice a certain integrity. Does her pastiche of Faulkner mean that Morrison gains no critical distance on his text? No, but that distance arises not intertextually but intratextually. Having reproduced one version of Faulknerian masculinity, potentially tragic in its sense of fatality and intention, Morrison fashions a way to avoid that tragedy. The above rhetorical flight of Gray's, the double of Charles Bon's, is grounded when LesTroy returns home. He tells Gray that he will accept the young man as a son if he can act like a son but warns, "don't bring me no whiteboy sass" (*J* 173), an expression that works to deflate Gray's "Faulknerian" tragic rhetoric.

The scene examined above points to a difference between Morrison's and Acker's acts of critical appropriation. Oddly, Acker's close parody of Faulkner's language is more nearly monological, in M.M. Bakhtin's sense, than the more open dialogism of Morrison's rewriting.[25] In other words, when Acker rewrites Faulkner, she says, in effect, "This is what Faulkner means." And what he means means little more than the patriarchal oppression of women. If there is little that could be termed "dialogue" in Acker's use of Faulkner, there is even less between author and reader; one either accepts or rejects Acker's misinterpretation of Faulknerian masculinity. Morrison, however, in activating the Faulknerian intertext, invites the reader to participate in a reexamination of his work. The only clear intersection between *Absalom, Absalom!* and *Jazz* may be the way Golden Gray's pain parallels Charles Bon's. But having made this move, Morrison authorizes the reader to think in the space between the two novels. If one is less certain of the precise moments where Morrison consciously gestures to Faulkner (since unlike Acker's, Morrison's are not line-by-line revisions), one nevertheless feels as though meaning is a shared enactment. So my movement from father (Charles) to son (Etienne) is less sure but certainly in the spirit of Morrison's more generous act of misreading Faulkner.

If one accepts the Faulknerian resonance in Morrison's narrator, then there is a striking passage, one underscoring the metafictional nature of her narration, when the narrator stops to comment on her construction of the story. She claims to have gotten the portrayal of Golden Gray wrong in a way that eerily recalls Morrison's discussion of Faulkner's delayed and disguised portrayal of race in *Absalom*, a portrayal that she characterized in the *Paris Review* interview, quoted earlier, as "*not the point anyway*":

> What was I thinking of? How could I have imagined him so poorly? Not noticed the hurt that was not linked to the color of his skin, or the blood that beat beneath it. But to some other thing that longed for authenticity, for a right to be in this place, effortlessly without needing to acquire a false face. . . .
>
> Now I have to think this through, carefully, even though I may be doomed to another misunderstanding. I have to do it and not break down. Not hating him is not enough; liking, loving him is not useful. I have to alter things. I have to be a shadow who wishes him well, like the smiles of the dead left over from their lives. (*J* 160–61)

The repeated pronouns in this passage—"he" and "him"—seem not simply to describe the relation between narrator and character but perhaps also to point to a commentary from one author to another. In this moment, Morrison appears almost to speak in coded form of her revision of Faulkner. Whether Morrison here stands to Faulkner as the narrator does to Golden Gray, it is in Morrison's second, revised portrayal of Golden Gray that the figure who seems to be altered is Charles Bon's son, Etienne.

If LesTroy demands that Gray choose between black and white identity, this father's articulation of the need to choose seems predicated on the choice Etienne Bon has already made. Like Golden Gray, Etienne is presented with a clear choice between black and white, but how he chooses sets him apart in Faulkner's depiction of racially mixed characters. Faulkner's most fully developed black male characters of mixed race choose whiteness as the core of their identity. (When they do choose blackness, as Etienne Bon does, it is portrayed as a terrible mistake.) Lucas Beauchamp in *Go Down, Moses*, for example, fixes his genealogical pride in his descent from Carothers McCaslin, the man who has raped his grandmother and great-grandmother.[26] Etienne chooses blackness through an identification with his mother, but only to emphasize his cultural wounding; Gray also finally chooses blackness, ostensibly through an identification with a black father, though in fact it is as much his union with the voiceless African American woman, Wild, that creates identity.

Morrison, initially, leaves Gray's decision much less clear than Etienne's, but through Joe Trace's quest for acknowledgement from Wild, Joe's absent mother, the reader discovers the material trace that reveals Gray's choice. (Joe Trace, one of the central figures of the novel's plot of the present, must be read through his relation to his lost mother, so that his desire for acknowledgement from his mother also comments on and revises Charles Bon's desire for acknowledgement from his father.) The personal items and male clothing belonging to Golden Gray that Joe discovers in Wild's cave reveal that Golden has chosen blackness through cohabitation with Wild.

In this regard, Wild works to reclaim the figure of the nameless black woman whom Etienne Bon marries. Clearly one of Faulkner's most embarrassing representations of race (even acknowledging its source as Mr. Compson), this woman, who never is given a voice, is described as "coal black and ape-like" (*AA* 166). Etienne's choice of blackness, an act that seems to defy black masculine identity even while proclaiming such identity, suggests a racial self-loathing; his marriage to the African American woman, as Mr. Compson imagines, is done to injure Judith, the white woman who urges him to pass for white. His defiance of the white woman who helped raise him serves as an ongoing act of vengeance against white culture. Golden Gray, however, learns to love the black woman whom he initially found disgusting. Once again, "Faulknerian pastiche" seems to be an appropriate way to name Morrison's use of language when she records Gray's immediate nausea at the sight of the obviously pregnant "berry-black woman"; his revulsion at the "black, liquid female" (*J* 144–45) almost exactly duplicates Joe Christmas's fear and loathing of women. Gray, however, is able to put aside his youthful sense of injury and move past his fear of the feminine. As a result his choice of blackness becomes an act of love, one in which he accepts a new identity and creates his earthly paradise with Wild. Finally, then, Morrison's portrayal of Gray's choice to accept black manhood helps map the limits of Faulkner's ability to represent African American masculinity in *Absalom*. But it is a mapping that never fails to acknowledge the value of the territory being mapped.

We are left, then, in this comparison of two postmodern appropriations of Faulknerian textuality with an odd situation: Acker's parody performs the cultural work of Jameson's pastiche, while Morrison's pastiche of Faulknerian discourse actually historicizes in a fashion that Hutcheon ascribes to postmodern parody. In other words, Acker's intentional and overt parody of Faulkner serves only to erase the possibility of historical thinking by reducing the aesthetic past to an affectless sameness, while Morrison's pastiche of the Faulknerian sentence engages and revises history, implicitly inviting the reader to participate in this work of revision.

Pastiche and parody, two related styles that suggest the intertextual element of all reading and writing, perhaps are not tied as inexorably to
the versions of postmodern politics ascribed to them by Jameson and
Hutcheon. Nevertheless, both tropes serve as useful starting points for
thinking about contemporary reimaginings of Faulkner's Yoknapatawpha,
as it increasingly becomes a territory to be remapped by postmodern
writers.

NOTES

A different version of this essay appeared earlier as "Parody or Pastiche? Kathy Acker,
Toni Morrison, and the Critical Appropriation of Faulknerain Masculinity," *The Faulkner
Journal* 15. 1–2 (Fall 1999/Spring 2000): 169–84; reprinted by permission of the author
and the University of Central Florida.

1. John Barth, "The Literature of Exhaustion," *The Friday Book* (New York: Putnam,
1984), 67–68.

2. Edouard Glissant, *Faulkner, Mississippi*, trans. Barbara Lewis and Thomas C.
Spears (New York: Farrar, Straus and Giroux, 1999), 254.

3. Linda Hutcheon, *The Politics of Postmodernism* (New York: Routledge, 1989), 57.

4. Linda Hutcheon, *The Poetics of Postmodernism* (New York: Routledge, 1988), 120.

5. Fredric Jameson, *Postmodernism, or, The Cultural Logic of Late Capitalism* (Durham: Duke University Press, 1991), 16–17.

6. What I hope to accomplish by reversing Jameson's and Hutcheon's articulations
of the cultural work of parody and pastiche, in part, is to illustrate the limits of using
these two tropes as a way to distinguish postmodernism from modernism. To identify a
text as either parody or pastiche is to make an interpretive leap. This leap may involve
the producer's intentions (or perhaps lack of intentions) for his or her text. Is Morrison's
use of Faulknerian rhetoric devoid of the satiric impulse, as Jameson might say? This is
a judgment call. Alternatively, what Jameson and Hutcheon's disagreement may come
down to is the question of who gets the reference. In that case, for those readers who
cannot hear the intertextual links to Faulkner—who simply do not get it—then both
Acker's and Morrison's novels both may be, in Jameson's terms, examples of pastiche—
"speech in a dead language." On the other hand, for readers who do register Faulknerian
resonances, then both Acker's and Morrison's novels—despite their differences—may
serve as parody, as Hutcheon would have it. In either case, whether positing a knowing
encoding author or an informed decoding reader, the interpreter must essentialize the
intertextual connection, such that one implicitly claims that text A's (e.g. Faulkner's)
existence in text B (e.g. Acker's or Morrison's) is a formally constitutive feature of text
B's parodic or pastiched nature.

7. Kathy Acker, "A Conversation with Kathy Acker" with Ellen B. Freidman, *Review
of Contemporary Fiction* 9.3 (1989): 13.

8. Kathy Acker, *In Memoriam to Identity* (New York: Grove Weidenfeld, 1990), 265;
all subsequent references to the text, cited parenthetically as *IM*, are to this edition.

9. I use the older title for Faulkner's 1939 novel rather than the corrected *If I Forget
Thee, Jerusalem* because *The Wild Palms* was the title Acker specifically invokes in her
novel's appropriation. In 1990, the older title was the only way she would have known
this Faulkner novel.

10. Kathy Acker, "The Path of Abjection: An Interview with Kathy Acker" with Larry
McCaffery, *Some Other Frequency: Interviews with Innovative American Authors*, ed.
Larry McCaffery (Philadelphia: University of Pennsylvania Press, 1996), 31–33.

11. Working with a different Acker novel, *Blood and Guts in High School*, Karen Brennan ("The Geography of Enunciation: Hysterical Pastiche in Kathy Acker's Fiction," *boundary* 2 21 [1994]: 242–68) describes the novelist's fiction as "hysterical pastiche" but notes that "Jameson's distinction is considerably vexed in Acker's writing" (251). Brennan instead argues that Acker "relies on both pastiche and parody—parody to subvert pastiche and pastiche to engender parody—vacillating hysterically between the two modes . . . to present a fiction of feminine subjectivity" (251–52).

12. William Faulkner, *Sanctuary* (New York: Vintage International 1993), 28–29.

13. John T. Matthews has fully developed this point; see "The Elliptical Nature of *Sanctuary*," *Novel* 17 (1984): 246–67.

14. Philip Cohen and Doreen Fowler, "Faulkner's Introduction to *The Sound and the Fury*," *American Literature* 62 (1990): 278.

15. William Faulkner, *The Sound and the Fury* (New York: Vintage International, 1990), 115–16; all subsequent references, cited parenthetically as *SF*, are to this edition.

16. Here I follow John T. Irwin's reading of this scene in *Doubling and Incest/Repetition and Revenge* (Baltimore: Johns Hopkins University Press, 1975), 38–39.

17. My sense of the problem with Acker's project is close to Colleen Kennedy's, who notes that she does not question Acker's "commitment to feminism or the virtue of [her] intent: rather, it is how successfully these simulations of pornographic sexual relations free women from object-status in the culture. . . . If not even the 'ultrasophisticated' reader can contain the simulation, what is left is violence" ("Simulating Sex and Imagining Mothers," *American Literary History* 4 (1992): 183–84).

18. Arthur Redding, "Bruises, Roses: Masochism and the Writing of Kathy Acker," *Contemporary Literature* (1994): 297.

19. While this is not the place to detail the history of feminist interpretation of Faulkner, in passing one might note that Minrose Gwin's *The Feminine and Faulkner* (Knoxville: University of Tennessee Press, 1990) was published the same year as Acker's *In Memoriam to Identity*. Since then, there have been a number of feminist studies of Faulkner. See for example Deborah Clarke's *Robbing the Mother: Women in Faulkner* (University Press of Mississippi, 1994) and Dianne Roberts's *Faulkner and Southern Womanhood* (University of Georgia Press, 1994). For discussions that suggest how little Acker picks up on the highly fraught representation of gender in Faulkner, see Frann Michael's "William Faulkner as a Lesbian Author," *The Faulkner Journal* 4.1–2 (1988–89): 5–18 and Minrose Gwin's "Did Ernest Like Gordon?: Faulkner's *Mosquitoes* and the Bite of 'Gender Trouble,'" *Faulkner and Gender*, ed. Donald M. Kartiganer and Ann J. Abadie (University Press of Mississippi, 1996), 120–44.

20. For a fuller treatment of Morrison's response to Faulkner, see my "Toni Morrison and the Anxiety of Faulknerian Influence," *Unflinching Gaze: Morrison and Faulkner Re-Envisioned*, ed. Carol Kolmerten, Stephen Ross, and Judith Wittenberg (Jackson: University Press of Mississippi, 1997) 3–9.

21. Toni Morrison, "The Art of Fiction CXXXIV," interview with Elissa Schappell, *Paris Review* 129 (1993): 101.

22. William Faulkner, *Absalom, Absalom!* (New York: Vintage International, 1990), 255; all subsequent references, cited parenthetically as *AA*, are to this edition.

23. Philip Weinstein also uses this passage as a clue to Morrison's rewriting of Faulkner; see *What Else But Love? The Ordeal of Race in Faulkner and Morrison* (New York: Columbia University Press, 1996), 147–48.

24. Toni Morrison, *Jazz* (New York: Knopf, 1993), 158; all subsequent references to the text, cited parenthetically as *J*, are to this edition.

25. Here I am thinking particularly of M. M. Bakhtin's reflections on the role of parody and parodic stylization in novelistic discourse: "In order to be authentic and productive, parody must be precisely a parodic *stylization*, that is, it must re-create the parodied language as an authentic whole, giving it its due as a language possessing its own internal logic and one capable of revealing its own world inextricably bound up with the parodied

language" (*The Dialogic Imagination*, ed. Michael Holquist, trans. Caryl Emerson and Michael Holquist [Austin: University of Texas Press, 1981], 364). Acker, as I hope to have suggested, does not grant Faulkner's discourse its internal logic. In Bakhtin's terms, then, Morrison's pastiche of Faulkner's language is closer to what he means by parodic stylization.

26. Some readers may object to my use of the word "rape," but the dynamics of master and slave make any notion of consent impossibly problematic.

Modernist Design, Postmodernist Paranoia: Reading *Absalom, Absalom!* with *Gravity's Rainbow*

MOLLY HITE

"You see, I had a design in my mind. Whether it was a good or bad design is beside the point; the question is, Where did I make the mistake in it, what did I do or misdo in it, whom or what injury by it to the extent which this would indicate?"
—WILLIAM FAULKNER, *Absalom, Absalom!*

If there is something comforting—religious, if you want—about paranoia, there is also anti-paranoia, where nothing is connected to anything, a condition none of us can bear for long [. . .].
Either They have put him here for a reason, or he's just here. He isn't sure that he wouldn't, actually, rather have that *reason*. . . .
—THOMAS PYNCHON, *Gravity's Rainbow*[1]

These two famous quotations, the first from a monument of modernist innovation, William Faulkner's *Absalom, Absalom!*, the second from arguably the most important postmodernist novel written in the U.S., Thomas Pynchon's *Gravity's Rainbow*, suggest that one way to relate modernism to postmodernism in literary narratives might be to consider the relations between design and paranoia. In Thomas Sutpen's question in the first headnote, design is the act of a single human agent planning a particular effect. Because the effect is a dynasty, however, the plan involves other human agents—and of course other passions, which in Quentin's and then Shreve's capping accounts ultimately destroy Sutpen's plot of patrilineal succession. In the second headnote, Pynchon's protean and relatively omniscient narrator observes how paranoia signals the agency of an unknown Them, who have Their reasons for Their machinations, and whose ineffable designs as a consequence may be preferable to a total absence of machinations. *Absalom, Absalom!* presents design as human, limited and fallible. *Gravity's Rainbow* presents paranoia as a response to conspiracy, or alternately to the ungrounded apprehension of conspiracy. We could hypothesize that paranoia signals design gone global and incognito; agency turned on the hitherto agent, who

57

has shifted from making things happen to suspecting that someone or something is making things happen *to* him or her. Such a development would accord with some accounts of postmodernist writing as a reflection or symptom of late capitalism, the information age, the digital revolution, or even a widespread First World incredulity toward master narratives.[2]

Except of course that design in *Absalom, Absalom!* is not the controllable, man-sized phenomenon that Thomas Sutpen (in what Grandfather Compson describes as his innocence) assumes. Design takes on superhuman attributes in all tellings of the Sutpen saga. It is ascribed to the agency of a vengeful God in Rosa Coldfield's version and acquires the whimsical but manipulative irony of classical Fate in Mr. Compson's version. It retains the suggestion of fatalism later in the more empathetic versions of Quentin and Shreve, although Shreve posits human plotters as well. Design and agency are large and amorphous concepts in *Absalom, Absalom!*, seeping into the narrative foundation (how much authority inheres in the different designs that tellers construct to make sense of the Sutpen story?) and informing these various versions with the appearance of overriding intention, although whose intention is unclear. Like *Gravity's Rainbow*, *Absalom, Absalom!* is deeply, perhaps irremediably uncertain about the extent to which a plot entails a motivated plotter and, more generally, about what the real story is among the various versions.

And like *Gravity's Rainbow*, *Absalom, Absalom!* insinuates that storymaking itself, the forging of connections into coherence and meaning, *is* paranoia. The drive to discern a structure behind events and then to have that structure function within the narrative as a force causing or even willing these events is a product of imaginative anxiety, of a need for "that *reason*. . . ." The desire for plots can become a desire for an archplotter. As a number of Faulkner critics have observed, the multiple narrators within the novel come up with the stories they want and need, which are also the stories they fear: in the case of Quentin Compson, the story that explains most is the story that seals his own fate. As some of the most perceptive of these critics have noted further, the multiple, palimpsestic versions related by the succession of narrators become more coherent and more explanatory as these versions move further and further away from what the novel presents as empirical grounding. Charles Bon's manipulative mother and her lawyer and the "negro blood" that makes Bon an unthinkable husband for Judith Sutpen are "facts" secured at best by circumstantial evidence. The projective identifications of the narrators and their readerly desires for a well-made plot taint any claim of the capping narrative to be the sought-after real story—that is, the ultimate revelation of what, within the fiction, counts as historical truth. Because what I call here the real story is so compromised that not only is any narrated version in doubt but the whole notion of "real" is thrown into question, critics of postmodernist writing have accorded special status to *Absalom, Absalom!* A case in point is the classic study *Postmodernist Fiction,* in which Brian McHale terms *Absalom, Absalom!* "limit-modernist" because it seems to press at the boundaries of modernist inquiry, raising questions not only about what can be known, but about what can exist.[3]

In reading *Absalom, Absalom!* with *Gravity's Rainbow* I, too, am concerned with the relation of Faulkner's great novel to postmodernist fiction, in particular postmodernist American fiction. But I am less interested in seeing how *Absalom, Absalom!* might be postmodernist, or near-postmodernist, or like postmodernism than I am in what McHale in another essay calls postmodernist text-processing strategies. Such strategies may arise from the reading of postmodernist writing, as McHale proposes in his exposition of how characteristically modernist text-processing strategies do *not* work for *Gravity's Rainbow.* I think, however, that postmodernist text-processing strategies also respond to the readerly needs of a particular period and a particular national context. McHale argues that most readers of the 1970s and '80s approached *Gravity's Rainbow* with preconceptions about how narrative fiction ought to work, and that these preconceptions were based on readings of modernist novels. He suggests that readers thus conditioned by modernist writing are by convention "paranoid," in a sense indicated in the quotation from *Gravity's Rainbow* I have used as a headnote—that is, they are driven to make connections, to construct links with the aim of getting the whole story or the big picture. He proposes that a postmodernist text-processing strategy might be characterized, on the contrary, by "anti-paranoia," in that it would forego making connections because the implications of such apparent connections are repeatedly undermined at other points in the text. In other words, a postmodernist reading (of *any* text, I would add, not just a postmodernist text) would not be primarily concerned to arrive at narrative coherence and closure, and would be commensurately more attentive to apparently stray or random details, loose ends in the plot, contradictions in characterization, narratorial obliquities, and so forth.

My own readings and rereadings of Pynchon's novels confirm a thematic and ideological aspect of such an "anti-paranoid" reading practice. In mid- to late-twentieth century modernist readings (the kind most U.S. readers learned to perform in high school and college), the elements most often subordinated to the demands of structural and thematic coherence involve social and cultural others—characters who *in the dominant society* (often of the reader, as well as of the fictional universe) are conventionally "minor characters" because they have little social, political, and economic power. This kind of modernist or "paranoid" text-processing strategy, aiming to achieve a vision of the novel as a coherent whole without much reflection on what assumptions affect the reader's own priorities, mimics mainstream ideologies in rushing to a synthesis that plays down the perspectives and desires of less socially valued people. In effect, such devalued people can be read as always already minor characters even when they play major roles, because they are so easy to judge only in terms of whether they aid or thwart the intentions of the more valued people. For this reason, a postmodernist version of negative capability, in which the reader attends to details without any irritable reaching after wholeness, is likely to reconsider conventionally "minor" actions and voices.[4]

Such a reading practice might be more concerned to open doors than to close them. In comparing the two novels I have begun with the way each thematizes and enacts a version of coherence that denies possibility: a "plot" (in at least two senses) that reaches absolute closure, a self-destructive society, a doomed human subject. Tendencies working against such coherence often take the form of a radically altered perspective on the action. At points where such a perspective intrudes, the effect may be confusion or irrelevance or liberation—or humor. And perhaps ironically, Faulkner's humor, far more than Pynchon's, offers exits from a pervasive romantic despair born of nostalgia for a lost innocence.

Paranoia and Patrilineage

In the headnotes, design is an acknowledged pattern or system, whereas paranoia embodies fallibility and incertitude, usually naming the delusion that there *is* a pattern or system. The contexts in which these quotations occur, however, complicate the opposition between the two modes of connection. The *Absalom, Absalom!* quotation is from an embedded first-person narrative, and moreover a first-person narrative ironized by the labyrinthine nature of its embedding. The passage represents Thomas Sutpen as actually speaking (inasmuch as he "actually speaks" anywhere), but the story passes through a relay of retellers, from Sutpen to Grandfather Compson, to Quentin's father (at least in part), to Quentin, to Shreve, who by the time he gains control of the story is the most evident figure for the reader. And in this relay Grandfather Compson is not simply the medium of communication but the co-narrator, inserting in his turn a critical gloss that reshapes the story Sutpen tells. In a passage about the explanation of his design that Sutpen offers, Grandfather Compson calls attention to "that innocence which believed that

the ingredients of morality were like the ingredients of pie or cake and
once you had measured them and balanced them and mixed them and
put them into the oven it was all finished and nothing but pie or cake
could come out" (211–12).

Still further, however, Grandfather Compson's moral authority to point
out the ingenuousness of this kind of measuring and planning is gro-
tesquely compromised by the much earlier scene in which Sutpen begins
the narration of his life story. In this scene, the two men are members of
a party formed to hunt down the escaped French architect, whom Sutpen
has hired to build the house his design requires. Such an outrageous
frame for Sutpen's initial reminiscence works in the novel as a brilliant
reductio ad absurdum of the power relation grounding slavery. Because
Grandfather Compson willingly joins Sutpen in tracking an employee
like escaped livestock (the same scenario, except that the escapee is a
black slave, grounds the overtly ironic "Was," the first story of the 1942
collection *Go Down, Moses*), readers are confronted with the category
mistake undergirding slavery as an institution. Human beings do not lose
their subjectivity even if treated like cattle or pigs. The episode, with its
uncanny "wild niggers" who are described as straddling the border between human and bestial and who, according to Grandfather Compson's
Conradian ruminations, might be planning to eat the French architect
(178, 206), is darkly hilarious—but not, finally, because of the gap between the barbarity of Sutpen and his slaves and the civility of the Compsons, the de Spains, and the Sartorises and *their* slaves. The juxtaposition
reveals more similarity than difference. The story told by Sutpen reveals
that he, too, is motivated by considerations of personal integrity and reverence for his ancestors. Grandfather Compson reports,

> "if he did not do it he knew that he could never live with himself for the rest
> of his life, never live with what all the men and women that had died to make
> him had left inside of him for him to pass on, with all the dead ones waiting
> and watching to see if he was going to do it right, fix things right so that he
> would be able to look in the face not only the old dead ones but all the living
> ones that would come after him when he would be one of the dead." (178)

Sutpen's ambition and ideas of probity, comically simple and disruptive,
express in demystified form the veneration of a past in which brute force
and trickery transformed people into possessions; and the possessions,
once remade and renamed, bestowed prestige on their possessors. What
these ancestors "pass on" is a history of possession, a kind of haunting. As
Joseph Allen Boone and Eric Sundquist have noted in recent revisionary
readings of *Absalom, Absalom!*, in the mid-thirties Faulkner was reexam-
ining and revising the quasi-mythic claim of white Southern landowners

to civility, and he was especially concerned with slavery and its legacy of segregation and race hatred. The flagrancy of Sutpen's assumptions is one means of keeping readers from accepting an economy in which one person can own another as simply sanctioned by historical practice.[5]

The epigraph from *Absalom, Absalom!* that prefaces my essay thus turns out to be multiply undermined when taken in context. By contrast, my second epigraph, from *Gravity's Rainbow,* appears to have a simple, stable narratorial framework. The source of the information about paranoia and its contrary, anti-paranoia, is the third-person extradiegetic narrator of the novel as a whole, a narrator who often takes the point of view of various characters but here assumes the authority of what in realist, naturalist and many modernist contexts we feel reasonably secure in terming omniscience. Other passages in the same sort of voice define paranoia as "the onset, the leading edge, of the discovery that *everything is connected*" (703), and describe the exemplary paranoiac under discussion, the New Englander Tyrone Slothrop, as having a "Puritan reflex of seeking other orders behind the visible, also known as paranoia" (188).

The paradox here is that the apparently reliable mode of narration in these passages from *Gravity's Rainbow* works ultimately to authorize extreme skepticism about apparent connections. It does so by suggesting that the act of interpretation itself is close to paranoia, and that paranoia is frightening not because it is delusionary but, on the contrary, because it is valid. In Pynchon's great novel, to recognize that "*everything is connected*" is to suspect in the same instant that someone or something has engineered the connections. An apprehensible design seems to imply a designer. To discover the design rather than to plan and execute it, as Thomas Sutpen wishes to do, is to acknowledge the possibility that someone else has significant but imperceptible control over one's own life. In other words, the blessed rage for order stops being blessed when the order is imposed secretly by somebody else. Design becomes conspiracy.

In an acute study of postwar U.S. thinking about conspiracy, Timothy Melley demonstrates that this suspicion of being controlled by others is a feature of American culture after World War II, not only in many postmodernist stories and novels but also in at least purportedly nonfictional books like J. Edgar Hoover's *Masters of Deceit* and Vance Packard's *The Hidden Persuaders.* Melley suggests that the range of audiences and political positions in these latter examples of popular social interpretation indicate that the whole idea of conspiracy has undergone a sea change in the twentieth century. Rather than being a plot undertaken by a small group of dissidents against an established authority (as we see, for instance, in Joseph Conrad's *The Secret Agent*), a conspiracy now becomes the plot on the part of the established authority itself, pitted against a minority or a solitary individual. Melley's analysis suggests a relevant analogy to the Oedipal situation in *Absalom, Absalom!* as well. In Faulkner's novel the retellings focus more and more on a situation in which the authoritative father kills or arranges the killing of the sons: a reverse *Totem and Taboo* scenario in which the progress and futurity guaranteed by the accession of the young is betrayed by the father, who in effect wins the Oedipal battle decisively. Because this father is mortal, however, his triumph is simultaneously a defeat for his dynastic line. In this respect, the plot on the part of authority decrees its own extinction, in that it leaves no heirs to possess its property and carry on its tradition. The crucial experience of the son—or in the more overtly social version, of the beleaguered solitary citizen or minority group—is extreme doubt about what sort of ability to judge and act freely actually exists. To put it another way, the crucial experience is the sensation of potency suddenly draining away. This experience is what Melley terms agency panic.

As the formulation in terms of drained potency insinuates, Melley sees such agency panic not only as a crisis in the concept of what a person is, but also as a crisis in the concept of what bourgeois masculinity is. U.S. theories making the individual the autonomous origin of action, judgment, and even identity—the subject practicing Self-Reliance, the self-made man—deal implicitly with male personhood, and moreover with male persons who have the social status and privileges that make it *rewarding* to claim responsibility for themselves. *Gravity's Rainbow* plays overtly with the ways such attitudes about agency are entangled with sexuality. The central mystery of the intricate and in some respects unmasterable plot is that the boobish, likable Tyrone Slothrop, a G.I. stationed in London during the closing days of the Second World War, finds sexual partners in exactly the locations subsequently hit by German V-2 rockets. This statistical *Liebestod*, in which a map of liaisons that Slothrop keeps out of a "fraternity-boy reflex" is point-for-point congruent with a map of rocket strikes, makes Slothrop's penetration of individual women a synecdoche for rocket explosions violating "Lady London" (*GR* 22, 215). Allied authorities on psychological warfare note the congruence and link it to a further fact of which Slothrop is ignorant—that as an infant he was the subject of an experiment in Pavlovian conditioning, in which an unidentified "Mystery Stimulus" was used to produce his erections. The experiment and stimulus in turn link Slothrop with a network of international corporations, which in return for his use as a lab animal sponsored and monitored his progress through Harvard and the echelons of the U.S. Army, to the point where his apparent role in provoking rocket strikes could also be a vast, terrifying experiment for purposes exceeding his understanding. His most intimate, personal, and private desires and actions are thus represented as being exactly the properties of his person that are under outside control—a situation summed up in one of Pynchon's disruptively interpolated songs, this one called "The Penis He Thought Was His Own" (216). Slothrop's "paranoia" in at least certain respects turns out to be the reasonable and rational response to a genuinely existing conspiracy.[6]

Slothrop is thus the antithesis of the self-reliant or self-made man. Like several other male characters in *Gravity's Rainbow*, he comes to wonder if he is a creature of his conditioning and for this reason essentially a construction of others. His situation motivates a 760-page, multicharacter quest aimed at arriving at a satisfactory explanation—not only for what makes Slothrop into a death-magnet, but by metaphoric *and* metonymic extension, for the forces shaping the trajectory of Western history, the devastations of the twentieth century, and an apparently unstoppable proliferation of corporate and technological systems into "structures fa-voring death" that seem destined, once they have reached a certain stage of development and self-perpetuation, to destroy the world despite any kind of human agency (167). The question of what draws both women and bombs toward Slothrop, most concentrated in the question of what the Mystery Stimulus is, expands until it has apocalyptic resonances. The text works to implicate its readers, both as textual interpreters and as inhabitants of a world that Pynchon's anti-mimetic, hyperbolic, conven-tionally and tonally disruptive text gestures toward. The narrative asks what is happening, what went wrong, and who or what is responsible. At the same time, it thwarts attempts to imagine what sorts of answers such questions could have. As the implications grow vaster, the search for "other orders beyond the visible" (242)—a project also identified as a reflex, this time a Puritan one—suggests how critical reading practices can lead to something like agency panic. Just as the questing characters within the novel come to doubt that the designs they apprehend have any real existence, readers find themselves unable to make satisfying or final connections among elements of the plot, while at the same they suspect that such connections are of supreme importance and must be made.

One unexpected link between *Gravity's Rainbow* and *Absalom, Absa-lom!* that emerges from this skeletal summary is that the crisis of agency Thomas Sutpen experiences also involves control of his penis. After the death of Charles Bon, Sutpen *"must have seen himself as the old wornout cannon which realises that it can deliver just one more fierce shot and crumble to dust in its own furious blast,"* to cite Quentin's wonderfully obscene assimilation of sexual impotence to the discourse of Civil War history (148, italics in the original). The design of patrilineage assumes an ability to produce a son instead of a daughter, a presumption that makes the situation of *"just one more fierce shot"* something of a crap-shoot. More generally, the design of patrilineage entails a degree of control over one's offspring; or one's "get," as Shreve insists, emphasizing the agency assumed by the patriarch as intrinsic to the dynastic project. The most evident failure of control in *Absalom, Absalom!* is the father's inability to make his sons behave as he wishes.

Sutpen's inability to control his "get" is the stuff of classical tragedy—cognate with the dark irony through which Oedipus fulfills the prophecy of the Delphic oracle by trying to *avoid* fulfilling that prophecy. Classical tragedy lends unexpected credence to Sutpen's query, "Where did I make the mistake in it, what did I do or misdo in it, whom or what injure by it to the extent which this would indicate?" The "mistake" Sutpen presumes could well be the essential *hamartia*, or "tragic error" that according to Aristotle is the key to a well-made tragic plot. Deriving from the notion of "missing the mark," *hamartia* need not imply that the agent making the erroneous choice is morally culpable (as is the case in the Renaissance and Victorian idea of "tragic flaw"). Judged by the values of the surrounding culture, Sutpen is different only because he makes clear that standards of aristocratic breeding and female subordination work to guarantee a clear line of patrilineal descent in a society founded on racial distinction. Although Grandfather Compson pronounced Sutpen naive or morally deficient in attributing calamity to some initial mistake, Sutpen's question grants unexpected pathos to the newcomer who understood the system too well and exposed its brutality in the process of acting according to its principles. He was only trying to be a founding father.[7]

Sutpen's question is "Why me?" It directs attention once again to a more encompassing moral question that implicates the collective Confederate South, a question Quentin at the beginning of the book appropriates only half-ironically from Rosa Coldfield: "why God let us lose the War" (6). *Absalom, Absalom!* presents the institution of slavery, the *hubris* of a hierarchy based, as Quentin observes, on "the divine right to say 'Go there' conferred upon them by an absolute caste system" (276), and the miscegenation and incest that characterized the intersection of family and slavery in antebellum Southern practice, as if suggesting possible or partial answers to the larger ethical question of why God or some other overwhelming juridical power let the South lose the war. As the story expands into more global and mythic registers, acquiring a series of ironic reversals that draw the history of the Old South into complex interaction with classical and biblical tales of brothers killing brothers and fathers killing sons, the dominant theme is the justice of punishing the children for the sins of their fathers. By the time the outsider Shreve takes on the task of imagining Charles Bon, he has fully accepted as the governing premise of the story that succeeding generations pay the moral debts of their progenitors, even to the point of their own annihilation (260).

Who or what ordains and enforces this retributive code? Or, to bring the question back to its most urgent embodiment within the novel, from what does Quentin Compson suffer? Why does he carry the burden of desire, remorse, and guilt? Is he somehow fated to hate the South and, by synecdoche, himself, or has he internalized this purported legacy in a way that could possibly have been averted? To put the question still another way, is there an imaginable outside to the closed, or terminal design of patrilineal succession in which, as Quentin muses, ultimately a man never outlives his father? (222)

In *Gravity's Rainbow*, patrilineal succession threatens to close or terminate on an even more cosmic scale. As the central white man, the Nazi Lieutenant Weissmann, explains to the lover and surrogate son whom he is about to sacrifice, "Fathers are carriers of the virus of Death, and sons are the infected . . . and, so that the infections may be more certain, Death in its ingenuity has contrived to make the father and son beautiful to each other" (723). The homosocial daisy chain in which Charles loves Thomas, Thomas loves Henry, and Henry loves Charles, which circles around the ostensibly passive, featureless, and mute body of a woman, Judith, passes on fatality like a patrilineal STD. In *Gravity's Rainbow* the same structure of family romance becomes a national and then an international circuit of corporate, financial, military, and technological connections, drawing Western and finally global civilizations into the self-absorbed, self-annihilating trajectory of a history seeking its own end. Pynchon's great novel is the fall of the house of Sutpen writ large— and further historicized in the wake of another devastating war. It is the latest chapter of a chronicle to which Faulkner made significant contributions, of First World masculinity and its discontents.

Pynchon indicates the many respects in which the story of the father who sacrifices his own son is old and, in many respects, foundational in Western culture. It is the story not only of David, Amnon, and Absalom, but also Kronos and his sons and Abraham and Isaac. Most of all, it is the central event of the Christian myth, in which the father uses the son for his own ultimate purposes and the son cries out, in a voice that could be Charles Bon's, "My God, my God, why hast thou forsaken me?" As the narrative reconstructions proceed, Quentin realizes the extent to which he himself is implicated in *Absalom, Absalom!*'s story of the war in which the South sacrificed its "get" and promise for the future to an ideal of agrarian aristocracy and racial purity always already betrayed by the fathers who created and upheld it. Thomas Sutpen is not essentially dif-

ferent from the de Spains, Sartorises, and Compsons, who represent aristocracy and gentility in the region of Jefferson. He is simply one
generation too late, an uncomfortable reminder to other plantation own-
ers that their way of life is not only founded on but also sustained by a
violence supposedly antithetical to culture. Quentin's own incestuous desire to "protect" the purity of his sister stands revealed as an integral
element of the murderous circuit that seems to have deprived him of
both potency and agency. "Nevermore of peace," he thinks, and the
phrase could be a dirge for the moribund Old South that sired him and
kept him entangled in its legacy of unforgiveness, outrage, and storytelling (298–9). In multiple senses, neither this South nor Quentin will rise
again.

Outsides and Others

Fatality haunts both *Absalom, Absalom!* and *Gravity's Rainbow* as part
of the general nostalgia that keeps fathers and sons conniving at their
oedipal plots. Both novels to a degree romanticize a mythic past that was
betrayed by history—or to use Pynchon's great metaphor of Gravity, by
the one way direction of Western time, which inaugurated a Fall from
innocence that was also a downward plunge toward annihilation (*GR* 139,
413). In *Absalom, Absalom!* the golden age is of course the antebellum
South. In *Gravity's Rainbow*, where history is the story of the increasing
exploitation and technological manipulation of the earth and most of its
inhabitants, the mythic past is less locatable; but one lyrical high point
late in the novel presents a pretechnological and in a literal sense prehis-
toric vision of "the World just before men. Too violently pitched alive in
constant flow ever to be seen by men directly." This vital, sensuous, coherent world organism could exist only until the arrival of "human consciousness, that poor cripple, that deformed and doomed thing." In the
overall scheme of Pynchon's novel, the dominant version of "human consciousness, that poor cripple"—Western civilization—carries to completion the filicidal, genocidal and finally suicidal design of patrilineal
transmission: "*It is our mission to promote death*" (720).

Despite its almost endless tonal shifts, narratorial self-questionings,
and comic deflations, however, *Gravity's Rainbow* is more univocally
committed to nostalgia for a prelapsarian harmony than is *Absalom, Absalom!* When Pynchon's narrator celebrates the defectors from Western
modernity who travel "into the rests of the folk-song Death (empty stone
rooms), out, and through, and down under the net down to the uprising"
(720), or at other moments laments the impossibility of returning to unity
with nature, the tone is passionate and far from parody. In contrast, the

mood of inevitability saturating Faulkner's great novel is so lush, hyperbolic, and self-indulgent that it slides easily into humor, not only in the scenes where Thomas Sutpen reduces the hitherto genteel Southern institutions of home, family, and courtship to their pragmatic bare bones, but also on other occasions when the various narrators show their pleasure in the tidy machinations of authorial Fate. Indeed, in the developing story, fatality often seems to follow the conventions of popular novels, especially the kind of sentimental novel about the Civil War that flooded the South from Reconstruction well into the twentieth century (Margaret Mitchell's *Gone with the Wind*, published the same year as *Absalom, Absalom!*, is the best-known example). Faulkner's unpublished short story "Evangeline," an early version of the Henry-Judith-Charles love plot, uses two flippant present-day narrators to emphasize how a local story of a Sutpen "ghost" is expected to embody popular stereotypes. The scene in which Bon first rides home with Henry is a mutual construction in which the two speakers compete in piling up the clichés:

> "Now, get it. The two young men riding up to the colonial portico, and Judith leaning against the column in a white dress—"
> "—with a red rose in her dark hair—"
> "All right. Have a rose. But she was blonde."[8]

By the time the events of "Evangeline" get to the Civil War, the two narrators are claiming points for supplying or avoiding a predictable element of a generic plot:

> "Oh, the war," I said. "I think this should count as just one: Did Charles save Henry's life or did Henry save Charles' life?"
> "Now I am two up," Don said. "They never saw each other during war, until at the end of it." (587)

Of course, *Absalom, Absalom!* manages to incorporate both scenarios of heroic rescue. Mr. Compson reports that Henry saved Charles, while much later Shreve finds a more adequate narrative logic in the thesis that Charles saved Henry (98, 275). In such turns and counterturns, the vengeful or simply malevolent power manipulating the Sutpens and the South to their destruction seems identical to a set of hackneyed literary conventions, some going back to the Bible and classical tragedy, others familiar from recent popular fiction.

The parody and humor that unsettle nostalgia in *Absalom, Absalom!* are important means of insisting that there are other ways to live in, and with, a South "peopled with garrulous outraged baffled ghosts" than to be a ghost oneself (4). Comic hyperbole and deflation suggest limits to the miasma of romantic hopelessness produced and inhabited by Rosa

Coldfield and three generations of storytelling Compsons. By giving the climactic version of the story to Shreve, the one narrator who is an outsider not only to the South but also to the U.S., Faulkner gave the Sutpen story dramatic coherence while stressing that there is an outside to this particular doom-laden account of why the South lost the war and why, as an apparent corollary, Sutpen's lone surviving descendant is African American. The transgressive "Let me play now" with which Shreve takes over the narration (224) signals a different approach to recounting history, one in which eyewitness accounts, physical evidence, and conjecture are reinterpreted or even replaced by virtuoso fabulation. In engaging in narrative "play," Shreve is concerned not with historical truth but with narrative integrity and effect. As a consequence, he pieces together a brilliant story, supplying missing motives and on occasion missing characters. And in a striking abdication of omniscience, the third-person narrator at two points deems these insertions "probably true enough," although we are not told enough for what, or why "probably" is the nearest we can come to an authorized version of the real story (268).

Because he is the one narrator who is not Southern (and not Yankee either: as a western Canadian he suggests possibilities beyond the persistent binaries of North-South, black-white, brother-lover, father-son), Shreve can center his version of the Sutpen story on Charles Bon. Only such an outsider to U.S. racial paranoia could both supply the climactic miscegenation motif and ventriloquize a character who by the standards of the narrative present is still a "nigger." In taking the point of view of Charles Bon and assigning this young man his own "spot of negro blood" (247) as the legacy of Sutpen's purported tragic error, Shreve updates and further historicizes the Sutpen family romance. Eric Sundquist has explained how Bon's sacrifice is tied to the particular contingent conditions of slavery in the U.S. South, in which miscegenation was pervasive but unspeakable and in consequence incest between master and slave could not "count" as incest because the cross-racial breeding by definition could not have occurred.[9] The sudden transformation of Bon into an inadmissable other, in accordance with the one-way logic of the "one-drop rule," cancels out his blood relation to Henry. Shreve has him say that he is no longer Henry's brother precisely *because* he is, as Shreve has him say, *"the nigger that's going to sleep with your sister"* (286). If he is that "nigger," he cannot claim he is going to sleep with *our* sister. The presumption would be so breathtaking as to make the statement unintelligible.

In moving Bon to the center of the narrative, Shreve also updates and historicizes the story in another way. His version presents the paternal design from the point of view of its unknowing victim, so that Bon's central mode of being is a paranoia that, in a Pynchonesque development, turns out to be fully justified. Shreve's "play" with the character produces a young man oddly similar to Pynchon's Tyrone Slothrop. Shreve's Charles Bon is obsessed, as Slothrop is, with the question of *who made him* and with an impending moment "which would reveal to him at once, like a flash of light, the meaning of his whole life" (*AA* 250).[10] Again like Slothrop, Bon comes to realize there is something important he does not know about himself, something causing some people to study him or shun him. Passionately awaiting the recognition that will secure his identity by placing him within an overall design, this Bon, again like Slothrop, is betrayed by his sexual desire, a desire that initially seems to seek the daughter and second son as substitutes and revenge for the withheld love of the father, but that becomes disturbingly powerful as it becomes inextricably associated with death. Shreve's Charles Bon wanders in all innocence into the Sutpen plot, led by the Penis He Thought Was His Own.

But as Shreve constructs the story, the design has become a conspiracy, and therefore Bon cannot really be in it by accident. As Shreve sets up the causal links (as if in response to Mr. Compson's readerly objection, "It's just incredible. It just does not explain" [80]), he seems to work from the premise that a plot cannot have full explanatory force unless it is informed throughout by intention—that is, unless it is a conspiracy. And so he comes up with the two characters of Bon's mother and Bon's mother's lawyer, who can provide an airtight reason for Bon's belated appearance at the new, backwoods University of Mississippi, where in due course Bon meets Henry Sutpen. In a flight of paranoiac fabulation, Shreve anticipates *Gravity's Rainbow* by even suggesting the lawyer has control over Bon's sexuality. Speaking of the morganatic marriage Bon had apparently contracted in New Orleans, Shreve could be speaking of the relations between Slothrop and his shadowy corporate masters when he hypothesizes, "maybe he even had a spy in the bedroom like he seems to have had in Sutpen's; maybe he even planted her" (242).

In Shreve's story, both mother and lawyer have their own motives for setting up an encounter that will lead to the deadly standoff between the brothers and the collapse of Sutpen's projected dynasty. The lawyer's motives are among the most credible to twentieth-century readers: he wants to make a lot of money. But what causes the mother's plotting? Shreve is quite clear about the cause, but it is in a different category from the lawyer's motive—what Aristotle calls a formal cause, logically entailed by the essence of the being (the kind of explanation that would maintain that a dog barks because it is in its nature to do so), rather than the more familiar efficient cause that is the basis of scientific and social science reasoning. The mother nurtures and grooms her son for the sacrifice, not out of intelligible motives, but because of what she is—an embodiment of vengefulness, "who couldn't to save her life have told you or the lawyer or Bon or anybody else probably what she wanted, expected, hoped for because she was a woman and didn't need to want to hope or expect anything" (243). Shreve's authority for women as good haters seems to be Mr. Compson interpreting Rosa Coldfield, although Shreve provides the added twist that this mother's sole, sustained aspiration for her only child is to use him as bait.[11] Rather than providing plausible intentions, Shreve motivates the mother's key role in the conspiracy plot by citing her nature. Women are just like that.

Thomas Sutpen described the pragmatic reasoning that allowed him to abandon his first wife: "I found that she was not and could never be, through no fault of her own, adjunctive or incremental to the design which I had in mind, so I provided for her and put her aside" (194). As Grandfather Compson observed, such disregard for ethics and legality demonstrated Sutpen's "innocence" that civilization is anything more than a matter of mapping out the means to desired ends. But the self-absorption of the scheme, and of course the notion that certain human beings exist only as tools—a notion underlying not only slavery but the chattel status of conventionally privileged Southern white women—are more widespread than this criticism might indicate. Shreve's capping invention of the single-mindedly vengeful mother is only one of many instances in which women in *Absalom, Absalom!* serve as "adjunctive or incremental to the design" that not only Thomas Sutpen, but also Mr. Compson, and finally Quentin and Shreve have "in mind." Female characters emerge as subjects in *Absalom, Absalom!* only to be swept up into the obsessive storytelling about fathers and sons, in which the design governing the fall of the house of Sutpen seems more and more to predestine the fall of the house of Compson. Yet progenitive control does not fail only because the father cannot dictate the behavior of his sons. The very existence of daughters points to a block in the circuit of patrilineal transmission. Female "get" cannot perpetuate the dynastic line. The daughters thus trouble the tendency to read the story entirely in terms of the dynastic line. Along with the multiple and dubitable narrators, they are powerful evidence that uncertainty is fundamental to the structure of this novel, and that the structure has room for multiple stories that could be entwined with, but that also could be in conflict with the plot of patrilineal succession.

"What about the girls?"

In *Gravity's Rainbow*, a novel similarly preoccupied with masculinity and the circuit of patrilineal transmission, female characters also intervene at points to suggest a radically different construction of events. Far more than the women in *Absalom, Absalom!*, the women in *Gravity's Rainbow* embody nostalgic alternate modes of thinking and acting: astrology, witchcraft, and various other non- or anti-rational ways of making connections and interacting with the world. But the moments in which Pynchon's female characters prompt a genuine change in perspective are different from such thematized treatments of feminine difference as stereotypically preconscious or prescientific. One of the most important of these moments occurs when a young woman attached to the group investigating Slothrop's prophetic erections wakes up one night and whispers, "what about the girls?" (87).

In context, the question blows open a whole corridor of doors. When the focus is on masculinity and its implications—which include dominance and the death drive—the investigation clearly centers on Slothrop as lure for or prophet of eventual rocket strikes. The phenomenon under discussion is Slothrop's erections, which connect somehow to the stimulus used in the Pavlovian experiments of Slothrop's early childhood. But if the focus is "the girls," the women who are on hand and willing to have what seems to be satisfying and even romantic sex with Slothrop—in locations where rockets subsequently fall—there is a further fortuitous and indeed somewhat magical phenomenon to account for. How do sudden, unmotivated erections produce young, sexual women and intimate liaisons? Furthermore, with this focus the event to be explained is not an erection and its consequences, but rather a force with the uncanny ability to seek out and kill young women. Slothrop's hypothesized "love . . . sexual love, with his, and his race's, death" (738) is mediated by a violent misogyny—if not on Slothrop's part, certainly on the part of the rocket and, by Pynchon's extension, the history of scientific and technological development. The reflection suggests a whole reading of *Gravity's Rainbow* that centers on major "girls" of the novel: not on the thematic positions they enact or embody, but on ways their desires, motivations, and character development might indicate alternate readings.

What about the girls in *Absalom, Absalom!*? Faulkner's chronology suggests that Quentin and Shreve complete their version of the story within a year of the historical moment when, as Virginia Woolf hyperbolically proposed, "human character changed." One index of this change, Woolf went on to assure her readers, was that canonical texts began to elicit strikingly different readings. "Read the *Agamemnon*," she counseled, "and see whether, in process of time, your sympathies are not almost entirely with Clytemnestra." Woolf issued this challenge to point up the important reversals characterizing modernity. In this enterprise she was even further ahead of her time: the reading that finds a point of view and sympathetic motivations for Cytemnestra uses text-processing strategies closer to those Brian McHale termed postmodernist. A reading that finds its sympathies with Faulkner's Clytemnestra attends to details of characterization, motivation, tone, and presentation that resist being pulled together into the "organic" whole too often assumed to be the goal of modernist writing—in this case, into the tragic master-plot of fathers and sons. And postmodernist text-processing strategies might lead us to read messier, less final, and commensurately more open "real stories" within or alongside the airless, futureless loops of history-as-fate or history-as-conspiracy, which are ultimately the master narratives of *Absalom, Absalom!* and *Gravity's Rainbow.*[12]

If your sympathies in *Absalom, Absalom!* are with the sister and slave Clytemnestra, you may notice how much she is represented in terms of opacity and impenetrability, qualities that to white observers even of Quentin's generation signalled an intrinsic absence of subjectivity. She accordingly operates most clearly as a symbol of the father and of blackness, a "coffee-colored" image of Sutpen who carries out his will. Yet her moments of articulation are unexpected gashes in the text. They indicate she is also fully present: a thinking, feeling, and decision-making agent behind the official story of fathers, sons, and their adjuncts and increments. Her closing statement to Quentin about Henry, "Whatever he done, me and Judith and him have paid it out," is a sudden opening-out of the text, forcing the recognition that she must be saying "*our* brother, *our* sister, *our* father" (296). Almost spoken here is the forbidden language of kinship that asserts the fundamental likeness denoted by family resemblance: the equivalent possession by all kin of some points of view, memories, and stories. To see such evidence of subjectivity in Clytie is to glimpse the possibility of an account fundamentally different from her father's, Grandfather Compson's, Mr. Compson's, Quentin's, Rosa's, or even Shreve's.

Clytie accordingly overflows the roles of adjunct and integument. By a similar token, so does Judith. The incident John Irwin calls the primal scene of the Sutpen family romance, in which the young Henry is carried off "screaming and vomiting" while Clytie and Judith remain together, unmoving and impassive, in the loft above the yard where their father has fought and conquered one of his "wild" slaves (21–2), entails strikingly different models of filiation than Oedipal sonship. What sort of person is a daughter in this new Oedipal configuration? What does it mean if the daughters seem to resemble the father more than the son does? How do these clearly signaled likenesses trouble the social categories of gender, race, social status, and inheritance that govern the fictional universe—or at least govern some narrators' understanding of this fictional universe?[13]

Judith goes through so many transformations in the various narrators' retellings that she exists in irreconcilably multiple versions. The young Judith who "instigated and authorized" the carriage driver to make the family team of horses bolt, and who watched her father fighting one of his own slaves without any of her brother's signs of revulsion, needs to be imaginatively related to the grown woman who is also extraordinary, although in different ways (18). The depth and complexity revealed in her reported speech to Mrs. Compson about countering the fateful or conspiratorial "Ones that set up the loom" by making "at least a scratch, something, something that might make a mark on something that *was* once for the reason that it can die someday" (101), has little evident connection to Mr. Compson's version of Judith, the young woman who with her brother is a "single personality with two bodies both of which had been seduced almost simultaneously by a man whom at the time Judith had never even seen," or more radically, "the blank shape, the empty vessel" required to facilitate a particular version of events (73, 95). Still less can she be reconciled with the passive, compliant Southern belle of Shreve's story, whose appeal to Bon is summed up by the simile of lemon sherbet:

> "like when you have left the champagne on the supper table and are walking toward the whiskey on the sideboard and you happen to pass a cup of lemon sherbet on a tray and you look at the sherbet and tell yourself, That would be easy too only who wants it [. . . .] [but then] you find that you dont want anything but that sherbet and that you haven't been wanting anything else but that and you have been wanting that pretty hard for some time—besides knowing that sherbet is there for you to take." (258)

Judith as palate cleanser has no thoughts or desires about her consumption. She is entirely the object of appetite. Indeed, at many points in the retellings, readers will lose the cohesiveness of the narrative if they ask themselves what Judith or Clytie can know or feel or be thinking.

One could argue (or just assume) that Clytie and Judith are minor characters, not intended to carry the burden of subjectivity that such questions imply. The clear models for such a conception of character are the accounts of the male narrators, who all substitute their own reifying premises for Rosa's initial insinuations about how Sutpen's demonic nature passed intact to the female "get" (16–22). But it is hard to call such characters minor when their unknown thoughts and feelings are so central to the plot, if not to the discourse, of all its narrators. In the tale Rosa tells Quentin in chapter 1, both Clytie and Judith are set up as alien, potentially malign, and complex to the point of being unfathomable. After Rosa's elaborate foreshadowing, however, they recede into the background of the father-son plot, emerging as developed characters again only in chapter 5, when Rosa resumes the narration, describing the aftermath of Bon's death and her own incomprehension in words that assert the Sutpen sisters' willed resistance to communicating rather than emptiness. In Rosa's anguished and outraged recounting, Clytie has a "sphinx face"and Judith is "a woman more strange to me than to any grief for being so less its partner" (109, 120). Rosa has a direct interest in (and acquaintance with) the Sutpen daughters. Her narrative is strikingly different from the versions of the Compson men and Shreve, in that she views Clytie and Judith as powerful. In the male narrators' versions, the Sutpen women generally embody qualities and functions. They emerge as three-dimensional characters only on the few occasions they utter those disruptive remarks that indicate they have had points of view all along.

By contrast, Henry gains substance because of Mr. Compson's curiosity and Quentin's projective identifications, while Bon is only an object of desire and an impetus for speculation about the plot until Shreve takes him on and gives him a belated set of motives and manipulators. That is, narratorial self-interest creates emphasis that shifts attention away from gender and/or racial others. But as we have seen, narratorial self-interest also sabotages the claim of narrated stories to be something like objective truth or the last word. At the same time that readers are seduced by the claims of the story to be a supreme fiction, they are bombarded with reminders that this fiction is one of many possible, and that no version can claim final authority.

Coming to Conclusions

In both *Absalom, Absalom!* and *Gravity's Rainbow*, the supreme fiction is about the end of a world. *Gravity's Rainbow* achieves one of the most emphatic conclusions in literary history by dramatizing a conclusion of the reader's world as well as the characters'. On the last page, the narrator shifts to a form of address that casually sweeps readers into the outermost frame of the fictional universe, invoking "us, old fans who've always been at the movies (haven't we?)." In context, the phrase "at the movies" (which in its figural sense indicts readers for living within a realm of mass-market fantasies) locates readers inside a movie theater over which is poised the Third Reich's great contribution to weapons technology, the

V-2 Rocket, in all likelihood loaded with the U.S.'s own great technologi-cal advance from World War II, the atomic bomb. This rocket is "falling, nearly a mile per second, absolutely and forever without sound" until it "reaches its last unmeasurable gap above the roof of this old theatre, the last delta-t" (760). The intimate, confidential, elbow-nudging tone of this extraordinary passage connotes uninvited penetration into readers' psy-chic processes, a sort of narratorial rape. The overwhelming import is that no one is safe because no one is outside the plot that, in achieving closure, closes down the future.

In *Absalom, Absalom!* the supreme fiction about the end of the Old South seems to entail the end of its most recent son and heir Quentin Compson. Quentin cannot hate his filicidal patrimony without hating himself and becoming its latest filicide. Moreover, a conspiracy of literary conventions determines the shape and conclusion of his life. His fate is sealed by the account of his suicide in *The Sound and the Fury*, published seven years before *Absalom, Absalom!* The plot in which he figures is thus a perfect design, already closed, always a plot *against* him. The Old South, too, is dead, moving and speaking only through its ghosts, without any possibility of resurrection.[14] Not only have its claims to gentility, ci-vility, and innocence been exposed as hypocrisies, but its defining condi-tion of racial separation is from its founding moment a lie. Like innocence, racial "purity" is a product of denial. As Shreve suggests at the conclusion, the racial threat to the white South is not evident contam-ination, a "spot of negro blood" showing up against a white field, but rather a condition in which skin defined as "black" by "one-drop" stan-dards will "bleach out again like the rabbits and the birds do, so they wont show up so sharp against the snow" (302).

In this closing evolutionary fantasy, blackness is not something that impinges on white people from outside, and which they can accordingly guard themselves against. Rather, it is implicitly the prior condition, which can then "bleach out again" in response to an environment in which whiteness offers greater chances of survival. The early versions of the Sutpen story tried to assume a worldview in which blackness is the clear other of whiteness. But the undermining of Sutpen's design by growing intimations of an invisible "blackness" within—first in the situa-tion of Bon's octoroon wife, then more damningly in the thesis of Bon's own African ancestry, which makes him an impossible Sutpen brother *or* husband—creates a more paranoid racist understanding of blackness, on the lines of "They're everywhere!" And of course "they" were, histori-cally, everywhere, including in the heart of the land-owning white family in the Old South. The rape of slave women by the master was central to the institution of slavery in the U.S. The shadow family was as much a part of the Southern way of life as the "pure" wife and legitimate children in the big house. Shreve's reference to a possible African genesis for the whole human species is a biological metaphor for a social fact. Although the color line has been a recurrent source of turmoil in American history, color has not stayed in line. Ostensibly "white" people might imperceptibly, secretly *be* black people, even without their own knowledge.[15]

Just as Shreve can empathize with a "nigger" Charles Bon, he can identify himself with the racially blurred subject he imagines. In predicting "I who regard you will also have sprung from the loins of African kings," he suggests an alternate patrilineage and aristocracy that claims rather than repudiates blackness. The framework suggests a wider range of interpretation for the last remaining Sutpen, Charles's grandson Jim Bond. On one hand a figure of idiocy and retardation who enacts nineteenth- and early twentieth-century eugenic theories about how "mixing" leads to degeneracy, Jim on the other hand recalls Quentin's brother Benjy Compson in *The Sound and the Fury*, whose ostensibly simple-minded perceptions cut through hypocrisies about love, shame, and loss. Both Benjy and Jim Bond are vatic figures, "howling" their grief in the background of tragedies brought about by inhumane social conventions. Both look forward to the unnamed young woman of the penultimate story in *Go Down, Moses*, "Delta Autumn," who might unite the two strains of the McCaslin family and insure its continuity but who in Ike McCaslin's horrified cry of recognition is a "nigger." This woman resembles Benjy only in cutting through societal prohibition, asking , "Old man . . . Have you lived so long and forgotten so much that you dont remember anything you ever knew or felt or even heard about love?" (*GDM* 257). In the great sequence of works that includes *Light In August, Absalom, Absalom!*, and *Go Down, Moses*, Faulkner was increasingly concerned with how love inevitably blurs racial boundaries.[16]

If love is the ultimate means of reconciliation, however, mistakes are a more immediate way to undermine some of the damage inherent in designs of patrilineal succession. A major subplot of *Gravity's Rainbow*, in effect an alternate version of the *Absalom, Absalom!* story, concerns two important characters, one European, one half African, who are sons of the same father. Throughout the novel the white son intends to kill the black son. But at what should be the climactic moment of encounter, the two pass without recognizing each other. The narrator comments, "This is magic. Sure—but not necessarily fantasy. Certainly not the first time a man has passed his brother by, at the edge of the evening, often forever, without knowing it" (*GR* 735). In a reversal of Aristotelian *hamartia*, ignorance averts tragedy. The magic of missed connections betrays the fantasy of a coherent plot—a plot of one brother against the other. The moment of reprieve is local and provisional in the overall structure of the novel, but it suggests how the Sutpen story might be read not as fatality but as radical contingency. The logic that successive narrators discerned or created to make sense of an event that had already happened did not, after all, determine the original characters. Henry Sutpen might easily have failed to kill Charles Bon.

NOTES

1. *Absalom, Absalom!* (New York: Vintage International, 1990), 212; hereafter cited in the text as *AA*. *Gravity's Rainbow* (New York: Viking-Penguin, 1973), 434; hereafter cited in the text as *GR*.

2. The most influential descriptions of a postmodern era or condition are Fredric Jameson, *Postmodernism, or the Cultural Logic of Late Capitalism* (Durham: Duke University Press, 1992), and Jean-François Lyotard, *The Postmodern Condition: A Report on Knowledge* (Minneapolis: Minnesota University Press, 1984).

3. The *locus classicus* for the subjective motivation of narrators and the uncertainty attaching to the "invented" stories is Donald Kartiganer, *The Fragile Thread: The Meaning of Form in Faulkner's Novels* (Amherst: University of Massachusetts Press, 1979), 69–105. Kartiganer, however, sees the radical uncertainty of the narrative as part of the quintessentially modernist "attempt to construct a significance of fictions without giving up the sense of a fundamental discontinuity between art and life" (69). McHale agrees that for the most part the "dominant" of *Absalom* is modernist, but sees a shift to an ontological, rather than epistemological, mode of questioning in chapter 8, where, he argues, the certainty of the events chronicled becomes irrelevant. Brian McHale, *Postmodernist Fiction* (London: Routledge, 1987), 8–11.

4. Modernist or "paranoid" text-processing strategies include the New Criticism, which had so much to do with early and persuasive interpretations of Faulkner's novels, but are not confined to New Critical practice. McHale discusses the two kinds of text-processing strategy in "Modernist Reading, Postmodern Text: The Case of *Gravity's Rainbow*" (1979), rpt. in Brian McHale, *Constructing Postmodernism* (London: Routledge, 1992), 61–86. My study, *Ideas of Order in the Novels of Thomas Pynchon* (Columbus: Ohio State University Press, 1982), employs modernist readings in my own extended (and later) sense. For a revision of some of my own preconceptions about *Gravity's Rainbow*, see my "Feminist Theory and the Politics of *Vineland*," *The Vineland Papers*, ed. Geoffrey Greene (Normal, Il.: Dalkey Archive Press, 1993), 134–52. In linking postmodernist reading to the socially and culturally marginal subject, I am especially indebted to Phillip Brian Harper, *Framing the Margins: The Social Logic of Postmodern Culture* (London: Oxford University Press, 1994). Naomi Schor considers strategies very much like those I am calling postmodernist in *Reading in Detail: Aesthetics and the Feminine* (New York: Methuen, 1987).

A less "paranoid," or postmodernist methodology that finds passages and details interesting precisely inasmuch as they do *not* fit in with a holistic and presumptively sanctioned vision of what everything adds up to might be said to underlie many of the feminist, African Americanist, Marxist, postcolonialist, and historicist criticism of Faulkner over the last two decades. See especially Carolyn Porter's intelligent "*Absalom, Absalom!*: (Un)Making the Father," *The Cambridge Companion to William Faulkner*, ed. Philip M. Weinstein (Cambridge: Cambridge University Press, 1995), 168–96.

5. William Faulkner, "Was," *Go Down, Moses* (New York: Vintage, 1996), 7–26, hereafter cited in the text as *GDM*. Patrick O'Donnell is especially acute in arguing that this story sequence is postmodernist in its opposition to the fatality characterizing earlier, modernist fiction. I return to this point at the conclusion of this essay. See "Faulkner and Postmodernism," *The Cambridge Companion to William Faulkner*, 31–50.

Eric Sundquist, *Faulkner: The House Divided* (Baltimore: Johns Hopkins University Press, 1983), 96–130; Joseph Allen Boone, *Libidinal Currents: Sexuality and the Shaping of Modernism* (Chicago: University of Chicago Press, 1998), 298–322.

6. Timothy Melley, *Empire of Conspiracy: The Culture of Paranoia in Postwar America* (Ithaca: Cornell University Press, 2000). The chapter on *Gravity's Rainbow*, "Bodies Incorporated" (81–106), has been especially important to my rethinking of Pynchon's great novel.

Sigmund Freud, *Totem and Taboo: Some Points of Agreement between the Mental Lives of Savages and Neurotics*, trans. James Strachey (New York: Norton, 1962). The reversal of the *Totem and Taboo* plot is of course the basis of several great Greek tragic cycles, among them the Oedipus plays, which notoriously deal with the fall of a house and a dynastic line because of a "tragic error" (*hamartia*) made by an initially successful progenitor. I shall return to the analogue of the Greek tragedies later in the essay. It is interesting to note, however, that such tragedies display what Melley has seen as a view of agency revived with great anxiety in North America after World War II, in that a conspiracy on the part of some large force like Fate, abetted by plans of the father to sustain his own power, tends to destroy an entire family. In *Gravity's Rainbow* the "family" becomes all humanity, and the "fathers" are the governmental and corporate ruling class who abet a Fate inherent in the requirements of profit-making and technological development.

7. On *hamartia*, see especially *The Poetics of Aristotle*, trans. Preston H. Epps (Chapel Hill: University of North Caroina Press, 1982), where *hamartia* is rendered "inadequacy or positive fault" (24–5, n. 18), and Nancy Sherman, "*Hamartia* and Virtue," *Essays on Aristotle's Poetics*, ed. Amélie Oksenberg Rorty (Princeton: Princeton University Press, 1992), 177–96.

8. "Evangeline," *Uncollected Stories of William Faulkner*, ed. Joseph Blotner (New York: Random House, 1979), 587.

9. Shreve is not free of racism, of course, only of the impossible, fully paranoid version of racism that we see in the Mississippi narrators. He happily uses the epithets "nigger" and "black bastard" far more freely than any of the other characters, evidently taking ebullient pleasure in brandishing terms that for the others constitute an elaborate code, to be employed in particular contexts with particular connotations (Rosa's "Take your hand off me, nigger," addressed to Clytie, is a key example). I want to suggest here that Shreve is so much an outsider to the (of course racist) threat of racial contamination that he can enjoy imagining himself thus contaminated. For an acute consideration of Shreve and the various racist positions in the novel, see Thadious M. Davis, *Faulkner's "Negro": Art and the Southern Context* (Baton Rouge: Louisiana University Press, 1983), 179–238.

We see other consequences of this combination of latitude and prohibition in *Go Down, Moses*, where Carrothers McCaslin perpetuated the slave McCaslin line by fathering a child on his own mulatto daughter.

10. Slothrop's father sold Slothrop "like a side of beef" to the psychologist Laszlo Jampf and the chemical cartel funding Jampf's experiments. Once Slothrop discovers this information, he sets off on a quest for data on what sort of experiment used him and what, exactly, the stimulus was. This information should lead him to understand the structure (in many senses) that controls and incorporates him.

11. Shreve cites Mr. Compson's relevant remark: "besides, your father said that when you have plenty of good strong hating you dont need hope because the hating will be enough to nourish you" (243).

12. Virginia Woolf, "Mr. Bennett and Mrs. Brown," *Collected Essays* (1923; I cite from the 1924 revised version, "Character in Fiction," *The Essays of Virginia Woolf: Volume Three, 1919–1924*, ed. Andrew McNeillie (San Diego: Harcourt Brace Jovanovich, 1987), 420–38.

Astradur Eyesteinnsen has documented how much "organicism" and other values ascribed to modernism generally historically derived from New Critical *readings* of modernist work. *The Concept of Modernism* (Ithaca: Cornell University Press, 1990).

13. See especially John T. Irwin, *Doubling and Incest, Repetition and Revenge: A Speculative Reading of Faulkner* (Baltimore: Johns Hopkins University Press, 1975).

14. In a letter written in 1933, Faulkner explained, "Quentin Compson, of the Sound & Fury, tells it, or ties it together; he is the protagonist so that it is not complete apocrypha. I use him because it is just before he is to commit suicide because of his sister, and I use his bitterness which he has projected on the South in the form of hatred of it and its people to get more out of the story itself than a historical novel would be. To keep the hoop skirts and plug hats out, you might say" (quoted in Joseph Blotner, *Faulkner: A Biography* [New York: Random House, 1974], 830).

15. For a detailed study of slavery and "miscegenation" in Faulkner's *Absalom, Absalom!*, see Sundquist. For information on the "shadow" (i.e., mulatto) family of William Faulkner's great-grandfather, the Confederate General William Clark Falkner, see especially Joel Williamson, *William Faulkner and Southern History* (New York: Oxford University Press, 1993).

In *Gravity's Rainbow* the Nazi Lieutenant Weissmann ("white one") has the nickname of "Dominus Blicero," deriving from " 'Blicker,' the nickname the early Germans gave to Death. They saw him as white: bleaching and blankness" (322). The iconography of the novel aligns racial whiteness with sterility, death, and hell.

16. In a superb essay on Rosa's narrative position within *Absalom, Absalom!*, Linda S. Kauffman notes the "niggardly debit-credit mentality" informing all the male narrators' accounts and reads Shreve's vision of Jim Bond as remainder: "one might argue that instead of lack, there is always something left, something from which human existence can replenish itself, as in a few thousand years we may replenish the human race from the loins of African kings." *Discourses of Desire: Gender, Genre, and Epistolary Fictions* (Ithaca: Cornell University Press, 1986), 267, 270.

"I'm the man here": *Go Down, Moses* and Masculine Identity

TERRELL L. TEBBETTS

The concerns in Faulkner's fiction often emerge from what we might call a metaconcern for Faulkner—the difficult need of many characters to claim an acceptable personal identity while at the same time handling exterior claims on their identity—particularly those of the past and of the community, including the family. As a modernist, Faulkner maintained an essentialist view on the question of personal identity, with a number of characters claiming a core, an essence, an innate foundation which they want to build their characters on, which they want to live and act in accord with. But much of his best fiction also anticipates the postmodern questioning of individual identity, particularly when the fiction deals with the power of exterior circumstance to influence identity—to define and circumscribe it, to fragment it, or to prop and support it. *Go Down, Moses* follows a series of works that examine these conflicting understandings of identity and provides Faulkner's last major consideration of them. In doing so, it gives readers a complex and perhaps unresolved final look, in particular, at Faulkner's take on masculine identity.

Some characters in Faulkner's fiction preceding *Go Down, Moses*—such as Sarty Snopes in "Barn Burning" and Bayard Sartoris in *The Unvanquished*—speak directly to Faulkner's metaconcern with identity, regularly steering between modern and postmodern understandings. Twenty years after the events in "Barn Burning," for example, when Sarty concludes, " 'If I had said they wanted only truth, justice, he would have hit me again,' "[1] he expresses his understanding of the conflict between modern essentialist and postmodern social/familial constructions of identity. On the one hand, the power of social construction recognized by postmodern thought looms large. His family, in the person of his father Abner, demands that he " 'stick to your own blood or you ain't going to have any blood to stick to you' " (*CS* 8), and Sarty tries to comply, fighting the boy who calls his father a barn burner. His character—his values and his behavior—come from outside himself. If this urge to comply were his only urge, Sarty would fully embody psychologist Kenneth Gergen's postmodern vision of identity, one that has received some notice since *The Saturated Self* appeared in 1991. Gergen argues that postmodernism is having an "apocalyptic" impact on the West's understanding of the self: "the very concept of personal essences is thrown into doubt," he writes, for "Selves as possessors of real and identifiable characteristics— such as rationality, emotion, inspiration, and will—are dismantled."[2] Or again, "In the postmodern world there is no individual essence. . . . One's identity is continuously emergent, re-formed, and redirected as one moves through the sea of everchanging relationships" (139). Those relationships, Gergen explains, are the only "self" one is likely to know, for in "the final stage in this transition to the postmodern . . . the self vanishes fully into a stage of relatedness" (17). With "selves" no more than "manifestations of relationship," relationships themselves come to hold "the central position occupied by the individual self for the last several hundred years of Western history" (146–7).

It would be perverse, of course, to claim Faulkner as a thoroughgoing postmodernist when most would agree with André Bleikasten's assessment that "Faulkner was a modernist, after all, or at the very least assumed by most readers to be one."[3] Most would especially find it easy to accept that Faulkner's concerns with identity are modernist, agreeing with Philip Weinstein that the fiction wrestles with Lockean views of identity, the tragic characters, in particular, exhibiting "radically failed self-ownership."[4] Perhaps predictably, then, Sarty Snopes's urge to comply with his father's construction of his identity is not at all his only urge. Feeling "pulled two ways like between two teams of horses" (17), Sarty asserts an identity separate from his father's seeking support in the laws that Abner violates, abstract laws that offer Sarty not only refuge but a warehouse of principles other than and larger than Abner's, a warehouse he can draw from to begin constructing a distinct identity he can own:

> "Hit's big as a courthouse" he thought quietly, with a surge of peace and joy whose reason he could not have thought into words, being too young for that: "They are safe from him. People whose lives are a part of this peace and dignity are beyond his touch. . . ." (10)

The story ends in tension, with little resolution of these conflicting ways of understanding identity: is Abner, the embodiment of the postmodern relational self, dead or alive? Will Sarty's flight lead him to successful modernist self-ownership? Sarty's outset at dawn is suggestive but still indefinite.

The Unvanquished brings Bayard's struggle with essentialist and relational constructions of self to a resolution rare in Faulkner's fiction, one that highlights the lack of resolution elsewhere. Only after Bayard Sartoris sees how not just to honor but also to deny his family's and society's claims on his identity can he claim personal ownership of that identity, saying "Then I was free."[5] He expresses his modern, essentialist drive toward individual self-fashioning in speaking to Aunt Jenny: " 'I must live with myself' " (240). The "self" Bayard seeks to live with suggests a core identity, a skeleton on which he intends to build both the muscle of fuller personal identity and the skin of public identity as well, choosing both by individual will. If this were the total story, it would be as simple as James Mellard makes it: "No one, these days, would reasonably dispute that William Faulkner is a modernist."[6] It is not that simple, however. Bayard also moves toward a relational construction of who he is. He accepts the claims of family when he identifies himself as "The Sartoris" (214). And he accepts larger social claims when he acknowledges that " 'I want to be thought well of' " (243)—especially by George Wyatt and the other veterans. Bayard resolves those conflicting constructions of his identity in his confrontation of Redmond. A kind of whole identity emerges encompassing a core and also a relational identity. Even so, the novel as a whole reaches no final resolution. Its lack of resolution lies in Drusilla and Ringo, both torn with tension in the struggle between their self-definitions and society's construction of their identities based on gender and race, relational identities Diane Roberts and others rightly see as "binary."[7]

Few characters in Faulkner's major fiction articulate this metaconcern with identity as directly as Bayard Sartoris does. Yet many of them demonstrate Bayard's contradictory needs to fashion their own identities around a perceived essential core and to live within the relational constructions of their given times and places, within the strictures of family, town, county, and region, strictures frequently based on gender and race. Few of them find Bayard's direct way of resolving the conflict; most are like Ringo and Drusilla—or like Sarty Snopes, choosing one identity and facing permanent, painful loss of the other, "crying 'Pap! Pap!', running . . . panting, sobbing 'Father! Father!' " (24), running out of the Snopes tribe, out of Yoknapatawpha County, and out of Faulkner's fiction.

Few characters in *Go Down, Moses*, in particular, resolve the conflict over identity as neatly as Bayard does. Instead, they confront conflicts between their need to construct an individual identity and their need for a relational identity in times and places that demand conformity to familial and racial roles destructive of the individual identities they might construct for themselves. And most notably, perhaps, in this novel they confront gender roles—male gender roles. Like Drusilla, Ringo, and

Sarty, like many characters in the major fiction, they find only partial resolution.

The modern/postmodern identity conflicts centered on family in *Go Down, Moses* are as strong as any in the earlier major fiction. If we consider the novel's opening and closing chapters, we see a shift away from a balance of core and community identity, a shift toward loss of any identity whatsoever. Turl's attraction to Tennie and Miss Sophonsiba's for Uncle Buck open the novel with a comic romp that gives Turl what he sought and presages Miss Sophonsiba's eventual triumph as well. If individual identity determines attraction and desire, then the black man and the white woman claim their identities and assert them. If marriage channels individual drives into the family and toward the community, then Turl's victory and Miss Sophonsiba's promised one suggest a balance of modernist self-construction and postmodern relational construction, one that Bayard would applaud. But *Go Down, Moses* closes with something altogether different. Butch Beauchamp, descendant of black and white Mc-Caslins, dies outside the community—an outlaw, an enemy of the people, simultaneously identified and denied by the same label: cop killer. He also dies abandoning his self-constructed identity, confusing the census taker by dropping whatever name he had been living under in his exile:

> "Wait." The census-taker wrote rapidly. "That's not the name you were sen— lived under in Chicago."
> The other snapped the ash from the cigarette. "No. It was another guy killed the cop."[8]

What is a lost name but a lost identity? What is self-constructed identity if it can be discarded so casually? And Beauchamp loses his patrilineal family as well. Not a single McCaslin greets the body or mourns the loss of this last McCaslin seen in *Go Down, Moses*. Why does Lawyer Stevens arrange for the body's return and why do the Worshams mourn but to point out through their presence the absence of the McCaslins? Where is Roth Edmonds? Where is Isaac McCaslin? Where is Butch's own grandfather Lucas Beauchamp, more McCaslin than any of them? How could the novel end with a clearer picture of the dissolution both of McCaslin identity and of the McCaslin family? Butch Beauchamp, the last McCaslin descendant speaking and acting in the novel, is a kind of anti-Bayard, neither well thought of by others nor living with himself. He is not even living! He is like Benjy Compson at the end of *The Sound and the Fury*, his death like Benjy's wailing, presaging an end without redemption. Even more, he is like Jim Bond at the end of *Absalom, Absalom!*, howling his own and his family's demise into the black of the night. In failing to negotiate Bayard's narrow path, Butch Beauchamp has destroyed himself; in making the path so very narrow, crooked, rocky, and steep for its black son, his family has destroyed both him and itself. Butch Beauchamp, dying without the identity he formed for himself but also without the family that so clearly formed him, embodies the novel's journey from modern individual identity to postmodern relational identity to no identity at all. Each of the other male characters in *Go Down, Moses* participates in the novel's journey in his own way.

Roth Edmonds's journey is a rich one to start with. Two important episodes in the novel highlight the conflicts of this McCaslin's heart: his separation from Lucas, Molly, and Henry Beauchamp in "The Fire and the Hearth" and his rejection of his lover and child in "Delta Autumn." In "The Fire and the Hearth," Roth's rejection of Henry represents his adoption of the racial constructions of his white family and the white community he lives in, at the price of his own heart's desire for brotherhood with his black cousins. In moving Henry out of his bed and onto the pallet, the narrator tells us, Roth succumbs to "the old curse of his fathers, the old haughty ancestral pride based not on any value but on an accident of geography" (107). Facing a choice between his fathers' cursed values—denial and separation—and his own truer one—love for his brothers—Roth chooses his fathers' curse: he "never slept in the same room again and never again ate at the same table" (109) with his Beauchamp kin. But his choice brings with it "a rigid fury of the grief he could not explain [and] the shame he would not admit" (109). It thus resolves nothing; indeed, it throws his identity into crisis. On the one hand, Roth's need to love emanates from a presumed core, something like Sarty's core longing for justice. On the other hand, his fathers' demands both construct and destroy him as surely as father Abner would Sarty. Roth joins society in its doomed construction of him precisely at the point when he denies Henry, who can say what Roth cannot: " 'I aint shamed of nobody. . . . Not even me' " (110). Roth becomes a postmodern unit in the McCaslin line, anything but a modernist product of self-definition, another example of Weinstein's "failed self-ownership." The novel sees the failure as a terrible loss.

Roth remains the postmodern McCaslin-unit in "Delta Autumn." He has come to embody thoroughly the very fathers who tore him apart in "The Fire and the Hearth." Specifically he has made himself into the avatar of Lucius Quintus Carothers McCaslin, the forefather whose name he bears, Roth short for Carothers, and whose features and expression he likewise bears: "It was the youngest face of them all, aquiline, saturnine, a little ruthless, the face of his ancestor too" (321). He treats his nameless mistress just as old McCaslin treated Eunice and Tomey, denying her and her son, paying them off with a sheaf of banknotes as surely as old

McCaslin tried to pay off Tomey's Turl with his legacy, which Ike has already judged as being *"cheaper than saying My son to a nigger"* (258). Roth fails Ike McCaslin's dictum that " 'most men are a little better than their circumstances give them a chance to be' " (329), having become nothing more than his heritage would have him. Neither Roth nor we readers will ever know what identity Roth might have claimed had he been as strong as Bayard Sartoris in encompassing both individual and societal constructions of his identity. But we can see the remnants of an abandoned identity, remnants contributing to a very conflicted heart. They live in the hostile misery driving Roth in "Delta Autumn," in his "harsh, restrained, furious impatience" (338–9). Those remnants notwithstanding, Roth has become an empty space, a void represented by five of his final words in the novel: " 'No . . . no . . . nothing . . . nothing . . . no' " (339). His fathers begot and then annihilated him, as he has begotten and now annihilates his own son. In conferring a familial identity, they destroy an essential one. How right that his expression is "saturnine," old Saturn (Cronos) having devoured his children one by one. Faulkner does seem to be a thoroughgoing modernist at this point, creating a character whose acceptance of a postmodern relational identity brings suffering and loss to himself and others.

If Roth has denied a core identity in becoming an avatar of his forebear, Ike McCaslin at first seems to differ from Roth. Ike seeks peace; Roth is always angry. Ike prefers the wilderness, which critics identify with the feminine, while Roth runs the plantation, a masculine reshaping of the earth. Ike appears to be celibate, while Roth is sexually rapacious, their difference clear in Legate's words: " '[Roth's] got a doe in here. Of course a old man like Uncle Ike cant be interested in no doe, not one that walks on two legs—when she's standing up, that is' " (321). If Roth is old McCaslin's avatar, Ike seems like his anti-avatar, as much old McCaslin's opposite as Roth's. He certainly intends to claim an individual identity free from old McCaslin and his curse when he repudiates his inheritance, the McCaslin plantation, and chooses the wilderness instead: " 'I am free' " (285), he tells his cousin; " 'Sam Fathers set me free' " (286). He sounds like a Sarty Snopes, rejecting his father's construction of his identity, setting out upon a journey of self-construction. Many critics have responded to such a possibility, seeing what R. W. B. Lewis calls "the miracle of moral regeneration" in Ike's story.[9] He even sounds like Bayard Sartoris when he explains his repudiation as something " 'I have got to [do] because I have got myself to have to live with for the rest of my life' " (275). That "self" Ike intends to live with may well be such a regenerated one, the modernist one that Roth rejects.

But it is not unambiguously so. What about the ways Ike's life does not differ from but rather matches Roth's? Their settings may match more than readers first think, Roth's plantation and Ike's wilderness being perhaps more alike than different. Do we need the narrator of "Race at Morning" to remind us that "the hunting and the farming wasn't two different things at all—they was jest the other side of each other"?[10] Their family relationships may match, as well: in "Delta Autumn" both are wifeless and childless, once Roth repudiates his son. More importantly, they join in denying and sending away Roth's mistress and child, their cousins. And they join in receiving the woman's rebuke: " 'you dont remember anything you ever knew or felt or even heard about love' " (346). And has not Ike McCaslin already denied his own wife when he denied her his farm and through that act also denied his responsibility for the plantation and the lives of those living on it? A number of critics have thought so—Olga Vickery, for example, seeing in Ike's repudiation "an attempt to evade . . . his own responsibilities,"[11] Arthur Kinney seeing in Ike a young man who refuses "individual responsibility,"[12] and Alan Friedman seeing that refusal not as regenerative but as "morally disastrous."[13] The words of Ike's denial support such critics in their particularly telling echo: " 'No,' he said. 'No:' and she was not looking at him . . . 'No, I tell you. I wont. I cant. Never' " (300). Ike's "No" and "Never" spoken to his wife sound indistinguishable from Roth's "No" and "Nothing" intended for his mistress, as if Ike like Roth has been constructed and annihilated, becoming an empty space without identity.

No wonder Roberts finds Roth and Ike both representative of the "masculine hegemony" in "Delta Autumn."[14] In seeking to become the opposite of old McCaslin, Ike may have become his mirror image, as controlled by him as Roth is. Is that why he and Roth are equally absent from the last chapter, from the homecoming of their kinsman Butch Beauchamp so obviously bereft of identity? Has Ike realized and claimed an essential identity? Or has he remained a unit in a relationship, no more than his grandfather's anti-avatar? As Gwendolyn Chabrier points out, there is a "psychological pattern of the son identifying with the grandfather rather than the father."[15] Has Ike done so inversely, twisting himself 180 degrees from sick and thus still remaining sick, becoming what he rejects?

Even the freedom Ike claims seems compromised in its source. Sam Fathers, the man who Ike thinks has freed him from his grandfather's curse, seems better equipped to ensnare Ike than to free him. Sam has a strongly masculine descent as signaled by his ultimately patronymic name, "which in Chickasaw had been Had-Two-Fathers" (160). One of several suggestions carried by such a name is that the second father has replaced the mother, erasing her influence on her son. If one father can construct and annihilate a son, what can two fathers do? One of Sam's fathers is "Doom," from the French "Du Homme." He is not just a man; he "became in fact The Man" (160), the essence of masculinity divorced from the feminine. Instead of giving birth and nurturing life, Doom brings death through the white powder, the anti-milk he places in the mouths of puppies and presumably his cousin's son. Like old Carothers, he sells his child and the child's mother into slavery.

Has Sam Fathers freed himself from his own familial curse? If he is to free Ike, would he not have had to free himself first? He has left the McCaslin plantation for the wilderness, as Ike will do in his way. But has this movement freed him if hunting and farming are indeed just two sides of the same thing? When Cass Edmonds compares Sam to "an old lion or bear in a cage . . . born in the cage and . . . in it all his life" (161), he may be more right than he knows. The cage is not the mixed blood of his mother, as Cass thinks, but the "warriors' and chiefs' blood" (162) that Cass exonerates, or rather the shaping influence of his fathers' exclusive vision of masculinity. The novel makes the connection when Sam gives old Ben the ominous title borne by his father—"the man" (190). Old Ben, the "epitome and apotheosis of the old wild life" (185), the incarnation of all Sam has fled the plantation to seek, is as much "the man" as Doom was. And Doom was a peer of old Carothers; he even sold Sam to old Carothers. So how is Sam free? How can he free Ike by introducing him to this kind of wilderness? Are not wilderness and plantation both mere blank tablets upon which human beings write the plots and characters of their own creation, for better or for worse?

Even if Ike is seeking in the wilderness a feminine alternative to The Men shaping him, the family curse still seems to fall upon him. In embracing the wilderness, Ike betrays the woman he marries as his grandfather betrayed Eunice in embracing Tomey. Critics have sensed such betrayal, Daniel Hoffman suggesting such a reading, for example, when he writes that Ike "takes the wilderness as his true bride."[16] Ike speaks the annihilating "no" and "never" to this betrayed wife, and she, whose name Ike never utters and thus whose identity he never sees, pronounces the doom due betrayal: " 'And that's all. That's all from me. If this dont get you that son you talk about, it wont be mine' " (300–1). She has simply cut out the middle man, annihilating the son before conception, since Ike would beget and shape that son only to betray and annihilate him anyway, as if Sam Father's also unnamed mother had prevented his begetting to prevent his sale into slavery. Or put it this way: in betraying his wife, Ike annihilates his son before he ever begets him.

Go Down, Moses resolves little regarding identity in its portrayal of Ike McCaslin. Ike may be right in claiming that he is "free," that he has found what modernism sees as a core identity and has constructed a life suitable to it, but he gives readers like Rosemary Bradford Grant reason to write that "Ike knows the truth; but it has not set him free."[17] Yet if relational identity has supplanted core identity again, Faulkner's fiction still seems the straight-forwardly modern. Being a unit in a relationship means destruction and loss.

If Roth Edmonds's and Ike McCaslin's negotiations of the path between modernist self-fashioning and Gergen's postmodern vision of relational identity seem unsuccessful, Lucas Beauchamp's journey contrasts with theirs. But it contrasts subtly, for at first Lucas Beauchamp seems as much like old Carothers as his cousins do. Like his forebear, Lucas loves money. He is the one descendant of old McCaslin who not only takes but demands his inheritance, his and his brother's too:

"The rest of that money. I wants it."

. . . .

"All of it? Half of it is Jim's."
"I can keep it for him same as you been doing." (105)

And despite Roth's ownership of the plantation, Lucas also is the one descendant of old McCaslin who actively seeks a way to turn the land into gold, farming it with a metal detector as well as a steel plough, seeking to raise buried bullion as well as cotton, actively and inventively farming it in both cases, trying to make the earth produce something hidden to others but glimpsed by him. If Roth has become an avatar of old McCaslin and Ike possibly an anti-avatar, Lucas sometimes seems to be not an avatar but the archetype of the old patriarch: Lucas Beauchamp is *more like old Carothers than all the rest of us put together, including old Carothers*" (114). A unit in a familial relationship.

Once again, however, this is not the whole story. The most important way that Lucas Beauchamp resembles old Carothers, ironically, is in a characteristic that makes him both an archetype of old Carothers and at the same time fully himself, a member of his family and yet at the same time self-constructed. His cousin Ike tells us of that characteristic not once but twice: Lucas "*fathered himself, intact and complete, contemptuous, as old Carothers must have been*" (114–15), Ike muses, and he later reiterates that Lucas is "by himself composed, himself selfprogenitive and nominate, by himself ancestored, as, for all the old ledgers recorded to the contrary, old Carothers himself was" (269). Lucas would seem to have negotiated the very path that Bayard wound down. He is a version of his forefather and thus very much within the family, but he is most essentially like that forefather in being self-created, having constructed an identity out of a core—free from family while the essence of the family. Lucas Beauchamp rather than Ike would seem to be the McCaslin who is truly "free."

If Lucas Beauchamp's relationship with his McCaslin kin suggests such a possibility, we can test it by examining his relationship with his wife and children. When Lucas's hunt for gold in "The Fire and the Hearth" brings him to the verge of divorce, he comes close to denying his wife Molly just as his cousins deny mistress and wife, the separation of man from woman in *Go Down, Moses* suggesting male acquiescence to a postmodern familial identity that destroys them even as it forms them. When Lucas insists to Roth that " 'I'm a man. . . . I'm the man here' " (116) and then again " 'I'm going to be the man in this house' " (117), he claims the title worn by Doom, the enslaver of his mate, the begetter and annihilator of his son, the equal of old Carothers. If Lucas is going to follow the Doom/McCaslin gender construction as Roth followed its racial one, Lucas will suffer the same destruction and loss. As a unit in the McCaslin line, he will separate from a kind relationship he needs in order to be whole.

This Doom/McCaslin denial of the female may spring from what Jung describes as the ego's denial of anima. In fact, Jung helps a great deal with all three of these cousins at this crisis. Particularly helpful is his insistence that when the masculine ego attempts to assert its strength by denying anima it actually denies itself the very resource it needs to grow into its own full strength as part of a harmonized whole, the Self. The anima "conveys the vital messages of the Self,"[18] and it thus plays the essential "role of guide, or mediator, to the world within and to the Self."[19] Without a connection to Self, the masculine ego remains alienated and, in its alienation, incomplete.

Though the threatened divorce brings Lucas to the verge of such alienation and failure, he is the one cousin who pulls back from it. If his cousin Ike "retreats to the comfort of an inflexible plan," into a "dream world,"[20] and if in doing so Ike has "retreated into his dreams while excluding his wife from it,"[21] Lucas does the opposite. Lucas enters the courtroom to reclaim his wife: " 'We dont want no voce,' Lucas said. 'I done changed my mind' " (124). Lucas follows his changed mind with changed behavior, relinquishing the metal detector in order to keep his wife. He even has to insist on relinquishing it when Roth tempts him to keep it and use it on the sly: " 'No. Get rid of it.' . . . 'No,' Lucas said. 'Get rid of it. I dont want to never see it again' " (126–7). Lucas's negatives—no, no, dont, never—are ironic parallels of Ike's negatives to his wife and Roth's to his mistress. Lucas repudiates the thing in order to claim the wife.

Lucas's relinquishment of the metal detector foreshadows Ike's repudiation of watch, compass, and gun later in the novel (though earlier in chronology). All are masculine tools for dividing, shaping, controlling the feminine wilderness of time and space. The cousins seem much alike in giving up their masculine tools for the greater good of feminine connection. They both seem stronger individuals for the relinquishment. Yet what a difference in the aims of their relinquishments. Ike relinquishes his tools to enter the wilderness and look upon the bear: "the wilderness coalesced. It rushed soundless, and solidified—the tree, the bush, the compass and the watch glinting where a ray of sunlight touched them. Then he saw the bear" (200). But are we not taken aback that, for all the reputed femininity of the wilderness, when it coalesces, it does so for Ike in the form of an old male bear, one that sounds very much like old Carothers McCaslin, called like him his own "progenitor" (202)? Doreen Fowler seems right to point out that Old Ben "functions in the text as a kind of elusive fatherhead."[22] Is Ike relinquishing his masculine tools to behold his model as anti-avatar of his grandfather, the patriarch of the wilderness that he will substitute for the patriarch of the plantation? Sam Fathers himself, the priest of the wilderness, describes the bear that embodies the supposedly feminine wilderness in words that sound as much like a description of old Carothers as of old Ben: "He dont care no more for bears than he does for dogs or men neither. . . . Because he's the head bear. He's the man" (190). Precisely. When the supposedly feminine wilderness coalesces, it metamorphoses into a man. Is it not the spirit of this old bear that Ike holds to when he excludes his wife from his dream, just as Roth holds to the spirit of old Carothers when he denies his mistress? And, as Linda Wagner-Martin pointed out at the 1998 Faulkner and Yoknapatawpha Conference, the old bear leads Ike back to the masculine tools he supposedly relinquished.

On the other hand, when Lucas relinquishes his tool, the metal detector, he chooses his wife over his dream of patriarchy: though Lucas has used Sam Fathers' words in claiming to be "the man here" (116) and "the man in this house" (117), by the end of "The Fire and the Hearth" he has acceded to Molly, realizing that " 'Man has got three score and ten years on this earth, the Book says. He can want a heap in that time and a heap of what he can want is due to come to him. . . . But I am near to the end of my three score and ten, and I reckon to find that money aint for me' " (127). It is possible that, while Ike masculinizes the wilderness in old Ben and leaves himself broken and alone, Lucas more truly enters the feminine, cementing his connection to Molly and thus completing himself as "the man." Perhaps in Lucas and Molly Beauchamp readers find what Jay Martin says Faulkner's fiction searches for: "an example of a harmonious marriage as proof that these impulses [masculine and feminine] could be joined naturally and without contradiction."[23] Men who become relational units in exclusive white patriarchies deny relationship with the black and the female alike. Yet to be full, the white male seems driven—by his core identity?—toward relationship with black cousins and female lovers. As a unit in an exclusive white, male relationship, the white and the male will fail. As a unit in inclusive relationships with the black and the female, the white male constructs a whole self. The core seeks not singularity but plenitude. The modernist essence fulfills itself only in postmodern relationship.

Such a complex understanding of identity would seem to be at the heart of "Pantaloon in Black." The story assaults the exclusive binary relational constructions of identity that have seduced Roth and perhaps Ike. The story rejects the polarization of male and female in its depiction of Rider and Mannie. As an individual Rider is a full expression of essential masculinity, as manly a man as Faulkner could believably create. He is big—"better than six feet" and "better than two hundred pounds" (131). He is physically powerful—"handling himself at times out of the vanity of his own strength logs which ordinarily two men would have handled with canthooks" (133–4)—so powerful he is literally an unstoppable force, uncontainable, twice "stepping over the three-strand wire fence without even breaking his stride" (133), ripping the "steel barred door" of his cell "out of the wall, bricks hinges and all" (153). He is sexually powerful with women, earning his name presumably by having bedded countless "women bright and dark and for all purposes nameless he didn't need to buy" (134). He is socially powerful with men, "head of the timber gang itself" at the age of twenty-four (133). If there is an essential masculine identity, Rider has claimed it.

And yet it is not enough. For "when he saw Mannie, whom he had known all his life, for the first time," he discards his former being: "Ah'm thu wid all dat" (134). His identity changes so utterly that when he loses Mannie he thinks of the man who lived with her as "somebody else" (135). Rider has been two different men, and his agony is that he needs to be the full, second self so much that he will die to regain the relationship that gave him that self, crying "lemme go wid you, honey" to Mannie's apparition and finding a way to do exactly that through the remaining days of his life. This most masculine man became another man when he found and married his Mannie, his loving relationship with Mannie "manning" Rider more fully than he could ever "man" himself. Masculine and feminine poles move dramatically to the center in Rider's story, Rider's essential masculine identity completing itself only in his social relationship with his wife. Rider has an essential selfhood and claims it to the fullest. His fullest selfhood, however, blooms only when he also becomes a unit in an inclusive relationship. Faulkner the modernist joins Faulkner the postmodernist.

If this vision were the sole, unambiguous truth regarding masculine identity in *Go Down, Moses*, the novel would hardly leave us in the tense unresolve we sense in it and in so much of Faulkner's greatest work. It is again the last chapter, "Go Down, Moses," that makes this marriage of modernist and postmodern identities something other than the novel's sole truth, that thus leaves readers with the novel's final unresolve. If Lucas Beauchamp, like Rider (who took Lucas as his model), has fashioned an identity encompassing both a modernist core and the postmodern vision of a self constructed through relationships—in his case, through the influence of the strong female identity of Molly Beauchamp—why is he not beside Molly mourning the death of his grandson, the last McCaslin seen in *Go Down, Moses*? In fact, Faulkner goes to some trouble to absent Lucas from the chapter. Not only does Lucas never appear as a character, not even as a passenger in the car carrying his wife in the funeral procession, but even his *name* never appears. The first two times the chapter mentions Lucas, he is called only "the old Negress' husband" and "her husband" (355), suggesting that, though the absent Lucas still lives, he lives with a postmodern identity derived from his relationship with his wife. In the third and final mention, Gavin Stevens calls Lucas by the wrong name—"old Luke Beauchamp" (359), his identity so tenuous even his name will not stick.

Why this carefully constructed and surely significant absence? Is Lucas's identity, after all, no more encompassing than that of his equally absent his cousins, his masculine core abandoned, absorbed into the feminine in a kind of Lacanian regression where, as Fowler points out, attaining a "complete self" means returning to "no self" (7)? Has Lucas been destroyed by returning to the feminine as his cousins were by denying the feminine? Is Lucas as empty of core identity as Darl Bundren, shaped by the rain, as self-annihilating as Quentin Compson and Joe Christmas? Surely not, we may argue. But why not? Or is Lucas deliberately absent from his wife's mourning, denying his wife for a final time and denying his grandson as well? If so, he joins old Carothers, Ike, and Roth in destroying his masculine core in the very act of trying to protect it against the claims the feminine. His disappearing name and his absence look like annihilation. Surely not, we may think. But why not? What resolution might we attempt here? Is this the novel that Wagner-Martin says it is, with Faulkner "making pronouncements,"[24] writing a "statement about responsibility"[25] where he "forces the reader to know"?[26] Or does it culminate a series of fictions, arriving with them at uncertainty, its competing notions of identity in tense unresolve?

NOTES

1. William Faulkner, "Barn Burning," in *Collected Stories* (New York: Vintage: 1995), 8. All further references will be to this edition and will appear in the text.

2. Kenneth Gergen, *The Saturated Self: Dilemmas of Identity in Contemporary Life* (New York: Basic Books, 1991), 7. All further references are to this edition and will be cited in the text.

3. André Bleikasten, "Faulkner and the New Ideologues," in *Faulkner and Ideology*, ed. Donald M. Kartiganer and Ann J. Abadie (Jackson: University Press of Mississippi, 1995), 12.

4. *What Else but Love? The Ordeal of Race in Faulkner and Morrison* (New York: Columbia University Press, 1996), 92.

5. William Faulkner, *The Unvanquished* (New York: Vintage, 1991), 228. All further references are to this edition and will be cited in the text.

6. "Realism, Naturalism, Modernism: Residual, Dominant, and Emergent Ideologies in *As I Lay Dying*," in *Faulkner and Ideology*, 217.

7. *Faulkner and Southern Womanhood* (Athens: University of Georgia Press, 1994), 84.

8. William Faulkner, *Go Down, Moses* (New York: Vintage, 1990), 352. All further references will be to this edition and will be cited in the text.

9. R. W. B. Lewis, "The Hero in the New World," in *Bear, Man, and God: Seven Approaches to William Faulkner's "The Bear,"* ed. Francis L. Utley, Lynn Z. Bloom, and Arthur Kinney (New York: Random House, 1964), 323.

10. *Uncollected Stories* (New York: Vintage, 1997), 309.

11. *The Novels of William Faulkner: A Critical Interpretation* (Baton Rouge: Louisiana State University Press, 1964), 326.

12. "Delta Autumn: Postlude to 'The Bear,' " in *Bear, Man, and God: Seven Approaches to William Faulkner's "The Bear,"* 390.

13. *William Faulkner* (New York: Ungar, 1984), 134.

14. *Faulkner and Southern Womanhood*, 87.

15. *Faulkner's Families: A Southern Saga* (New York: Gordian, 1993), 24.

16. *Faulkner's Country Matters: Folklore and Fable in Yoknapatawpha* (Baton Rouge: Louisiana State University Press, 1989), 129.

17. "The Concept of Space As It Relates to the Self in Faulkner's 'The Bear,' " *Teaching Faulkner* 11 (1997): 5.

18. Carl G. Jung, et al., *Man and His Symbols* (Garden City, N.Y.: Doubleday, 1964), 188.

19. Ibid., 183.

20. Kinney, 388, 390.

21. Vickery, 133.

22. *Faulkner: The Return of the Repressed* (Charlottesville: University of Virginia Press, 1997), 128.

23. "Faulkner's 'Male Commedia': The Triumph of Manly Grief," in *Faulkner and Psychology*, ed. Donald M. Kartiganer and Ann J. Abadie (Jackson: University Press of Mississippi, 1994), 150.

24. Linda Wagner-Martin, *New Essays on "Go Down, Moses"* (Cambridge: Cambridge University Press, 1996), 8.

25. Ibid., 7.

26. Ibid., 6.

Revising *The Sound and the Fury: Absalom, Absalom!* and Faulkner's Postmodern Turn

DOREEN FOWLER

According to the critical consensus, Quentin Compson commits suicide because he longs to escape time and change into a world of timeless verities. It has not always been recognized, however, that Quentin associates enduring values with unquestioned male authority. Quentin looks backward with nostalgia to a time when he imagines that male will held unchallenged sway, a time before the abolition of slavery, a social institution that promoted the myth that power is naturalized in the white male body. Near the end of his interior monologue, presumably as he is about to commit suicide, Quentin personifies death as a patriarch, a man like Grandfather. Because the passage reveals Quentin's deep investment in patriarchal power, I quote it in full:

> It used to be I thought of death as a man something like Grandfather a friend of his a kind of private and particular friend like we used to think of Grandfather's desk not to touch it not even to talk loud in the room where it was I always thought of them as being together somewhere all the time waiting for old Colonel Sartoris to come down and sit with them waiting on a high place beyond cedar trees Colonel Sartoris was on a still higher place looking out across at something and they were waiting for him to get done looking at it and come down Grandfather wore his uniform and we could hear the murmur of their voices from beyond the cedars they were always talking and Grandfather was always right.[1]

As Quentin perceives patriarchs like Grandfather and Colonel Sartoris, they walk the sky like gods. He associates Grandfather with symbols of authority—desk, uniform, and "a high place." This "high place" is Quentin's dream-fantasy inscription of transcendence of human limitations. As Quentin envisions him, Grandfather, the slaveholder and Confederate General, seems to possess power over life and death, a power equal to death's. Accordingly, Quentin conceives of death as a man like Grandfather, Grandfather's friend. Alternatively stated, Quentin imagines Grandfather as a site of transcendence, immune to and immutable as death.

Quentin introduces this personification of death with the words, "It used to be I thought," a prefatory phrase that imputes his dream of patriarchal power to the past. By ascribing this image of transcendence to the past, Quentin may be tacitly acknowledging that his image of Grandfather is the child's fantasy of the father's absolute power. But I contend that the child's dream of the father's deathlike power informs *The Sound and the Fury*, and that this dream has particular force in Southern fiction because it was once fostered by slavery, a historical institution in the American South that represented some white men as masters.

Of course Quentin's assertion that Grandfather "was always right" runs counter to all postmodernist notions of the instability of meaning. The work of Saussure, Derrida, and other theorists undermines traditional conceptions of truth. If we cast Quentin's vision of Grandfather in terms of contemporary language theory, Grandfather, for Quentin, represents the transcendental signifier, that is, the signifier that stands outside of a chain of signifiers and imbues the chain with meaning. But, according to poststructuralist thought, the transcendental signifier does not exist. In fact, while Quentin professes a belief in Grandfather's ability to guarantee stable, unchanging meaning, he himself, like his father and brothers, is unable to represent such meaning.

In *The Sound and the Fury* Quentin Compson struggles to be the kind of powerful patriarch he imagines Grandfather to be, but all his attempts end in humiliating failure. He fails to preserve Caddy's purity, his task as self-appointed surrogate-father; he fails to prevent her marriage to the odious Head; he fails to restore the little Italian girl to her father; he fails to carry out his plan of joint suicide with Caddy; and he fails ignominiously when he challenges both Dalton Ames and Gerald Bland. In sum, he fails utterly to be the strong figure of authority of his fantasy, and he is shadowed by the specter of impotence, embodied in Benjy, the castrated, helpless man-child. In identifying the source of Quentin's despair, Faulkner alluded to "the basic failure Quentin inherited through his father, or beyond his father. It was a—something had happened somewhere between the first Compson and Quentin. The first Compson was a bold ruthless man who came into Mississippi as a free forester to grasp where and when he could and wanted to, and established what should have been a princely line and that princely line decayed."[2] Arguably, what happened between the first Compson and Quentin is the dissolution of ways of thinking that prevailed from the Renaissance through the modern period—specifically, the interrogation of the received notion that language somehow represents meanings that exist independent of language. Faulkner explains that his novel is about the decline of a princely line; I propose that the novel is a site of conflict between a belief-structure that posits "princely" figures like Grandfather and a modernist/postmodernist view that contests such beliefs.

Grandfather is not the only figure whom Quentin visualizes dwelling in "a high place" above the sound and the fury that threatens to engulf Quentin. Observing Gerald Bland row, for example, Quentin imagines Bland "rowing himself right out of noon, up the long bright air like an apotheosis, mounting into a drowsing infinity" (120). Similarly, as Quentin describes them, Spoade and Ames also seem to emanate a static quality. But, if Quentin believes that these men inhabit a coherent world with a solid foundation and a hierarchy of meaning, Quentin himself is unable to locate fixed principles and stable meanings. For Quentin, all things appear to be "shadowy, paradoxical . . . without relevance inherent themselves with the denial of the significance they should have affirmed" (170). In other words, Quentin struggles with a distinctly postmodern apprehension of indeterminacy.

Quentin Compson, a central character of *The Sound and the Fury*, is a central mediating consciousness in Faulkner's 1936 novel, *Absalom, Absalom!* Faulkner selected Quentin, along with two other characters from *The Sound and the Fury*, Shreve and Mr. Compson, to narrate chapters of *Absalom*. Given that Quentin had committed suicide in *The Sound and the Fury*, Quentin's narrative presence made it necessary to predate the later novel, that is, to make the present time of the later novel earlier than Quentin's death in June of 1910. Despite this awkwardness, Faulkner selected Quentin, along with Shreve and Mr. Compson, to tell the story of Thomas Sutpen, and, as John T. Irwin has ably demonstrated, the effect of this choice was to create intertextual resonances between the two novels.[3] I propose to juxtapose the two related texts here to examine a notable development in Faulkner's postmodernist technique. A postmodern text questions and unsettles what Lyotard calls "the totalizing master narratives of our culture," with which we order experience.[4] I propose that *Absalom, Absalom!* interrogates the South's master narrative—the patriarchal order—in a way that *The Sound and the Fury* does not.[5] While *The Sound and the Fury* is demonstrably subversive in both form and content, I find a crucial lapse in the novel's self-reflexivity. To illuminate this lapse, I invoke a characteristic of postmodernism identified by Linda Hutcheon. According to Hutcheon, postmodernism always involves "a critical revisiting of the past never a nostalgic return."[6] In *The Sound and the Fury*, Quentin and his father nostalgically yearn for the days of Grandfather, when, they imagine, the patriarch's authority conferred meaning and identity. Further I suggest that *The Sound and the Fury* stages "a nostalgic return" of the past: Ames, Bland, and Spoade are represented in the novel, without self-reflexive irony or parody, as

"princely" figures; images of stasis consistently attend them and metaphorically pose the claim that they, like Grandfather, are immune and
immutable.

Absalom, Absalom!, on the other hand, "critically revisits the past." In
Absalom, with Quentin Compson narrating, Faulkner exposes as fraudulent the image of patriarchal power that Quentin espouses in *The Sound
and the Fury*. Faulkner reveals this fraudulence by means of a subtext
that investigates and demystifies the cultural structuring of subjectivity
and meaning. I propose to foreground this subversive subtext, and to
begin with Sutpen's beginning, that is, with Sutpen's birth as a subject
in the cultural order, which is narrated by Quentin and Shreve in chapter
seven. The model of identity that informs this entrance into subjectivity
and culture is profoundly at odds with essentialist notions of a unified,
coherent, autonomous self. Rather identity is represented here and elsewhere in the novel as socially constructed in loss, a distinctly postmodern
and, more specifically, Lacanian, notion.

Faulkner, of course, almost certainly did not know the work of Jacques
Lacan; however, I want to show that *Absalom*, and particularly Sutpen's
birth into cultural meanings, can be interpreted in terms of Lacan's theory of identity. In my reading, this correspondence signifies that Faulkner intuited what Lacan codified; that is, Faulkner's own intuitive
understanding of the instability of identity corresponds to Lacan's theory
of the fractured self.

To say that Lacan's theory is complex would be an understatement.
But I propose only to outline the most general overview of this Lacanian
model. The crux of Lacan's theory is that subjectivity arises out of alienation.[7] Lacan holds that in the beginning, before the rise of subjectivity,
we exist as part of one continuous totality of being. In this early stage of
development, we experience no lack and no sense of difference, and,
precisely for this reason, the child has no sense of a separate identity. In
this phase, which Lacan calls the imaginary, there is no "I" and no
"other," and, Lacan insists, the two concepts come into existence together. For identity and cultural meanings, there must be difference, and
this difference occurs only when the child, in obedience to the father or
someone who represents what Lacan calls the paternal metaphor, performs a splitting, represses a part, and the resulting absence opens up
the space that makes it possible to define the self apart from the other.
This moment of rupture is the all-important moment in Lacanian theory,
the one moment that matters; it is the moment when subjectivity is constituted in loss. The newly formed subject now enters the world of cultural orderings, or what Lacan calls the symbolic order, but the price of
subjectivity is high. Subjectivity is constituted of lack, and the subject,

now self-aware, is aware of its own absent center and is driven by desire to fill the void, to ascend to the place of the Father, whom the child deludedly believes is complete, powerful, and autonomous, in short, what Lacan calls the phallus.[8]

Faulkner's rendering of the rise of subjectivity in the little boy, Tom Sutpen, seems almost uncannily to narratize Lacan's often inscrutable theorizing about identity. In chapter seven of *Absalom*, Quentin relates to Shreve a story that has been passed down to him from Sutpen through Grandfather and Father. It is the story of the founding moment in Sutpen's life, the moment when the little boy was turned away from the front door of the planter's big white house. This event is the all-important event in Sutpen's life; it is the moment of origin. In a very real sense, all that occurs thereafter in the novel devolves from this event; and this event corresponds to the one moment that matters in Lacanian theory, the oedipal moment when subjectivity is born in loss.

Before Sutpen is turned away from the front door of the planter's house, he is decidedly not self-aware. As he approaches the planter's door, young Sutpen was "no more conscious of his appearance . . . or of the possibility that anyone else would be than he was of his skin."[9] Concomitant with this lack of self awareness is a lack of awareness of difference. In the world that the boy has inhabited up to this time, "the land belonged to anybody and everybody and so the man who would go to the trouble and work to fence off a piece of it and say 'This is mine' was crazy" (179). He "had never even heard of, never imagined, a place, a land, . . . all divided and fixed and neat with a people living on it all divided and fixed and neat because of what color their skins happened to be and what they happened to own" (179). Before he is turned away at the door, Tom Sutpen exists unaware of self and unaware of cultural hierarchies. In sum, he exists in what Lacan calls the presymbolic or imaginary, a register of being without difference or cultural meanings and without a sense of an "I" distinct from an "other."

At the front door of the planter's big white house, Sutpen experiences alienation; the liveried slave, who represents the planter within the house, tells Sutpen to go around to the back door. With the slave's words, Sutpen becomes aware of difference, specifically, his difference from the planter, and Sutpen's subjectivity is born in a moment of trauma and loss:

> [The slave at the door] was just another balloon face . . . , looking down at him from within the half closed door during that instant in which, before he knew it, something in him had escaped and—he unable to close the eyes of it—was looking out from within the balloon face just as the [planter] . . . , whom the laughter which the balloon held barricaded and protected from such as he, looked out from whatever invisible place he (the man) happened to be . . . at

the boy . . . , he himself seeing his father and sisters and brothers as the owner, the rich man . . . must have been seeing them all the time—as cattle . . . , with for sole heritage that expression on a balloon face bursting with laughter. (189–90)

Sutpen is describing the moment when he becomes self-aware; he sees himself now as the planter sees him and his family—as brutes. In accordance with Lacan's model of identity, this awareness is accompanied by loss—"something in him had escaped,"—and throughout this passage an identification of self-awareness with an absent center is strikingly represented by the profuse balloon imagery. The liveried slave is "another balloon face"; Sutpen now looks out of a "balloonface"; the planter is "barricaded and protected from such as he" by the balloon; Sutpen's sole heritage, he sees now, is that "expression on a balloon face bursting with laughter." The balloon image stunningly renders a poststructuralist notion of subjectivity. A balloon marks a boundary; but within that boundary there is nothing; thus the balloon aptly images Lacan's subject constituted of lack. The subject comes into being by a sundering that marks off a boundary, but, like the balloon, what the boundary "barricades and protects" is airy nothing, the yawning gap created by the sundering. The subject, Juliet Mitchell tells us, is "not an entity with an identity, but a being created in the fissure of a radical split."[10] The balloon image, with its absent center, images the fissure from which the subject speaks.

In the oedipal moment the child severs a former dyadic unity with the mother and the world. This violent sundering is also represented in Faulkner's text. After the rejection at the door, Sutpen goes to "a kind of cave" and sits "with his back against the uptorn roots" (188). The cave, an archetypal symbol for the womb, here represents existence prior to birth into subjectivity and culture; the "uptorn roots" figure the violent severing of a former continuous being.[11]

In the cave, Sutpen develops his "design." He goes to the cave to decide what to do "because he knew that . . . he would have to do something about it in order to live with himself for the rest of his life" (189). As Sutpen considers a course of action, he seems stymied. A split subject, he debates himself: "*But I can shoot him*: and the other: *No. That wouldn't do no good*: and the first: *What shall we do then?* and the other: *I dont know*: and the first: *But I can shoot him*. . . . and the other: *No. That wouldn't do no good*" (190). Young Sutpen continues to dismiss as futile the only course of action that seems open to him when suddenly the very circularity of his reasoning leads him to a blinding (and I use the word advisedly) conclusion. Quite simply, he deduces that the planter is completely beyond his retaliation, beyond his reach. He concludes that *"there aint any good or harm either in the living world that I can do to him"* (192). In other words, he determines that the planter transcends *"the living world."* This deduction is of cataclysmic import to the young boy, and rightly so, for with these words he infers the planter's inviolability; in Lacanian terms, Sutpen attributes to the planter the always mythical phallus.

Sutpen's innocence is frequently remarked in *Absalom*; "His trouble," Quentin says, "was innocence" (178). However, this innocence remains undefined in the text. In my reading, Sutpen's "innocence" is precisely his childish, naive belief in the cultural fiction that the patriarch in the big white house is autonomous and complete. "Instruct[ed]" by his innocence (192), his belief in the planter's unassailability, Sutpen formulates his "design," and this design is nothing more than the slavish imitation of a culturally constructed model of power, a patriarchal model. He must acquire what the planter has, "money, a house, a plantation, slaves, a family—incidentally of course, a wife" (212); he must do what the planter did: he must turn others away from the door of the big white house. In sum, we have witnessed Sutpen's induction into a social order that constructs him.[12] This induction into the the social order exemplifies Lacan's pronouncement that the child is inserted into "a symbolic order that pre-exists the infantile subject and in accordance with which he will have to structure himself."[13]

Thomas Sutpen is most decidedly not a postmodernist within a postmodernist text. Postmodernism maintains that there are no natural hierarchies; Sutpen embraces the cultural myth of a "natural" patriarchal order. Postmodernism claims that there is no ultimate authority to ground meanings; Sutpen believes in the absolute authority of the white planter. Perhaps the key characteristic of postmodernism is its insistence that we interrogate the totalizing master narratives of our culture. Even when his design fails, still Sutpen never questions the master code of his culture, the patriarchal tradition; Sutpen's only question is rather how did he fail exactly to duplicate the cultural model. Years later when he sees that he has not achieved inviolability within the walls of his big white house, he goes to Grandfather, a trained legal mind, to help him locate his error in the imitation of the patriarchal ideal. "You see," he tells Grandfather, "I had a design in my mind. Whether it was a good or bad design is beside the point; the question is, Where did I make the mistake in it, what did I do or misdo in it, whom or what injure by it to the extent which this would indicate" (212). I repeat: Sutpen's "trouble," according to Quentin, is innocence. His innocence is his willingness to accept as universal "truth" the fictions of culture.[14]

In *Absalom*, a perception of the patriarch as above *"the living world"* is consistently deconstructed. We have already seen how Sutpen's birth into culture corresponds to a Lacanian model of identity. I propose now briefly to show that another Lacanian notion, his theory of the gaze, also functions in *Absalom* to subvert a traditional conception of the subject's autonomy. According to Lacan, the subject "is not so much a representer as a representation."[15] Juliet Mitchell explains what Lacan means: "the identity that seems to be that of the subject is in fact a mirage arising when the subject forms an image of itself by identifying with other perceptions of it."[16] In accordance with this postmodern view, in *Absalom* identity is represented as an illusory image projected by a viewer. For example, Wash Jones sees Sutpen in much the same way that the young Sutpen looked at the planter or Quentin of *The Sound and the Fury* views Grandfather. Jones's word for Sutpen is "big": *"He is bigger,"* Jones says, *"than all them Yankees . . . , bigger than this whole county"* (230). But, if we examine the text closely, we observe that Sutpen's outsized stature is always a function of the viewer's perception: "he was the biggest thing in their sight" (290). Relentlessly the text underscores that Sutpen's bigness is merely an image. What Jones sees, we read, is "the fine proud image of the man on the fine proud image of the stallion" (230). Similarly Sutpen is able to locate an image of himself as supreme patriarch in Jones's granddaughter's gaze. When Sutpen returns from the war, he finds that he has not lost "absolutely all"; for there still "remain[s] to look at him with unchanged regard" one girl "who had been a child when he saw her last, who doubtless used to watch him from window or door as he passed unaware of her as she would have looked at God probably" (291). This passage is remarkable for its emphasis on looking. What remains to Sutpen is Milly's "unchanged regard"; in her gaze, he is elevated, transfigured; and, at some level, Sutpen himself knows this for he searches out the one gaze that, mirror-like, reflects back to him the image he longs to see.

I have said that in *Absalom* the first principle of the patriarchal order, the patriarch's legitimating authority, is discredited. This work of unsettling the patriarchal master narrative ultimately moves toward a climactic deconstructive moment, what J. Hillis Miller calls "the mise en abyme"; that is, the moment when the bottom drops away and there is a powerful recognition of the absence of any center.[17] This moment occurs when Wash Jones overhears Sutpen demean and reject his granddaughter, Milly, who has just given birth to Sutpen's daughter. To apprehend fully the impact of this scene we should recognize that, in a novel full of doubles and doubling, Jones is Sutpen's double. Jones's history reprises Sutpen's. The pivotal moment in Sutpen's life, the moment when he was turned away from the front door of the planter's house by the liveried slave, is a repeated motif in Jones's life; Jones is never allowed by Clytie, Sutpen's slave daughter, to enter the front door of Sutpen's house. Sutpen idealizes the image of the planter in the big white house; Jones reveres Sutpen. *"If God Himself was to come down and ride the material earth,"* Jones muses, *"that's what He would aim to look like"* (226). Finally, both men identify with the idealized image of the patriarch. Sutpen devotes his life to a slavish imitation of the planter while Jones sees Sutpen as "his own lonely apotheosis . . . gallop[ing] on the black thoroughbred" (226) and thinks: *"Maybe I am not as big as he is and maybe I did not do any of the galloping. But at least I was drug along where he went"* (231).

The deconstructive moment occurs as Wash waits for Sutpen outside the cabin where Milly lies with her newborn daughter. Even as Jones is "still hearing the galloping, watching the proud galloping image merge and pass . . . forever and forever immortal" (231), standing outside the cabin, he overhears Sutpen "speak his single sentence of salutation inquiry and farewell to the granddaughter, and Father said that for a second Wash must not have felt the very earth under his feet while he watched Sutpen emerge from the house" (231). "[F]eeling no earth, no stability" (231), Wash has entered the postmodern world, which Derrida describes as "a world of signs without error, without truth, without origin, . . . without security."[18]

Jones now sees that Sutpen and all his kind lack substance; they are, he says, a "set of bragging and evil shadows." Wash goes on to say that these men, "men of Sutpen's own kind, . . . men who had led the way, . . . who had galloped also in the old days arrogant and proud," are mere "symbol[s]"(232), an identification that anticipates Ihab Hassan's definition of the postmodern self as "a language animal . . . a creature constituting himself, and increasingly his universe, by symbols of his own making."[19] As well, Jones comes to see that meaning is not inherent and "true" in an absolute sense, but rather arbitrarily assigned by men. As he waits for men like Sutpen and Grandfather to come for him after he has killed Sutpen, he understands that there is no refuge, no place that is "beyond the boundaries of earth where such men lived, set the order and rule of living" (232). The story of Thomas Sutpen, the story that obsesses Miss Rosa, Mr. Compson, Quentin, and Shreve, has moved unerringly toward the climactic moment of Sutpen's death and unmasking. Throughout the novel the narrators have repeatedly remarked that Sutpen appeared to be posing or concealing something. For example, Sutpen's beard, we have been told, "resembled a disguise" (24). In death,

Sutpen is unmasked, and Jones recognizes that the mask, the pose, is what is; behind the mask is nothing.[20]

We must not think, however, that it is Sutpen alone who has been unmasked. Jones's shattering pronouncement of fraudulence is not directed solely at Sutpen. Lest we should conclude that it is only Thomas Sutpen, the parvenu, the self-made man, who is a sham, Jones clearly issues a blanket indictment of all Sutpen's kind, as he pointedly observes that that "they (men) were all of a kind throughout all of the earth which he knew" (232).

Ihab Hassan has said that the postmodern impulse is characterized by a "will to unmaking."[21] This anarchic impulse manifests itself in *Absalom* when Wash Jones slashes the throats of his granddaughter and her newborn baby and then, the scythe raised above his head, runs straight into the waiting gunbarrels of men like Sutpen. As he runs, Jones makes "no sound no outcry" (234). Hassan has written eloquently of the signification of silence. Silence, Hassan writes, carries "the incalculable potential of the negative." "Silence fills the extreme states of the mind—void, madness, outrage, ecstasy, mystic trance—when ordinary discourse ceases to carry the burden of meaning." "Silence de-realizes the world."[22]

It is instructive to read Jones's anarchy as foil and counterpoint to Sutpen's "innocence." Sutpen constructs himself in accordance with the planter image to "ri[eve] free" (210) his descendants from brutehood. Jones's anarchy also proposes to "rieve free" his progeny from the brutehood assigned to them by an arbitrary social ordering. Both men destroy their descendants to save them. Jones's anarchy, then, becomes the mirror image of Sutpen's complicity in the social order; and, here as elsewhere in the novel, ostensibly opposite acts merge, and the reader is made aware of a collapse of difference.

This loss of difference, like all the events of *Absalom*, is a narrated event; in this instance, the narrator is Quentin, who ultimately comes to see that all difference is a function of representation. In concluding, I want to focus on the critical role of the narrators in *Absalom* and, particularly, Quentin's role. The subversion of patriarchy that I have mapped out here is a function of the narrators' construction of meaning. As Donald Kartiganer and others have observed, each of the narrators constructs a different version of the Sutpen story that reflects his or her own needs and desires.[23] By having character-narrators represent Sutpen's story, Faulkner, in a postmodern move, foregrounds the role of representation, and I propose that, at the end of his telling and as a consequence of his telling, Quentin comes to understand that the difference necessary for meaning exists within the representation and nowhere else.

Throughout the second half of the novel, chapters six through nine,

Quentin, along with Shreve, has constructed the Sutpen story from a position outside of the narrative; but, at the novel's conclusion, Quentin enters the narrative, and the roles of narrator and character merge. The end of the Sutpen saga becomes Quentin's story, as Quentin, months after the event occurred, finally describes breaking into the old Sutpen place with Miss Rosa on a night in September of 1909. Because the narration of these events is withheld until the last pages of the novel, it appears as if the whole Sutpen story is a prologue to this exposition.

Quentin and Miss Rosa break into the decaying Sutpen mansion to answer this question: "What is it [Clytie's] got hidden there? What could it be? And what difference does it make?" (291). As if to delay the answer until the last possible moment, Quentin describes what he and Miss Rosa find in Sutpen's house only after he narrates escorting Miss Rosa home and returning to his own home:

> . . . when he turned at last toward the house he did begin to run. He could not help it. He was twenty years old; he was not afraid, because what he had seen out there could not harm him, yet he ran; even inside the dark familiar house, his shoes in his hand, he still ran, up the stairs and into his room and began to undress, fast, sweating, breathing fast. 'I ought to bathe,' he thought: then he was lying on the bed, naked, swabbing his body steadily with the discarded shirt, sweating still, panting: so that when, his eye-muscles aching and straining into the darkness and the almost dried shirt still clutched in his hand, he said 'I have been asleep' it was all the same, there was no difference: waking or sleeping he walked down that upper hall between the scaling walls and beneath the cracked ceiling, toward the faint light which fell outward from the last door and paused there, saying 'No. No' and then 'Only I must. I have to' and went in, entered the bare stale room whose shutters were closed too, where a second lamp burned dimly on a crude table; waking or sleeping it was the same: the bed, the yellow sheets and pillow, the wasted yellow face with closed, almost transparent eyelids on the pillow, the wasted hands crossed on the breast as if he were already a corpse; waking or sleeping it was the same and would be the same forever as long as he lived." (297–8)

Quentin at last reveals what is concealed in the dark house, and, by implication, what is buried in the unconscious mind. The scene he describes is characterized by elision. In this scene, everything is running down and running together. There are no definable units; everything appears to be shot through with everything else. Dissolution and disintegration are denoted by yellow, the color of decay. Described as "transparent" and "yellow," like his yellow sheets and pillow, Henry seems to be dissolving into his surroundings. This sense of disintegration is fostered by language that appears deliberately to confuse the animate with the inanimate, as in the construction, his "almost transparent eyelids on the pillow." The fundamental and seemingly irreducible binary opposition, the life/death binary, here appears to be breaking down, as life fuses with death. Henry is neither fully dead nor fully alive, but somewhere in between. As well, in a novel replete with vicarious identifications, here Quentin merges with Henry. Henry lies in bed poised betweeen life and death in an image formed in Quentin's mind as he lies in bed poised between sleep and wakefulness. Pronoun confusion also fosters a sense of dissolving identity. "He" in the passage refers ambiguously both to Henry and Quentin.

In this climactic image, identity is breaking down. Identity and meaning depend on difference. As Ferdinand de Saussure points out, a sign's meaning depends solely on its difference from other signs.[24] In the words of Terry Eagleton, "signs [are] themselves only because they are not some other sign."[25] But in this image out of the unconscious mind, signs cease to be themselves, cease to differ. The question Quentin posed before he went out to the old Sutpen place was "what difference does it make?" This image is his answer. The image is the language of the unconscious, and Quentin's image leaks a buried recognition that existence is one, fluid, and continuous; and identity and meaning are human constructions. "[T]here was no difference," Quentin realizes; "waking or sleeping it was the same."

If this postmodern awareness arrives too late for Quentin, who, in *The Sound and the Fury*, in June of 1910, commits suicide so as to join Grandfather in his "high place," it does not arrive too late for Faulkner.[26] In *The Sound and the Fury*, Quentin laments the demise of patriarchal authority. In *Absalom*, Faulkner exposes that authority as man-made sleight of hand. *Absalom, Absalom!* at last lays to rest the dream of patriarchal power that haunted *The Sound and the Fury*. Through writing fictions, through the process of constructing meanings with language, Faulkner has come to see that all meaning is similarly constituted; that is, Faulkner has come to understand that meaning does not exist outside of our representations, but rather meaning is constructed by the representation. Having finally banished the insidious fantasy of the father's deathless power, having recognized the immeasurable power that our own representations exert over our lives, Faulkner now can move on to explore the world men and women make with their words.

NOTES

1. William Faulkner, *The Sound and the Fury* (New York: Vintage International, 1990), 176. Subsequent references will be to this edition and will be noted parenthetically within the text.

2. *Faulkner in the University*, ed. Frederick L. Gwynn and Joseph L. Blotner (New York: Vintage, 1965), 3.

3. See John T. Irwin, *Doubling and Incest/Repetition and Revenge* (Baltimore: Johns Hopkins University Press, 1975).

4. Linda Hutcheon, *A Poetics of Postmodernism* (New York: Routledge, 1988), x.

5. Two valuable investigations of Faulkner's modernism should be noted here. In *Faulkner and Modernism: Rereading and Rewriting* (Madison: University of Wisconsin Press, 1990), Richard C. Moreland also sees *Absalom, Absalom!* as representing a turning point in Faulkner's career. Moreland argues that Faulkner's novels prior to *Absalom, Absalom!* are characterized by a Southern modernist view; that is, events are viewed either with irony or with nostalgia for a past purity. With *Absalom*, according to Moreland, Faulkner breaks out of an aesthetic dead-end typical of the Southern modernist. In *The Making of a Modernist* (Chapel Hill: University of North Carolina Press, 1997), Daniel J. Singal finds that, while *The Sound and the Fury*'s stream of consciousness technique mirrors the fluid instability characteristic of the modernist view, both Quentin and his father cling to the Cavalier myth of a Southern planter aristocracy.

6. Linda Hutcheon, "Beginning to Theorize Postmodernism," in *A Postmodern Reader*, ed. Joseph Natoli and Linda Hutcheon (Albany: State University of New York Press, 1993), 245.

7. As Juliet Mitchell explains, Lacan's notion of the self "is the obverse of the humanists." Mitchell writes: "Humanism believes that man is at the center of his own history and of himself; he is a subject more or less in control of his own actions, exercising choice." For Lacan, Mitchell continues: "The human animal is born into language and it is within the terms of language that the human subject is constructed" (4–5). See Juliet Mitchell, "Introduction," in Jacques Lacan, *Feminine Sexuality: Jacques Lacan and the "École Freudienne,"* ed. Juliet Mitchell and Jacqueline Rose (New York: Norton, 1982). For a fuller account of Lacan's theory of identity formation, see Jane Gallop, *Reading Lacan* (Ithaca. Cornell University Press, 1985) or Malcolm Bowie, *Lacan* (Cambridge: Harvard University Press, 1991).

8. The phallus is a difficult Lacanian concept. The phallus, Lacan insists, "is a signifier" (285). It functions as the signifier of a lack it serves to mask, and thus, because it masks lack, it is identified with the fullness of being that the subject lacks. See Jacques Lacan, *Écrits: A Selection*, translated by Alan Sheridan (New York: Norton, 1977), 281–91.

9. William Faulkner, *Absalom, Absalom!* (New York: Vintage International, 1990), 185. Subsequent references will be to this edition and will be noted parenthetically within the text.

10. Mitchell, "Introduction," *Feminine Sexuality*, 5.

11. Carolyn Porter observes that "the maternal element could be read as displaced onto the cave" (184). See "*Absalom, Absalom!*: (Un)making the Father," in *The Cambridge Companion to William Faulkner*, ed. Philip M. Weinstein (Cambridge: Cambridge University Press, 1995). As Porter's astute comment suggests, in this narrative, feminine elements appear to be displaced. Anne Goodwyn Jones and Molly Hite, on hearing this essay read, similarly observed that the conceptualization of the imaginary here appears to exclude the female. This displacement can perhaps be traced to the narrators; that is, this story is narrated by Sutpen and then retold by Grandfather, Father, and Quentin, and displacement of the feminine seems to characterize their narration of the imaginary.

12. John T. Irwin observes that young Sutpen "incorporates into himself the patriarchal ideal" (98). Irwin interprets this incorporation in terms of Freud's oedipal complex; that is, Sutpen is the son who must try to become the Father rather than kill him.

13. Lacan, *Écrits*, 234.

14. David Krause argues that Sutpen's innocence is that "he never doubts the accuracy of the text he reads," that Sutpen "assumes that the text from which the teacher reads, presumably like all texts, contains truth" (228). Krause's central concern is the act of reading texts; I would suggest that Sutpen similarly accepts the cultural narrative of patriarchy as somehow representing "truth." See David Krause, "Reading Bon's Letter and Faulkner's *Absalom, Absalom!*," *PMLA* 99.2 (March 1984).

15. Jonathan Scott Lee, *Jacques Lacan* (Amherst: University of Massachusetts Press, 1990), 155.

16. "Introduction," *Feminine Sexuality*, 5.

17. J. Hillis Miller, "Stevens' Rock and Criticism as Cure, I," *The Georgia Review* 30 (Spring 1976): 11–12.

18. Jacques Derrida, quoted by M. H. Abrams in "The Deconstructive Angel," *Contemporary Literary Criticism: Modernism and Post-Structuralism*, ed. Robert Con Davis (New York: Longman, 1986), 433.

19. Ihab Hassan, "Ideas of Cultural Change," in *Innovation/Renovation: New Perspectives on the Humanities,* ed. Ihab Hassan and Sally Hassan (Madison: University of Wisconsin Press, 1983), 29.

20. In a Lacanian approach to patriarchy in *Absalom, Absalom!*, Bleikasten contends that Thomas Sutpen is one of a series of failed fathers in Faulkner. These fathers fail because they are "dead, but not dead enough" to "act the role of the dead father" (143) who guarantees the law. See André Bleikasten, "Fathers in Faulkner," in *The Fictional Father*, ed. Robert Con Davis (Amherst: University of Massachusetts Press, 1981). I would agree with Carolyn Porter who takes Bleikasten's argument a step further and insightfully proposes that "Sutpen does not fail to function as a 'symbol of cultural order' but, rather, reveals the symbolic function on which that order depends" ("*Absalom, Absalom!*: (Un)making the Father," 192).

21. In *The Dismemberment of Orpheus: Toward a Postmodern Literature* (New York: Oxford University Press, 1971), as the title suggests, Hassan describes postmodernism as a decreative impulse. See particularly 3–23 and 210–71. As Hassan himself noted at the 1999 conference at which this essay was read, his later concept of postmodernism is much more inclusive. In 1980, Hassan writes: "We cannot simply rest—as I sometimes have done—on the assumption that postmodernism is antiformal, anarchic, or decreative; for though it is all these . . . it also contains the need to discover a 'unitary sensibility' (Sontag), to 'cross the border and close the gap' (Fiedler), and to attain, as I have suggested, a neo-gnostic immediacy of mind." See "The Question of Postmodernism," *Bucknell Review: Romanticism, Modernism, Postmodernism*, ed. Harry R. Garvin (Lewisburg, Pa.: Bucknell University Press, 1980), 21.

22. *The Dismemberment of Orpheus*, 12–13.

23. See Donald Kartiganer, *The Fragile Thread: The Meaning of Form in Faulkner's Novels* (Amherst: University of Massachusetts Press, 1979), 69–106; and Doreen Fowler, *Faulkner: The Return of the Repressed* (Charlottesville: University Press of Virginia, 1997), 95–127.

24. Ferdinand de Saussure, *Course in General Linguistics*, trans. Wade Baskin (1916) (New York: McGraw Hill, 1966), 67.

25. Terry Eagleton, *Literary Theory: An Introduction* (Minneapolis: University of Minnesota Press, 1983), 128.

26. It should be noted here that Faulkner uses Quentin as a character in other works written after his fictional death in *The Sound and the Fury*. Apparently the character he had created in *The Sound and the Fury* was useful to Faulkner in some profound way, and, for his own reasons, Faulkner continued to use Quentin as a central narrating consciousness in subsequent works. Quentin appears as a narrator not only in *Absalom, Absalom!*, but also in "That Evening Sun," published originally in 1931, and in "A Justice," first published in 1931. A story, "Lion" (1935), later rewritten as part of "The Bear," was originally a story related by Quentin. Early typescript versions of "The Old People" and "A Fool about a Horse" also appear to be narrated by Quentin Compson. See Joseph Blotner, "Notes," *Uncollected Stories of William Faulkner* (New York: Vintage, 1981), 690–2. It seems as if Faulkner elected to revoke Quentin's suicide or that, in Faulkner's mind, Quentin was not dead and that Quentin's telling changes Quentin as well as Faulkner.

Intertextuality, Transference, and Postmodernism in *Absalom, Absalom!*: The Production and Reception of Faulkner's Fictional World

MARTIN KREISWIRTH

> *I occasionally get just as tired of the slogan of "postmodernism" as anyone else, but when I am tempted to regret my complicity with it, to deplore its misuses and its notoriety, and to conclude with some reluctance that it caused more problems that it solves, I find myself pausing to wonder whether any other concept can dramatise the issue in quite so effective and economical a fashion.*
>
> FREDRIC JAMESON

Like many others, I am not entirely comfortable with the term postmodernism. Indeed, it is not a concept or designation that admits of comfort. Its definitional and performative disquiet has now even become part of its signification, or perhaps, of its appeal. Yet, whether at this late date, postmodernism is now conceived, as Richard Rorty has remarked, as the most overrated idea in recent history,[1] or merely vacuous, overdetermined, used "in so many ways that it has been rendered meaningless," as Arthur Asa Berger has observed,[2] it has become, willy-nilly, part of our intellectual furniture and we must learn to live with it, even if we have to move it around a bit, cover it up, or even push it into a corner. Like it or not, we, in some sense, meander in the maze of postmodernism, which, depending on one's vantage point, may be either beyond, or behind, or most probably, within what Geoffrey Hartman has called the maze of modernism,[3] since we apparently must always position ourselves in some relation to it.

What has been worrisome, however, are not the various attempts to examine this positioning per se, but some of the binary thinking and the sometimes unfortunate reductionism that has marked it, specifically in the modernism / postmodernism debate,[4] a debate that has come to have particular relevance for discussions of Faulkner and his career.[5] It is worth remembering that the intersecting histories of discursive forms and/or background sociopolitical periodization (and some of the difficul ties of this debate stem from an inability to separate the two) rarely allow us to make sure distinctions about modes of or assumptions about representation that undergird this or that genre, period, structure, or indeed way of life. Consequently, I am not going to argue that Faulkner, Yoknapatawpha, or, indeed, *Absalom, Absalom!* in particular, necessarily exploit certain conventions of postmodernism, rather than, say, those of modernism, or for that matter realism. Rather I want to show that in identifying filiations with *what have been defined today as postmodern tactics, or presuppositions*, we can see Faulkner as he is being filtered through the present, assuming various positions on a kind of moving continuum, from modernism to postmodernism and back again.

It has been long recognized that aesthetic postmodernism challenges much of modernist dogma—the centrality of the subject, the autonomy of art, its alienation from the world, and so forth. Yet, postmodernism just as clearly developed out of modernist strategies, seen most plainly, as one critic has put it, in its "self-reflexive experimentation, its ironic ambiguities, and its contestations of classic realist representation."[6] Nevertheless, postmodernism's inherent self-contradictions, unlike modernism's own, are emphasized to "such an extent that they become the very defining characteristics of the entire cultural phenomenon we label with that name."[7] In short, what I want to say is that there are certain singular features about Faulknerian textuality and, more importantly, intertextuality—particularly as it affects the construction and reception of Yoknapatawpha—that might helpfully be shown to be connected to what has been described, whether aptly or poorly, as postmodernism. Yet, at the same time, even these features are to some degree critically recuperated in a model of reception that, not surprisingly, seems to have something in common with what has been described, either aptly or poorly, as modernism. In Yoknapatawpha then, Faulkner, in some sense, may be seen to be rubbing what has been described as modernism and postmodernism against each other. In any event, I expect that looking at Faulkner through a postmodern lens may end up being more important for opening up the workings of his fictional construct—Yoknapatawpha—than for showing the ways in which these workings may or may not be connected to other texts (and conventions of their production and reception), however we want to label or periodize them. And conversely, postmodern proclivities may then also be seen to apply to a broader range of texts and discursive activities than those limited by the received formal and/ or historical components of the term.

For quite a long time now, critics have placed Faulkner precariously at the cusp between modernism and postmodernism.[8] In particular, *Absalom, Absalom!* is seen to teeter at this brink: it is undoubtedly affiliated with the formalism and the dominant interpretive ambiguities of modernism; nevertheless, it also offers a serious and critical questioning of representation, particularly, of historical representation that has become one of the few agreed upon hallmarks of much of cultural or aesthetic postmodernism. In this essay, I want to take this line a bit further. Notwithstanding the terminological reservations about postmodernism mentioned above, I want to show that the kind of interrogation of history linked with postmodernism is, in part, carried out, not just in *Absalom, Absalom!* (as certain critics have contended), but in the curious intertextual operations that underlie the production and reception of all of Faulkner's massive fictional world, operations that productively explore the borders of textuality itself. Yet, at the same time, I also want to point out that Faulkner appears unwilling to leave his admittedly unstable world fatally caught between the problematic representations of fiction and history, as many of his postmodern progeny will. He also, I want to argue, retains a kind of modernist blueprint for the reception of this world, one based on recuperation through transference. And even further, I want to show that these modes of production and reception are modelled in *Absalom, Absalom!*

First I think it is crucial to point out the peculiar character of Yoknapatawpha, Faulkner's immense fictional domain, and the particular operations of inter- or intratextuality that project it, especially since its unique nature as a multitextual imaginative construct is frequently misrepresented or ignored. In many ways, to be sure, Yoknapatawpha has much in common with multitextual fictional universes of the realist school (say Hardy's, Balzac's, or Trollope's) that are constituted by the perceived repetitions of elements from text to text. As possible-world literary theorists such as Marie-Laure Ryan, Thomas Pavel, or Lubomir Dolezel might say,[9] Yoknapatawpha can accurately be described as a large, textactual world, and, in its underlying logical makeup, not terribly different from those of its nineteenth-century predecessors. Like those worlds, Yoknapatawpha is constituted not by authoritative and authenticating narrative statements from a single novel or story, but from a collection of such utterances drawn together by the reader from a number of texts, linked by certain conventions, such as the fact that they are all offered under the name of the same author and that the characters, settings, or events—the logical *existents*—projected from them exhibit certain perceived commonalities. And this is still, for the most part, the dominant view of Faulkner's large-scale creation. The novels and stories that join to make up Yoknapatawpha, it is generally agreed, end up positing a comprehensive, harmonious, fictional universe, where we get the unproblematic fictional representation of a relatively well-defined place, with a recognizable population, and rich history.

Yes. But I want to go a bit deeper. In an earlier essay for a volume in this series, I argued that Yoknapatawpha is, in fact, quite an unusual kind of fictional world, a transgressive construct that ultimately refuses to project an entirely congruent, comprehensive text-actual or fictional world. In that essay I tried to show that there are admittedly small but critical cracks in the edifice that cause Yoknapatawpha to function differently from those more substantial multitextual fictional constructs of its precursors. And, further, that this strategy of destablization functions by means of a radical, particularly postmodern form of intertextuality, subtly working both to produce and challenge the construction of the fictional world itself.[10]

This double movement occurs at the text's deepest zones, in those basic elements that make up the narratively authoritative statements projecting the fictional world's "facts," the very building blocks of the larger text actual world. I'm referring here to the well-known but frequently ignored (or edited) contradictions and discrepancies in semantic details that undermine authenticating constructional conventions of the fictional world's *existents*, in, for example, characters' names and ages, in dates, places, and specifics of description that appear in different texts throughout the Yoknapatawpha corpus. There are numerous examples of this, but I'll remind you of just a few: Jack Houston's wife in *The Hamlet* is called Lucy Pate, in *The Town*, she's Letty Bookwright, in *The Mansion*, she goes unnamed; in *Sanctuary* Temple Drake is eighteen when she is raped, in *Requiem for a Nun*, she's seventeen; and, of course, as I pointed out in the earlier essay, there are many examples from *Absalom, Absalom!* that arise between the narrative proper and the appendices.

Inconsistencies such as these flout either what possible-world theorists call the logical law of noncontradiction or that of the rigid-designator controlling transtextual character identity. These inconsistencies cause disfunction at the level of the sign itself, the most basic level at which the data of the fictional world is logically posited, the one at which we are least likely to admit divergence and indecision. Above all, these types of incongruities force us to push the world constructing of Yoknapatawpha beyond a kind of accustomed "either/ or" thinking, replacing it with what Linda Hutcheon has called the postmodern logic of "both/ and."[11] This is a logic that admits no final resolution. In the fictional annals of Yoknapatawpha history (in what might have become Faulkner's *Domesday Book*), did the female Quentin climb down a pear tree or a rainpipe? Can we say? Did she climb down both the rainpipe and the pear tree? Is it the same Quentin in these instances? How do we determine the answer to these questions? Does it matter?

This contradictory logic controls the ways in which Yoknapatawpha is created between texts, and the kinds of uneasy, postmodern, relationships it establishes with the world outside the text. Admittedly, in the enormous body of fictional materials that project Faulkner's imaginative domain—the sixteen or so novels and numerous short stories—such semantic discrepancies may remain statistically or empirically inconsequential, overpowered, in some sense, by manifold intertextual continuities and repetitions. But, I think we must grant that they do obtrude rhetorically, particularly for those who are searching for a modernist aesthetic coordination that would result in a single, comprehensive text. Indeed, desires for such coherency are even further frustrated by authorial intention, as shown in Faulkner's many statements to his editors to leave "outrageous and paradoxical" contradictions stand, despite their instance that he do otherwise.[12]

As soon as attempts are made to tame Yoknapatawpha's unruliness, either by interpretive or editorial means, these disrupting symptoms of semantic discord tend to protrude. They, moreover, openly defy any attempt at traditional modernist rehabilitation by means of irony, ambiguity, or aesthetic autonomy. Instead, they act as reminders that Yoknapatawpha's multitextual conventions of fictional world construction are in fact unconventional, keeping mobile the workings of the intertextual, dare I say postmodern, "both/and"—that undecidable logical realm operating between inconsistencies that challenge representation and those connecting continuities that work to hold things together.[13]

In the language of possible-world semantics, these performatives, carried out by the reader in the larger intertext, or multitext within and between the Yoknapatawpha novels and stories themselves, logically exhaust the fictional *existent*. The point here isn't merely the instability of the particular "fact" of the fictional world—the consequences of, say, Charles Bon being born in New Orleans rather than Haiti aren't necessarily world shattering—but instead, that the semantic disruption meddles with the process of representation itself, drawing attention to it and to the impossibility of making a singular, logical determination. As such, the double gesture of maintaining a context of intertextual connection *and* its disruption neither brackets nor suspends the workings of representation, but, through what may come to be seen as a postmodern "strategy of interference,"[14] slightly displaces it, asking us seriously to consider what it means to represent. Moreover, and perhaps more importantly, this "both/and" logic operates beyond the conventions of individual textual borders in an amorphous in-between realm, and as such also asks us what it means to refer, to connect and corroborate, outside of textual boundaries.

This concern with the way in which elements from different texts may or may not connect with each other nudges Yoknapatawpha slightly away from the traditional modes of fictional world creating and toward the conventions of historical discourse, whose representations of past actualities—whose construed "facts," that is—are thought to be constrained by referential (or evidential) rather than purely textual or aesthetic conventions. Difficulties in stabilizing the referent are, of course, problems of factual discourse, of historiography, not of imaginative literature. Questions involving the possibility of multiple consturals of data at the level of the sign is the work of historical not fictional representation. While *existents* (agents, events) in the possible world(s) of the past are not *logically incomplete* like those of fiction,[15] they are empirically insufficient, incapable of becoming as complete as existents in the present actual world, dependent on frequently unavailable or contradictory data from various textual sources for their "constitution." While conceivable statements about them are not logically undecidable, much of their composition remains, in practical terms, unknown, or limited to conflicting information and interpretations.

Without the absolute authority of an authorial edict to set limits, the represented fact from the historical or past actual world can only be semantically steadied by making it fit with other corroborating representations. And thus, certain *existents* in Yoknapatawpha have the curiously extrafictional ability to have contradictory projections, based not on the novelistic world-creating conventions of fiction, but on those of historiographic representation, on, say, the discovery of divergent "evidence" or "data." In some sense, it may be that *existents* in all multitextual fictional worlds, while distinct from those in present actual worlds or even singular fictional worlds, generally resemble those from historical worlds, in that both are projected from incomplete textual data, requiring multiple sources for their constitution. Indeed, what Marie-Laure Ryan calls the "principle of minimal departure" would reinforce our reception of these irregular elements posited between Faulkner's texts as "conforming as far as possible" to representations of actual worlds, in this case, past actual worlds.[16] But, to place such nonfictive textual contradictions within an extensive and overarching context of fictional world creating, as Yoknapatawpha strategically does, pushes at the limits of fictional as well as nonfictional discursive formations and the kinds of "worlds" they posit, partaking, to some degree, in the conventions of both forms.

In my earlier paper, I went to great lengths to demonstrate that Yoknapatawpha's "both/and," historical/fictional world-making is actually inau-

gurated and modelled in *Absalom, Absalom!* I tried to argue that within
and between its own problematic textual boundaries—the chapters of the
novel proper, on the one hand, and the Genealogy, Chronology, and map
that appear as appendices, on the other—*Absalom, Absalom!* displays
many of the same kinds of contradictions (Bon's birthplace, Ellen Coldfield Sutpen's age, the causes of Judith and Charles's deaths, etc.) and
performs in miniature the same kind of intertextual world-making activity as Yoknapatawpha does at large: moments of self-contradiction open
up the possibility of alternative construals. In *Absalom, Absalom!*, as in
Yoknapatawpha more generally, the base-level stability of conventional
fictional constructs is thus denied, performatively inviting responses that
cross the borders between fiction and history, calling attention to the
indeterminate nature of both reference and representation. And, given
our postmodern vantage point, it might not be too farfetched to see these
multitextual world-making activities as sharing some of the conventions
of "historiographic metafiction," *the* postmodern literary form, according
to Linda Hutcheon, that puts "into question the authority of any act of
writing by locating the discourses of both history and fiction within an
ever-expanding intertextual network that mocks any notion of either single origin or simple causality."[17]

   Absalom, Absalom!, like Yoknapatawpha at large then, may plausibly be
associated with "historiographic metafiction," or, at least with the specific
kinds of postmodern cultural work that it performs. In this paper, I want
to claim that *Absalom, Absalom!* can be seen to do even more. It not only
establishes the specifics of the kind of Yoknapatawphan production I've
been describing, but also, through its self-reflexive dramatization of the
dialogic interrelationship of the narrators and their transferential interpretive activity, performs and models the pragmatics of Yoknapatawphan
reception—a strategy of reading and response that takes account of what
might be labelled as postmodern problems of reference and representation.

   As is well known, a good number of Yoknapatawphan texts (*Go Down,
Moses, The Sound and the Fury, As I Lay Dying, The Town, The Mansion*,
and so on) carry out their narrative work through represented conversational exchanges; they are all, in many different ways, "marriages of
speaking and hearing." It is in *Absalom, Absalom!*, however, that dialogue
becomes crucially dramatized and foregrounded: the stress here falls on
the verbal transactions themselves, and on the bodily interaction of the
conversational pair engaged in the transmission and reception of narrative materials—whether on Rosa and Quentin, General Compson and
Mr. Compson, Mr. Compson and Quentin, or, most notably, on Quentin
and Shreve. Indeed, as the novel progresses, more and more attention

is placed on the communicative act: beginning with chapter 6, self-conscious representation of the dialogic nature of narrative production claims equal attention with the production itself; the paired tellers and their tellings are just as narratively significant as the tale.

What hasn't been so commonly discussed, however, is just how the self-conscious dialogic structure of *Absalom, Absalom!* contributes not just to the novel's own subject matter and internal configuration, but to relationships beyond its own textual boundaries, particularly to the construction of Yoknapatawpha at large: how, for instance, the particular kind of narrative transaction that Yoknapatawpha calls for is both set up and modelled here, how this model might be usefully seen in terms of psychoanalytic transference, and, finally, how it might operate as a mode of reading or reception for the"both/and" multi-textuality of Yoknapatawpha.

Psychoanalytic transference might be described most simply as a displacement of the analysand's (or speaker's) unconscious ideas onto the analyst (or listener). In the "Dynamics of Transference," Freud writes that the patient's "unconscious impulses do not want to be remembered in the way the treatment desires them to be, but endeavour to reproduce themselves in accordance with the timelessness of the unconscious and its capacity for hallucination. Just as happens in dreams, the patient regards the products of the awakening of his unconscious impulses as contemporaneous and real."[18] The interpretive interaction of the two participants produces what Freud calls the "transference-love" that brings forth previously absent materials, but in radically distorted forms. These are then collaboratively acted out and "worked through" for both interpretive and therapeutic gains. Psychoanalytic transference thus invariably revolves around relationships of temporality, difference, fictiveness, and exchange, which, Freud points out, can be seen as central features of human interaction, beyond the analytic situation. It must not be supposed "that the phenomenon of transference . . . is *created* by psycho-analytic influence," Freud writes. Psychoanalysis "merely reveals it to consciousness. . . . Transference arises spontaneously in all human relationships."[19]

Psychoanalytic approaches to transference, in its more general and nonanalytic applications, have been shown to be a powerful tool for theorizing a transactive mode of reading and interpretation that retains modulations of difference and desire.[20] Yet, as important as these general speculations on textuality and interpretation might be for the subject at hand, I want to look at something more specific, at how transference itself is figured in the narrative structure of *Absalom, Absalom!*, and how this performs and models a pragmatics of reception, not just for this text, but for the intertextual relationships of the entire Yoknapatawphan canon.

Interestingly, Freud initially articulates his speculations on psychoanalytic transference in blatantly textual terms. Transferences, Freud writes, "are new *editions* or *facsimiles* of the impulses and phantasies which are aroused and made conscious during the progress of the analysis. . . . [A] whole series of psychological experiences are revived, not as belonging to the past, but as applying to the person of the physician at the present moment. Some of these transferences have a content which differs from that of their model in no respect whatever except for the substitution. These then—to keep to the same metaphor—are merely new *impressions* or *reprints*. Others are more ingeniously constructed; their content has been subjected to a moderating influence—to sublimation. . . . These, then, will no longer be new *impressions* but *revised editions*" (my emphasis).[21] "Intertextuality," of course, is now the name for the relationship between such editions, facsimiles, impressions, and reprints. "The act of transference," Sean Hand notes, "creates an intertextual space in which the story changes as it is listened to and worked on. . . . A search for the narrative's forgotten origin is replaced by a recognition of the active process of constructing the narrative."[22]

This process can be no more clearly seen than in the various threefold dialogues that take place in *Absalom, Absalom!* between Quentin and Shreve *and* the textual materials they are representing, materials themselves that emerge from other conversational exchanges. Through these various dialogical activities, affective associations are established between the interlocutors—Quentin and Shreve—and the "subjects" of their discourse—the Sutpens—whereby the interpretation of desire and the desire for interpretation merge—"the brain recalls just what the muscles grope for." A particularly significant instance of this transferential performance occurs (there are many) in the beginning of chapter 8, when the horizontal relations of the represented *tale*—those ostensibly between the Sutpen parent and "siblings" and between the "siblings" themselves—reach a certain level of intensity, and we see a concomitant heightening and merging in the vertical relations of the *telling*—between Quentin and Shreve:

> Shreve stood beside the table, facing Quentin again though not seated now . . . while both their breathing vaporised faintly in the cold room where there was now not two of them but four, the two who breathed not individuals now yet something both more and less than twins . . . not two of them in a New England college sitting-room but one in a Mississippi library sixty years ago . . . as free now of flesh as the father who decreed and forbade, the son who denied and repudiated, the lover who acquiesced, the beloved who was not bereaved

. . . not two of them there and then either but four of them riding the two horses.[23]

Here we do not witness a scene of reading, or of interpretation, or even of dialogue, but a scene that reproduces the eccentric form and energies of psychoanalytic transference, an emotionally charged activity of speaking and listening, "in which," as Hand puts it, "a narrative is composed from an interaction between at least two persons, who in fact always turn out to be more than two."[24] With the fictional Quentin and Shreve *standing in* for the fictional Sutpens *and* vice versa, the dialogue of the representa*tional* and represen*ted* is itself placed in dialogue, with the result that separation and difference, both textual and temporal, are transgressed. The circuit of love does not pass exclusively through individual subjects—through Bon, or Henry, or Sutpen, or Judith, or even Quentin or Shreve, but through generalized roles of human relationship—"the son," "the father," "the lover," and "the beloved." These seminal emotional relationships—though pointing towards the Sutpens—also, in this intertextual realm, just point; they remain signifiers, subject positions, unspecified and abstract, open to the libidinal desires of the tellers and listeners—both inside and outside the text.

Absalom, Absalom! stresses just this kind of transferential process in the numerous scenes in which Quentin and Shreve become bodily doubled and quadrupled in their narrative transactions with the Sutpens and the past.[25] A climax of this activity is reached later in chapter 8, when there occurs a kind of pause in the narrative re-creation—as if for theoretical self-reflection—and *transference-love* itself becomes the subject *and* object of Shreve and Quentin's speculations and pragmatics:

> "And now," Shreve said, "we're going to talk about love." But he didn't need to say that . . . any more than he had needed to specify which he he meant by he, since neither of them had been thinking about anything else; all that had gone before just so much that had to be overpassed and none else present to overpass it but them, as someone always has to rake the leaves up before you can have the bonfire. That was why it did not matter to either of them which one did the talking, since it was not the talking alone which did it, performed and accomplished the overpassing, but some happy marriage of speaking and hearing wherein each before the demand, the requirement, forgave condoned and forgot the faulting of the other—faultings both in the creating of this shade whom they discussed (rather, existed in) and in the hearing and sifting and discarding the false and conserving what seemed true, or fit the preconceived—in order to overpass to love, where there might be paradox and inconsistency but nothing fault nor false. (253)

Practically everything in this remarkably dense passage corroborates and makes explicit the kind of transferential relationship that I see *Absalom,*

Absalom! as setting up as a model for intertextual reception. Along with the foregrounded description of the production, reception, and working-through of absent narrative materials as the intertext of desire, there is, perhaps most conspicuously, the odd word "overpass" itself, which appears four times here in three different forms, but nowhere else in this text (or indeed in any other Faulkner text I can find). This word signifies both transgression and transference, operations that attempt to keep divisions between self and other, past and present, fact and fiction, the continuous and discontinuous, open and productive. Overpassing is a radically affective relationship, a bond, indeed, a kind of marriage, one that retains libidinal energies, and uses them to confront but not erase or ignore contradiction and discontinuity—those "both/and" intertextual elements that defy wholeness and linking repetition. In this way, transferential overpassing in *Absalom, Absalom!* thus performs in miniature the production and reception of Yoknapatawpha at large, providing, as it were, a guide for ways to read the unstable domain between history and fiction, both in this novel and in the larger multitextual domain.

Brian McHale has argued that *Absalom, Absalom!* is a kind of harbinger of aesthetic postmodernism since, at its climatic moment, it replaces what he sees as the epistemological (or modernist) dominant—where the text questions knowledge about the world—with the ontological (or postmodernist) dominant—where the text questions the world itself. Here is McHale on this point:

> In Ch. 8, Quentin and Shreve reach the limit of their knowledge of the Sutpen murder-mystery; nevertheless they go on, beyond reconstruction into pure speculation. The signs of the narrative act fall away, and with them all questions of authority and reliability. The text passes from mimesis of the various characters' narrations to unmediated diegesis, from characters "telling" to the author directly "showing" us what happened between Sutpen, Henry, and Bon. The murder-mystery is "solved," however, not through epistemological processes of weighing evidence and making deductions, but through the imaginative projection of what *could*—and, the text insists, *must*—have happened.[26]

McHale, however, ignores other kinds of information that perhaps may even strengthen his claim. What he doesn't mention is that the force of this "imaginative . . . *must* have happened" derives from the multiple affective relationships between the tellers and the told. To support this, I want to remind you of the particular passage in chapter 8 of *Absalom* to which McHale is referring, the climactic speculative (in fact transferential) recreation of a wholly absent past. Here are the opening few lines:

> He ceased again. It was just as well, since he had no listener. . . . Then suddenly he had no talker either. . . . Because now neither of them was there.

They were both in Carolina and the time was forty-six years ago, and it was not even four now but compounded still further, since now both of them were Henry Sutpen and both of them were Bon, compounded each of both yet either neither, smelling the very smoke which had blown and faded away forty-six years ago from the *bivouac fires burning in a pine grove, the gaunt and ragged men sitting.* . . . (280)

Again, we have a story of two who are more than two, where texts of fiction and history interact, where the provable merges into the fantasized, and where past and present dissolve into each other (remember the majority of this italicized "recreation" is in the present tense).

McHale, in one very important respect, misses the point here: the author does not directly show us what happened; rather, the narrator shows us the highly charged tellings and projected showings that are the result of the characters' transferential exchange. The text doesn't pass from mimesis of the various characters' narrations to unmediated diegesis; it very carefully depicts diegesis as wholly mediated, as a collaborative engagement between people and texts; and the signs of the narrative act do not fall away, but are, in fact, incorporated into the dramatized intertextual transaction. In this way, one could argue that *Absalom, Absalom!* not only points toward the ontological dominant, as McHale suggests, but also toward the intertextual dominant, openly played out in the spaces between texts and psyches, and between the historical and fictive.

This activity, however, seems somewhat different than that performed by the "either/or" logic of intertextual production alone. Here, reference and representation, certainly, are problematized; yet they become channelled through networks of interpersonal desire. In *Absalom, Absalom!*, the affective and subjective energies of the interlocutors (like perhaps those of the reader) seem to search for ways to move toward the recuperation and control of some of the waywardness of Yoknapatawpha's strategy of historical/ fictional representation. A model of reading seen as transferential "overpassing" shows that through a dialogue between psyches and texts the impossibilities of the "both/and" logic of Faulkner's imaginative world, while certainly not resolved, are somehow, confronted, perhaps even worked through. As Quentin and Shreve's conversational narration demonstrates, in *Absalom, Absalom!*, and between its own internal discursive divisions, as *in* and *between* this and other Yoknapatawphan texts, there may indeed be intertextual "paradox and inconsistency," but, by means of a pragmatics of transgression and transference, "nothing fault nor false."

If anything, this attempt at finding ways toward reconciling contradictions of reference and representation as they oscillate between history and fiction pushes the conventions of world-creating in *Absalom, Absa-*

lom! and Yoknapatawpha slightly back toward the presuppositions of modernism, where coherent aesthetic worlds may be created, even if only through the fictions of desire. But note, even here, the description of Quentin and Shreve's devising of the past does not positively say that truth, coherence, or correctness were or can be achieved, just that their negatives may not be: this remains a provisional, contradictory construct, not a place where everything is correct or true, but one "where nothing is fault nor false," one where things are "probably true enough."

When this model of transferential reception is placed against the disruptive postmodernism of intertextual production, we can understand why Yoknapatawpha and *Absalom, Absalom!* may, depending on one's vantage point, be seen to shift from a postmodern to a modern dominant. All in all, it may be that Faulkner was not enough of a postmodernist to leave unsettling questions of reference and representation without some suggestion for ways of working through them; yet, at the same time, not enough of a modernist to override them or reign in their critical energies. Surely, overpassing can only go so far toward attempting to confront the "both/and" logic of irresolvable textual contradictions. I don't want to say that from our current cultural position that the creator of Yoknapatawpha himself appears finally as "both/and": a modern postmodernist, a postmodern modernist, but I guess I don't not want to say it either.

NOTES

1. In Janny Scott, "Think Tank: Lofty Ideas that May be Losing Altitude," *New York Times*, November 1, 1997, 13.

2. Arthur Asa Berger, *Cultural Criticism: A Primer of Key Concepts*, (Thousand Oaks, Calif.: Sage Publications, 1995), 26.

3. Geoffrey Hartman, "The Maze of Modernism: Reflections on Louis MacNeice, Robert Graves, A. D. Hope, Robert Lowell, and Others," in *Beyond Formalism: Literary Essays, 1958–1970* (New Haven: Yale University Press, 1970), 258–79.

4. There has been an enormous amount of work done on postmodernism (and, indeed, postmodernity) in the past thirty years, certainly too much to begin to consider here. Some of the texts that I have found most helpful for my immediate concerns include Perry Anderson, *The Origins of Postmodernity* (London: Verso, 1998); Hans Bertens, *The Idea of the Postmodern: A History* (Routledge, 1995); Hans Bertens and Douwe Fokkema, *International Postmodernism: Theory and Literary Practice* (Amsterdam: J. Benjamins, 1997); Steven Best and Douglas Kellner, *The Postmodern Turn, Critical Perspectives* (New York: Guilford Press, 1997); Steven Connor, *Postmodernist Culture: An Introduction to Theories of the Contemporary*, 2nd ed. (Oxford: Blackwell, 1997); Ihab Hassan, *The Postmodern Turn: Essays in Postmodern Theory and Culture* (New York: Columbia University Press, 1987); Linda Hutcheon, *A Poetics of Postmodernism: History, Theory, Fiction* (New York: Routledge, 1988); Linda Hutcheon, *The Politics of Postmodernism* (London: Routledge, 1989); Fredric Jameson, *Postmodernism, or the Cultural Logic of Late Capitalism* (Durham: Duke University Press, 1991); Jean-François Lyotard, *The Postmodern Condition: A Report on Knowledge* (Minneapolis: University of Minnesota Press, 1985); Jean François Lyotard, *The Postmodern Explained: Correspondence, 1982–1985*, (Minneapolis: University of Min-

nesota Press, 1993); John McGowan, *Postmodernism and Its Critics* (Ithaca.: Cornell University Press, 1991); Brian McHale, *Postmodernist Fiction* (New York: Methuen, 1987); Brian McHale, *Constructing Postmodernism* (New York: Routledge, 1993); Joseph P. Natoli and Linda Hutcheon, *A Postmodern Reader* (Albany: State University of New York Press, 1993); Barry Smart, *Postmodernity* (London: Routledge, 1993); and Patricia Waugh, *Practising Postmodernism, Reading Modernism* (London: Edward Arnold, 1992). For a critique of some of the underlying presuppositions of this debate, see M. J. Devaney, *"Since at least Plato—" and Other Postmodernist Myths* (New York: St. Martin's Press, 1997).

5. On Faulkner and postmodernism, see, e.g., McHale in n.4 above; Richard Moreland, "Faulkner and Modernism," in *Cambridge Companion to Faulkner*, ed. Philip Weinstein (Cambridge: Cambridge University Press, 1995), 17–30; Patrick O'Donnell, "Faulkner and Postmodernism," in *Cambridge Companion to Faulkner* (Cambridge: Cambridge University Press, 1995), 31–50; and Gerhard Hoffmann, *"Absalom, Absalom!*: A Postmodernist Approach," in *Faulkner's Discourse: An International Symposium*, ed. Lothar Hönnighausen (Tubingen: Niemeyer, 1989), 276–92.

6. Hutcheon, *Poetics of Postmodernism*, 43.

7. Ibid.

8. See McHale in n. 4 above; and Hoffmann in n. 5 above.

9. On possible worlds and fictional worlds, see, e.g., Lubomír Dolezel, *Heterocosmica: Fiction and Possible Worlds, Parallax: Re-visions of Culture and Society* (Baltimore: Johns Hopkins University Press, 1998);Doreen Maitre, *Literature and Possible Worlds* (London: Pembridge Press,1983); Calin Andrei Mihailescu and Walid Hamarneh, *Fiction Updated: Theories of Fictionality, Narratology, and Poetics* (Toronto: University of Toronto Press, 1996); Thomas G. Pavel, *Fictional Worlds* (Cambridge: Harvard University Press, 1986); Ruth Ronen, *Possible Worlds in Literary Theory* (Cambridge: Cambridge University Press, 1994); and Marie-Laure Ryan, *Possible Worlds, Artificial Intelligence, and Narrative Theory* (Bloomington: Indiana University Press, 1991). Also see, Umberto Eco, *Six Walks in the Fictional Woods* (Cambridge: Harvard University Press, 1994); Kendall L. Walton, *Mimesis as Make-believe: On the Foundations of the Representational Arts* (Cambridge: Harvard University Press, 1990); and Nicholas Wolterstorff, *Works and Worlds of Art* (New York: Oxford University Press, 1980).

10. Martin Kreiswirth, " 'Paradoxical and Outrageous Discrepancy': Transgression, Auto-Intertextuality, and Faulkner's Yoknapatawpha," in *Faulkner and the Artist*, ed. Donald M. Kartiganer and Ann J. Abadie (Jackson: University Press of Mississippi, 1996), 161–80.

11. Hutcheon, *Poetics of Postmodernism*, 49.

12. See, e.g., Kreiswirth, 175.

13. Devaney has argued that many of what supporters of postmodernism view as "contradictions" or "paradoxes" are, by the principles of logic, neither, making a "both/and" construal unnecessary. Whether postmodern or not, the first order semantic discrepancies that I have been describing are indeed logical contradictions: an individual cannot be both seventeen and eighteen years old.

14. Hal Foster, quoted in David Herman, "Modernism versus Postmodernism: Towards an Analytic Distinction," in *A Postmodern Reader*, ed. Joseph Natoli and Linda Hutcheon (Albany: State University of New York Press, 1993), 169.

15. See, e.g., Dolezel, 22–3.

16. Ryan, *Possible Worlds*, 48–60.

17. Hutcheon, *Poetics of Postmodernism*, 129.

18. Sigmund Freud, *The Standard Edition of the Complete Psychological Works of Sigmund Freud*, ed. and trans. James Strachey et al. (London: Hogarth Press, 1958), 12:108.

19. Freud, *The Standard Edition*, 11:51.

20. See, e.g., Jessica Benjamin, *Shadow of the Other: Intersubjectivity and Gender in Psychoanalysis* (New York: Routledge, 1998); Harold Bloom, "Reading Freud: Transference, Taboo, and Truth," in *Centre and Labyrinth: Essays in Honour of Northrop Frye*, ed. Eleanor Cook, et al. (Toronto: University of Toronto Press, 1983), 309–28; Peter Brooks, *Reading for the Plot: Design and Intention in Narrative* (New York: Vintage, 1985), and his

Psychoanalysis and Storytelling (Oxford: Blackwell, 1994); Cynthia Chase, " 'Transference' as Trope and Persuasion," in *Discourse in Psychoanalysis and Literature*, ed. Shlomith Rimmon Kenan (New York: Methuen, 1988), 211–32; Jonathan Culler, "Textual Self-Consciousness and the Textual Unconscious," *Style* 18 (1984): 369–76; Shoshana Felman, "Turning the Screw of Interpretation," in *Literature and Psychoanalysis: The Question of Reading Otherwise*, ed. Shoshana Felman (Baltimore: Johns Hopkins University Press, 1982), 94–207, esp. 129–37; Jane Gallop, "Lacan and Literature: A Case for Transference," *Poetics* 13 (1984): 301–8; Sean Hand, "Missing You: Intertextuality, Transference and the Language of Love," in *Intertextuality: Theories and Practices*, ed. Michael Worton and Judith Still (Manchester: Manchester University Press, 1990), 79–91; Norman N. Holland, "Why This Is Transference, Nor Am I Out of It," *Psychoanalysis and Contemporary Thought* 5 (1982): 27–34; Roy Schafer, "Narration in the Psychoanalytic Dialogue," in *On Narrative*, ed. W. J. T. Mitchell (Chicago: University of Chicago Press, 1981), 25–49; Meredith Anne Skura, *The Literary Uses of the Psychoanalytic Process* (New Haven: Yale University Press, 1981); Susan Rubin Suleiman, "Mastery and Transference: The Significance of Dora,"in *The Comparative Perspective on Literature: Approaches to Theory and Practice*, ed. Clayton Koelb and Susan Noakes (Ithaca: Cornell University Press,1988), 213–23; and Laura Tracy, "Introduction: Transference Theory in Literature," in *Catching the Drift: Authority, Gender, and Narrative Strategy in Fiction* (New Brunswick: Rutgers University Press, 1988), 1–23. Also see, Steven J. Ellman, *Freud's Technique Papers: A Contemporary Perspective* (Northvale, N.J.: Aronson, 1991); and Aaron H. Esman, *Essential Papers on Transference* (New York: New York University Press, 1990).

21. Freud, *The Standard Edition*, 7:116.

22. Sean Hand, "Missing You," 79.

23. William Faulkner, *Absalom, Absalom!: The Corrected Text* (New York: Vintage International Edition, 1990), 236–7. All subsequent quotations from *Absalom* are from this edition.

24. Sean Hand, "Missing You," 79.

25. A transferential model—a story of two who always turn out to be more than two— can help explain this important but perplexing doubling, which has been virtually ignored by critics of *Absalom, Absalom!*

26. McHale, *Postmodernist Fiction*, 10.

Postvomiting: *Pylon* and the Faulknerian Spew

JOSEPH R. URGO

Vomiting does not have such a good name in contemporary human communities. The act is associated with eating disorders, over-indulgence in alcohol consumption, and, as a literary trope, with rejection and revulsion generally. It is markedly anti-social. Historically, the act has a pedigree. We may associate it with the decadence of the Roman empire, where the wealthy allegedly retired to the vomitorium and purged in order to continue the feast. Aesthetically, vomiting may signal cosmic or local rejection, a reification of existential nausea, signaling a character who is not at home in the world. Plenty of Faulkner characters throw up, to the point where critics have studied it. Gregory Forter, for example, links the vomiting in *Sanctuary* to Freud's 1925 essay on Negation, whose premise, "The world *begins* by being 'in me'—and it ends up by spilling out onto the floor," seems to have influenced Faulkner. He also reminds us of Walter Slatoff's suggestion that a typical Faulkner novel has a "vomitory tendency toward oxymoronical (anti) significance," a "tendency to 'say' things that it also does not say." [1] After listening to Temple, Horace vomits in *Sanctuary*; after watching his father fight his slaves, Henry vomits in *Absalom, Absalom!* These characters cannot hold down those things to which they have been exposed; they can't digest them and so they come up again.

Neither Horace Benbow nor Henry Sutpen can accept what they have been called upon to incorporate. However, their vomiting is unproductive and they both become incapacitated as a result. Horace does a pretty poor job in the courtroom, defending Temple; perhaps because he has not digested the logic of sexual representation and sexual assault into which he stumbles in *Sanctuary*. Henry Sutpen does a poor job as son and brother, too, because he has not digested the logic of the racial hierarchy embodied by his father's physical struggles in the barn. Had these characters digested these matters, of course, then they would have become implicated in the systems of power they represent, they would have found themselves on the inside, and not the outside, of social systems revealed to be so destructive. It's a kind of modernist fantasy to see oneself on the fringe, out there, removed from fault, at worst regurgitating the bland platitudes of a corrupted culture (like Temple's parroting of underworld epithets) but removed from complicity, like Darl Bundren, concluding comfortably, as his brother, Cash did, that "This world is not his world; this life his life."[2]

Metaphorically, regurgitation possesses connotations linking it to rote learning and the most unsophisticated, naïve forms of knowledge acquisition. It's not a good word in education. To regurgitate is to spoil the connection between mentor and student, and to cast doubt upon the intellectual legitimacy of the minds in question. (Shreve makes fun of Henry Sutpen, student at the University of Mississippi, calling him "Bayard . . . of the wilderness proud honor semestrial regurgitant").[3] If someone responds to your statement with the identical statement, you question that person's motives and suspect mockery, at best. If someone regurgitates the statements of another at a later time, you suspect theft, or dementia. When Temple Drake regurgitates, or parrots the language of gangsters, we grow suspicious of her actions and suspect she is not exercising her free will. She says things that she does not say, we might say. In *Absalom, Absalom!*, none of the narrating characters regurgitates; after Henry's spew there is no puking on the Compson porch, in the office at Miss Rosa's, or in the cold sitting room in Cambridge. On the contrary, most of what is consumed in those places is digested thoroughly and turned into some kind of fierce and assertive narrative energy.

Real puke is not like figurative regurgitation because it scarce resembles repetition. Vomit is revelatory. It reveals what happens to food in the process of digestion, which may not be unlike what happens to some of the ideas we hear, or interactions which engage us. Influence forestalled is like vomiting. Something enters and is expelled, and the stuff that is projected out is nothing at all like what went in. It's kind of sickening, really. It's like when Hagood, the editor, tells the reporter that "you never seem to bring back anything but information." All he does is vomit information, and it's never "the living breath of news" because "It's dead before you even get back here with it."[4] As info-vomit, what the reporter produces is partially processed, undigested, and vile. His work, in literary terms, is beneath mimesis; it is emetic. Hagood tells him this. He suggests that the newspaper, his newspaper, is suffering from a crisis in representation. "Can it be," he asks, that "you listen and see in one language and then do what you call writing in another?" (40). Well, nowadays, we would say yes, of course that's what he does. But that's because, I suggest, we are in the postvomit era.

Which brings me to the conference theme, Faulkner and Postmodernism. We are sure to come across multiple definitions of the term, post-

modern. "If there is a common denominator to all . . . postmodernisms,"
according to Hans Bertens, "it is that of a crisis in representation: a
deeply felt loss of faith in our ability to represent the real, in the widest
sense. No matter whether they are aesthetic, epistemological, moral, or
political in nature, the representations that we used to rely on can no
longer be taken for granted."[5] We can certainly include the representations we find, say, in a modernist novel like *Absalom, Absalom!* or in what
gets printed in what Faulkner calls the "diurnal dogwatch," or Hagood's
newspaper. These two sources are related, so hold on; Wait. Bertens continues, and distinguishes between modernism and postmodernism by arguing that "the self-reflexivity inherent in the modern project has come
to question modernity at large. In the last twenty years, modernity, as a
grand sociopolitical project, has increasingly been called to account by
itself; modernity has turned its critical rationality upon itself and has
been forced to reluctantly admit to its costs."[6] Postmodernism is modernist vomit. What modernism attempted to digest, to hold and to transform
into "the living breath" of some aesthetic, some grand sociopolitical project, ends up as spew, out in the open and revealed as historically in-
process and provisional, constructed, queer, and, in some quarters, vile.
We'll get back to this, so hold it in your stomach for a while: Postmodernism is modernist vomit. It's modernity that has turned its critical rationality upon itself, wrongsideout, to anticipate Faulkner, like some fierce
pseudoepochal orgasm.

Vomiting recurs like a bulimic carnival in *Pylon*. It seems to do some
good at first, before degenerating into parody. In the first narrative instance of ejection, the reporter feels wholly decentered, "his insides had
set up that fierce maelstrom to which there was no focalpoint, not even
himself" (103). As a result he stumbles down the stairs "swallowing and
swallowing the vomit which tried to fill his throat" (105). He is unsuccessful, and this leads Faulkner to one of the best descriptions of throwing up in literature: "he plunged out the door and struck a lamppost and
clung to it and surrendered as life, sense, all seemed to burst out of his
mouth as though his entire body were trying in one fierce orgasm to turn
itself wrongsideout" (109). The result of this gastronomic orgasm is, after
a good bit of unconsciousness, clarity.[7] After the reporter's purging, vision returns. In the restaurant the next day the reporter begins to "see"
his subject matter of his imagination more clearly than his immediate,
sensual surroundings. His physical existence gives way to his imaginative
powers: "Only the hangar was not the mirage but the restaurant, the
counter, the clash and the clatter, the sound of food and of eating; it
seemed to him that he could see the group: the aeroplane, the four dun-
garee figures, the little boy in dungarees too, himself approaching" (142).

This is not unlike Quentin Compson's assertion in *Absalom, Absalom!* ("If I had been there I could not have seen it this plain" [155]), as he comes to envision his Sutpen project. Of course, transcending one's time and place to achieve historical insight is a far cry from transcending the clash and clatter of the restaurant counter to envision an airplane a hundred yards away. One is high modernism; the other a kind of spew, a parody.

Not all vomiting in *Pylon* leads to insight; it's not a systematic trope in the novel. Jiggs vomits when Shumann tries to get him to eat that sandwich: "Shumann held him up, holding the sandwich clear with the other hand, while Jiggs' stomach continued to go through the motions of refusal long after there was nothing left to abdicate" (189). But Jiggs experiences no life-changing emission and seems to envision very little save the memory of his boots, unscarred. Similarly, the photographer at the crash site says, "I near vomited into the box while I was changing plates" (241), but he never does and he goes on taking those representational photographs, untroubled by his medium. So we can't identify vomiting or the urge to vomit in *Pylon* as a literary symbol and say, as critics do, that *this means this*. As Freud might have it, sometimes vomit is just vomit.

Sometimes, it's more, though. In the exchange the photographer has with the reporter about throwing up at the crash site, the link between vomiting and the media of news reportage is established.

> "You dont understand," the reporter said, in a peaceful baffled voice. "Let me explain it to you."
>
> "Yair; sure," the photographer said. "I still feel like vomiting too"; and then, the photographer:
>
> "You will have to call in with the buildup on it. Jesus, I tell you I feel bad too. Here, smoke a cigarette. Yair. I could vomit too. But what the hell? He aint our brother"; and then:
>
> "Yair," the reporter said. "Let's move. We got to eat, and the rest of them got to read." (243–5)

The mechanism of *Pylon* consists of these moving parts: airplanes and the people who jump out of them; bodies and the vomit that comes out of them; newspapers and the information that they project. To a lesser degree, there are busses and taxicabs, and people who enter and emit from them; elevators, offices and apartments, airplane hangars, and diners. The airplanes have received a lot of critical attention because, I think, that aspect of the text is fully digested. From the 1950s, when Donald Torchiana saw the flyers absurdly "caught in the machinery of the profit motive . . . with their disdain for money as such and their quixotic devotion to flying,"[8] to the 1990s, when John T. Matthews saw the novel as exposing "a tiered economy and society" that was dependent "on the violence of exploitation and oppression,"[9] critics have located social meaning in the digested subject matter of the novel. To further the legitimacy of such criticism, Faulkner's own flying is invoked, adding the truth of experience to the representation of barnstorming in the text.

But I'm not much interested in what the text represents, in those airplanes. Instead, what arrests my attention is the vomiting and the reporting, and, in the other direction, the connection between vomiting and narrative projection. "We got to eat," says the reporter, "and the rest of them got to read." There's a kind of slippage when the reporter and the photographer discuss explanations and vomiting at the crash site. The chapter title, "Lovesong of J. A. Prufock," implies some specific meaning to the reporter's "Let me explain it to you," but despite "the cups, the marmalade, the tea" in Eliot's poem, no one vomits there. No one even feels like it. On the contrary, it all stays down in the poem, "Till human voices wake us, and we drown."[10] It's this modernist sense of the whole, of digested completion, that *Pylon* vomits. Instead of measuring his life with coffee spoons, a fine and famous image, the reporter's is measured in spew, what he can and cannot hold, and in those phone calls he makes to Hagood, his editor.

Not all animal communities share the human revulsion for vomit. You may have seen your dog react to what it emits, for example. The biologist E. O. Wilson conducted a study of the physical regurgitation process inside a colony of black ants and found that throwing up plays an important part in the vitality of the ant community. Wilson and his colleagues located a forager ant and supplied it with some radioactive, traceable liquid, to see what happened to the food in its stomach, or crop. The scientists found that "portions of the food brought in by a single worker reached every other worker in the colony within twenty-four hours, after prolonged bouts of reciprocal feeding." The forager ant, taking and holding more than he needed in his crop, would regurgitate into the mouths of other ants who would, in turn, return the favor to other ants. "Within a week, all the colony members were carrying approximately the same quantity" of the original food in their stomachs. Biologists refer to the function of the single worker ant charged with delivering the living breath of food, so to speak, as possessing a crop which serves as the "social stomach" for the colony. Wilson points out further that all of this regurgitation is accomplished in the absence of a command center. "No individual—not even the queen . . . lays plans for the colony as a whole."[11] This is not unlike George Monteiro's sense (in 1958) that *Pylon* "proceeds without a moral center, without a perceiving intelligence";[12] an idea echoed twenty-three years later by Richard Pearce, who found the novel to proceed with "no organic design or controlling center."[13] Now, we must be wary of naturalist metaphors, as they have gotten human beings into trouble, from Social Darwinism through noble classes and master races. But I can't seem to help myself. In the conflation of eating, vomiting, calling in the story, and reading, we might recognize a link between the social stomach of the ant colony and the reporter's function as information processor. "We got to eat, and the rest of them got to read."

When the reporter vomits he loses hold on the myth of his centrality; when "his insides . . . set up that fierce maelstrom" he hurls himself into the postmodern presupposition that "there was no focalpoint, not even himself" (103). The absence of a command center fascinates the biologist as much as the absence of a moral center or center of perception attracts the literary critic—the absence of authoritative centers is in the air, we might say. John Duvall's postmodernist study of marginality in Faulkner dispenses entirely with centers, finding that "Pylon . . . highlights the recurring pattern in Faulkner's fiction of the 1930s—unions of men and women at the margins of the community."[14] Of course, if there is no center, no focal point, there can be no margins. The reporter's absent focal point signals a vomiting of the modernist quest to be located, as Dos Passos would say, at the center of things, or at the crossroads, where things come together, where they coalesce. In postmodern culture, the quest for the center is rejected not because it is unwanted but because it is impossible. Once we reject the subject itself as the center of its own experience, when there is "no focalpoint, not even himself," then our eyes are less fixed upon character as the source of moral or ethical value and more on that radioactive liquid—on the traces, the exchanges, the reciprocal feeding by which the colony, or the community, shares the substance on which it relies for its existence. In *Pylon* that substance is information, news, and Hagood's reporters possess the social stomach. We see "about the copydesk the six or seven men, coatless and collarless, in their green eyeshades like a uniform," and these men "seemed to concentrate toward a subterranean crisis, like so many puny humans conducting the lyingin of a mastodon" (209).[15] But what is news? The novel itself seems perplexed by the phenomenon of the social stomach; or, the information stomach possessed by Hagood's news operation.

A lot of critics are puzzled by Hagood's impatience with the reporter. The impatience, I think, stems from a lack of appreciation of vomit. Judith Wittenberg suggests that Hagood's demand for the living breath of news and then his rejection of imaginative interpretation is contradictory. "Mere information is inadequate, and so is high-flown fiction. True 'news' (the word, after all, from which 'novel' comes) lies somewhere in be-

tween. The problem of the writer is related to the problem of discovering
that elusive midline between data and fantasy and of infusing the 'living
breath' into a word-creation. It is a problem with which Faulkner would
deal on a much larger scale in *Absalom, Absalom!*"[16] That's right, but
Faulkner could not deal with this issue in *Absalom, Absalom!* until he
vomited it in *Pylon*. News reportage builds community, like an ant colony
where the ants engage in massive regurgitation until they all have the
same stuff in their stomach. A newspaper (or the TV news or MSNBC, if
we want to be up-to-date here) does the same thing intellectually, and
the reporter acts as the social stomach, vomiting his stuff into the minds
of readers. And literature—here is the nausea that Faulkner may well
have encountered in *Absalom, Absalom!*—does literature do the same?
We are a community of Faulkner readers into whose minds Faulkner has
vomited, repeatedly. By all accounts, *Absalom, Absalom!* is the largest,
most turgescent of the great novels. Is *it* the living breath of literature?
Recall Shreve's habit, in that novel, of "deep breathing" (235) while the
two roommates narrate the story of Sutpen, whose "breathing vaporised
faintly in the cold room where there was not two of them but four, the
two who breathed not individuals now yet something both more and
less than twins" (236). Characters in *Absalom, Absalom!* don't regurgitate
communally, but they come close. Does literature produce community?
Well, what are we doing here? "The best novel yet written by an American," as Faulkner described it upon completion,[17] constitutes as well as
reflects America, if we can manage to hold it down, that is.

In the course of writing *Absalom, Absalom!*, Faulkner put the manuscript aside to write *Pylon*. At Virginia in 1957 he explained,[18]

> I can't say just where it was that I had to put it down, that I decided that I
> didn't know enough at that time maybe or my feeling toward it wasn't passion-
> ate enough or pure enough, but I don't remember at what point I put it down.
> Though when I took it up again I almost rewrote the whole thing. I think that
> what I put down were inchoate fragments that wouldn't coalesce and then
> when I took it up again, as I remember, I rewrote it.

Putting it down and taking it up, not feeling passionate enough to hold
it down and getting only "inchoate fragments that wouldn't coalesce" and
so putting it down to write *Pylon*, the novel of vomit and representation,
and then going back and taking up the modernist masterwork and writing
it again, this time being able to put it down without, so to speak, putting it
down again. In his study of Faulkner and modernism, Richard Moreland
prefers exorcism to vomitism and speculates that "in writing *Pylon* Faulkner attempted to *exorcise* the relatively unfocused ironic bitterness of
cosmopolitan literary modernism in order to turn back to *Absalom* with

a more acutely concentrated critical attention to those cosmopolitan ironies' more specifically Southern cousins."[19] Maybe Faulkner got some
sort of intellectual stomach bug attempting that grand narrative, *Absalom,
Absalom!*

Critics have applied metaphors to explain postmodernism that are
reminiscent of early twentieth-century images of the kind of cultural and
historical illnesses that cause wars and other social upheavals. Contemporary critics disagree on the source, or cause, of our postmodern condition.
Jean-François Lyotard invokes an image of illness, not time, to place the
postmodern era. He argues that "Postmodern does not signify recent. It
signifies how writing, in the broadest sense of thought and action, is situated after it has succumbed to the contagion of modernity and has tried
to cure itself."[20] One symptom of this "contagion" is that the West repeatedly "arms itself with ideals, calls them into question, and rejects them."
Hence, postmodernism thrives on "the power of the negative" and the
incessant rejection of received tradition requiring "a full-blown nihilism."[21] This full-blown nihilism may be cast aesthetically as fully blown
lunch, for example, the turning of the totalities of modernism wrongsideout. It may result, on the part of the writer of fiction, in being unable to
put something down. In any case, just as vomit cannot be said to be what
happens to food organically or systemically—that is, it is not a process
that we understand to come properly *after* ingestion—the postmodern is
also not thought to follow temporally upon the digestion of the modern
era. Like vomiting, postmodernism is convulsive, always already possible, though indicative that something has gone wrong with the way we
understand systems to work. After ingesting modernism, a contagion
forces the incessant rejection of its ideals and assumptions by western
thinkers; what emits from this consciousness, postvomiting, is not modernism, but postmodernism.

Temporality remains problematic. Viewed as a matter of simple causality, one would say that vomiting is caused by ingestion. But ingesting,
like breathing, is a constant state of present-activity. Human beings are
always consuming—oxygen, images, ideas—and always producing; at the
very least, we produce carbon dioxide and noise. The idea of the modern
may well be tied to this sense of an ever-present now, the sheer nowness
of human existence. Vomiting, though, interrupts the normal processes of
ingestion and production by unmasking the human focal point as entirely
arbitrary, subject to operations that may be organic, but which are far
from immutable and eternal. Postmodernism works similarly on modernism, according to Perry Anderson. "Since the modern—aesthetic or historical—is always in principle what might be called a present-absolute,
it creates a peculiar difficulty for the definition of any period beyond it,

that would convert it to a relative past."[22] Once the modern, understood as the new or the *now*, is temporally digested and thus becomes the past, what happens to *now*? Like the oxygen and food we consume, the modern is always what we are becoming, in the present. But if we reject the modern, throw it up and no longer find ourselves able to digest its ethics, its narratives, its world view, then we are not beyond the modern but we are like the reporter, locked outside of our (modern) apartment, surrounded and coated in what we cannot, have not, and will not digest. Anderson concludes that "the makeshift of a simple prefix—denoting what comes after—is virtually inherent in the concept [of modernism] itself, one that could be more or less counted on in advance to recur whenever a stray need for a marker of temporal difference might be felt. Resort of this kind to the term, 'postmodern' has always been of circumstantial significance."[23] Vomit, no matter how vile, is a mixture of what we have ingested and what we always already were; postmodernism, no matter how interesting or vile it may be, is soaked through not only with modernism, but with the systems available to us for its processing.

Absalom, Absalom! may well be the grand narrative of twentieth-century American literature, the ultimate modernist project. But nearly everything that *Absalom, Absalom!* represents in the way of imaginative re-creation, characterization, faith in narrative reason, and authorial knowledge is undone in *Pylon*, where all that is hoped for in the grand narrative is discredited, rejected as un-coalesced spew, the incoherent dream and now the object of what the novel itself calls some "postgraduate certificate of excess" (135). Terry Eagleton describes postmodern consciousness as pure rejection. "Suspecting all assured truths and certainties, its form is ironic and its epistemology relativist and skeptical. Rejecting all attempts to reflect a stable reality beyond itself, it exists self-consciously at the level of form or language."[24] In *Absalom, Absalom!*, there intrudes an authoritative voice to endorse the inventions made by Quentin and Shreve, affirming their veracity; in *Pylon*, no voice (least of all the "apocryphal, sourceless, inhuman, ubiquitous" [36] voice of the public address system)—no voice exists in *Pylon* to tell us that the reporter or anyone else is "probably right" (*Absalom, Absalom!*, 268) about anything said or done in that novel.

Eagleton continues: "Knowing its own fictions to be groundless and gratuitous, [postmodernism] can attain a kind of negative authenticity only by flaunting its ironic awareness of this fact, wryly pointing its own status as a constructed artifice."[25] This *Pylon* does continually, pointing to repeated efforts to know the (groundless?) flyers through the print media, and not even bothering to affect barriers between its journalistic and novelistic ambitions. Thirty-five years ago, Olga Vickery compared storytelling in *Absalom, Absalom!* and *Pylon*, finding that selection, arrangement, and invention, hallmarks of the modernist narrative, were supplanted, in *Pylon*, by a haphazard presentation of conflicting facts and motivations, offered "in the hope that of they cancel out or at least modify each other, something of the real truth might emerge."[26] Alas, if there is a real truth in *Pylon*, the text offers no guidance or rationale for locating it and calling it "probably right."

Postmodern culture rejects what Quentin and Shreve worked all night in order to reinsert into the Sutpen story: linearity, plausibility, the logic of cause and effect, "the best of thought" (208), and "the best of ratiocination" (225). The two Harvard students are too sophisticated for Miss Rosa Coldfield's demonizing; they can see right through Mr. Compson's tragic sensibility; they can even penetrate Sutpen's self-promotion in the story he tells Quentin's grandfather. These are modern men, cosmopolites; they are at a New England college where regions are effaced and modern sensibilities cultivated. Shreve, of Alberta, Canada, and Quentin, of Yoknapatawpha, Mississippi, are part of each other's education; the references they ease about in—medieval romance, Greek mythology, Old and New Testament symbolism, world literature—are the contexts of modernism, and they are intended to supplant the certainties of Alberta and Mississippi by placing Alberta and Mississippi into their grand context. The modern Harvard sensibility transforms all such localities into objects of study (*"Tell about the South. What's it like there. What do they do there. Why do they live there. Why do they live at all"* [142]); such localities as Mississippi and Alberta do not qualify as subject positions, as centers, but are called regions, margins, outlying areas. Postmodernism responds by suggesting there is no center by which to adjudicate marginality; that marginality, not centrality, comprises our condition. Postmodern culture also rejects the very notion of the "high culture" represented by *Absalom, Absalom!*, with its biblical title and its participation in the tradition of elite narrative construction. In the vomiting, the Harvard students and the planter class are turned wrongsideout, and we have the quest for new boots, some jack, and the thrill of three-party sexuality.

It's a mistake to judge vomit by the standards of what it might have become had it stayed down. There is no effort in *Pylon* to raise the flyers to the level of high culture, no overarching Biblical paradigm of King Anybody having too many sons. Irving Howe described the novel as dramatizing "a situation which has already reached a dead-end . . . so that *Pylon* comes to seem a pale signature of another, unwritten, far more arresting book."[27] It's vomit. Instead of Quentin sitting for hours in Miss Coldield's office, *Pylon* opens with Jiggs staring a full minute at some cowboy boots in a shop window. Instead of carefully weighing images and ideas in the iron cold sanctuary of Harvard Yard, the reporter phones it in as it happens. Grandfather Compson gave Thomas Sutpen what he needed to gain a foothold in Mississippi; the reporter helps Shumann buy an airplane. It's all about to be there, in *Pylon*; but it's just grosser, unformed, and not so suitable for consumption. *Pylon* is seldom cited as exemplary Faulkner; it may be that *Pylon* is exemplary of nothing.

When we read how "the downfunnelled light from the desklamp struck the reporter across the hips" (38) as he stands over Hagood's desk, the image recalls Shreve at Quentin's desk in Cambridge, with Quentin "looking fragile and even wan in the lamplight" (236). But nothing creative or groundbreaking and no claims to any insight whatsoever into the human condition emerge from the copydesk. The tragedy of Charles Bon's affiliation emits, in *Pylon*, as the comedy of Jack Shumann's "couple or three sets of grandparents"(46); and Bon's projected desire for some sign from Sutpen degenerates into a game of "who's your old man today, kid?" (16). Quentin's anguish is signaled by the point where he is revealed to have been "not listening" to Rosa; the reporter also stops listening, but only when he's made up his mind and does not want to be influenced. Once, in his rush to regurgitate news, he ceases "not alone to listen but even to hear" (49) Hagood and then later, he stops listening to Laverne (168) once he's decided to help Shumann buy the airplane, over her objections. Quentin stops listening when there is something he cannot pass, something he cannot digest; the reporter stops listening when he does not want to be contradicted. The reporter experiences Quentin's insomnia (57), but unlike Quentin the reporter does not create shades but is himself "a citizen of the shadows . . . who from all outward appearances had been born there too" (79). Again, the reporter is not and cannot be the focal point; in *Pylon*, there is no subject position to occupy, no Harvard sitting room, no narrators who "slept in the same room" and who had "eaten side by side of the same food and used the same books from which to prepare to recite in the same freshman courses" (*Absalom, Absalom!*, 208).

There are no subject positions in *Pylon* and thus no intersubjective collaboration, no attempt to construct a community across time, though like an ant colony, much is happening: airplanes are flying, the show is going on, the newspapers are reporting. But *Pylon* works toward no grand "Continental Trough," or international narrative; its primary consciousness is as shadelike as its subject matter. *Absalom, Absalom!* features "a sort of geographical transubstantiation" that brings together its elite, Harvard narrators to enact the "geologic umbilical" of the North American Environment (208); *Pylon* features a topographical transubstantiation, "pocked desolation of some terrific and apparently purposeless reclamation" of land which possesses "a chimaera quality which for the moment prevented one from comprehending that it had been built by man and for a purpose" (13). In *Absalom, Absalom!*, human beings create stories to explain what happened on the land; in *Pylon*, human beings create land to accommodate the needs of "a yet unenvisioned tomorrow" (14). *Absalom, Absalom!* constructs a worldview informed and shaped (today we might also say colonized) by Harvard elite culture. Quentin is not telling about the South; it is Harvard that is incorporating the South and telling Quentin about himself, reconstructing him, as it were. No such grand structure undergirds *Pylon*; even the narrator is a corpse, "escaped into the living world" (17) not with a tale to tell, but in search of one to report; he works not for knowledge, but for stimulation, nothing more. As Hagood explains, the newspaper reports that which "creates any reaction excitement or irritation on any human retina" with no interest in narrative design—demonizing or ratiocinate, either. "[W]hat they want is not fiction, not even Nobel Prize fiction, but news" (48), Hagood says.

This may be why Faulkner resurrected Quentin, the suicide from *The Sound and the Fury*, to tie it all together in *Absalom, Absalom!* Quentin Compson "is the protagonist," Faulkner explained when he began the novel, "so that it is not complete apocrypha."[28] He is, like the reporter, virtually a walking corpse at the time of his appearance in the novel; nonetheless, or more so, it is Quentin's impending death that gives him such substance in the novel. The reporter also resembles Sutpen both in his decorating habits, as he "hunted down piece by piece the furniture which cluttered" his home (89), and in his background, as he "joined the paper without credentials or any past, documentary or hearsay, at all" (90). In his brief economic collaboration with Shumann, the reporter again resembles Quentin, who collaborates with Shreve to produce the Bon family lawyer. The reporter collaborates with Shumann to produce the crash that will kill the pilot, destroy the flyers' family, and end the narrative. The collaboration thus moves not toward creation but toward disaster (174), as if Quentin had gone out to the Sutpen house not to learn its secrets but to destroy it. Thus we may see Roger Shumann as "the antithesis of Thomas Sutpen, the father who denies a son he knows to be his own" when he accepts "the son he cannot know is his."[29]

The similarities are limited, though, as the exercise is something like comparing vomit to digested food transformed into something else, "cooked and et" as Vardaman says of his fish in *As I Lay Dying*, transformed into Pa and Cash and the rest of the family. *Absalom, Absalom!* begins where the reporter gets stuck. The reporter sees himself as a perennial Henry Sutpen, stuck in some sort of outer circle of rejected observation, trying to figure out what went wrong. Recall the scene where Ellen runs into the barn to see "Henry plunge out from [the hayloft] among the negroes who had been holding him, screaming and vomiting" at the sight of his father "naked and panting and bloody to the waist" (21), in the first pages of *Absalom, Absalom!* The reporter, similarly, "seemed doomed to look down at everyone with whom he seemed perennially and perpetually compelled either to plead or just to endure . . . and so permit him to see himself actually as the friendly and lonely ghost peering timidly down from the hayloft at the other children playing below" (169). He is stuck at the level of observation; indeed, he is known by everyone, as "a person of unassailable veracity" (232). His trouble, like Sutpen's, may be innocence as well. He lies once in the novel, in the process of getting Ord's airplane for Shumann. "I never told a lie in my life that anybody believed," he exclaims; "maybe this is what I have been needing all the time!" (218). It is the lie that produces the plane that produces the crash that completes the novel and allows Faulkner to return to *Absalom, Absalom!* News representation, though, with its strict and necessary delineation between fact and lie, can only regurgitate, it cannot and must not create. Think of how every few years some hapless reporter somewhere writes a story exposing some awful truth about a social issue, only to have the story discredited because the facts (some, all, any) were invented, not found. News is vomit, not digestion. Digestion lies about what it consumes; it transforms it into something else and discharges what it does not need, as waste. Vomit tells the truth about this process.

Absalom, Absalom! seeks to represent Sutpen and finds that the mimetic exercise is impossible, fraught by an incapacitating confrontation with modernist structures of representation: perspective, memory, motivation, narrative form, myth. Each of these structures threatens to erect something through which present knowledge cannot pass, leaving characters isolated and islanded in the present. In the barn, as a child, Henry sees his father, sees power represented in its most base and vulgar, unmediated form, and he vomits. What can be known, digested, absent mediation of some kind? *Absalom, Absalom!* repeatedly reveals how perspective influences representation, how memory is not reliable, how motivation cannot be separated from consequence, and how all narratives possess prior forms and structures that shape our knowledge of history and its twin, myth. Faulkner began *Absalom, Absalom!*, vowing, in February of 1934 in a letter to his editor, "To keep the hoop skirts and plug hats out" by using Quentin Compson as the protagonist, "to get more out of the story itself than a historical novel would be."[30] In August he wrote to the same editor to say that the book "is not quite ripe yet" though he has the title, *Absalom, Absalom!* In October 1934, Faulkner reports that

a new novel is underway based on an air story.[31] He would finish *Pylon*
by December 1934, virtually vomiting the chapters as he wrote them,
sending them (uncharacteristically) to Random House piecemeal. Like
Henry in the barn, Faulkner could not, at first, get (or keep) the unripe
grand narrative down. *Absalom, Absalom!* literally and figuratively embodies modernism while turning the processes of modernism wronside-
out, raising the grand sociopolitical project of modernist discourse to a
level at which it encapsulates itself and its points of fissure: The representational crisis faced and embodied by Quentin and Shreve is solved, finally, by the creation of secondary shades judged by the narrator, the
source of the grand narrative itself, as "probably true enough"—a statement that reverberates throughout Faulkner's apocrypha, across the map
of Yoknapatawpha and beyond, raising and suspending the *sine qua non*
of Faulkner's project: what is truth? Quentin is brought into the novel to
keep it from becoming "complete apocrypha" just as the lawyer is
brought into Quentin and Shreve's narrative to make it "true enough."
But true enough according to whom and in reference to what?

And so we vomit. As we might do in one of those "aeroplanes" from
the 1930s going too fast around the pylon, decentering us, and inebriat-
ing our sense of being grounded anywhere, we throw up. We examine
the spew. Now we are not looking at Sutpen anymore but over Jiggs's
shoulders we are staring at boots in a shop window, "the image of an
onlooker separated from his desired object, the inability of the observer
to reach out and *grasp* the thing that has caught his attention and whetted
his appetites," as Joseph McElrath says.[32] With the reporter, we are looking at Laverne and the male flyer-lovers and listening (or not listening)
to the voice of the announcer. The reporter is the main piece in the
vomit, described "as though made of air and doped like an aeroplane
wing with the incrusted excretion of all articulate life's contact with the
passing earth" (17). He wants to transcend representation and he can't.
His editor wants him to do the same but he can't articulate his desire and
doesn't really know what he means. Unlike *Absalom, Absalom!*, which
raises questions of representation to the level of grand narrative, *Pylon*
throws them up. Like postmodernism, which seizes upon the fault lines
in modernist discourse and examines them minutely, *Pylon* vomits the
very points of coalescence on which *Absalom, Absalom!*, as intricately
constructed discourse, depends.

Postvomiting, the reporter at first refuses to consume. He declines a
drink offered to him at the bar. "He felt profoundly and peacefully empty
inside, as though he had vomited and very emptiness had supplied into
his mouth or somewhere about his palate like a lubricant a faint thin taste
of salt which was really pleasant: the taste not of despair but of Nothing.

'I'll go call in now,' he said" (246). Postvomiting leads again to stable representation but not quite: postvomiting, like postmodernism, leaves representation forever tinged with self-consciousness and irony. Postvomiting, the reporter begins his refrain, "I have just got to try to explain to somebody" but finds that his "lungs [are] not large enough to accommodate the air which his body had to have" (263) in order to project, in order even to approximate the deep breathing on the level of the Harvard sitting room. Finally, with Jiggs, he takes a drink and throws it up immediately. Then he has his postvomit vision of Jiggs delivering the toy airplane to Laverne:

> "Maybe I will go and look," he thought, waiting to see if he were until suddenly he realised that now, opposite from when he had stood in the bedroom before turning on the light, it was himself who was the nebulous and quiet ragtag and bobend of touching and breath and experience without visible scars . . . as though it had not been a steam train which quitted the station two seconds ago but rather the shadow of one on a magic lantern screen until the child's vagrant and restless hand came and removed the slide. (289)

Postvomiting, the reporter becomes not Quentin, the anti-apocryphal narrator who receives the authorial benediction of creating *"out of . . . rag-tag and bob-ends"* shadows of people "quiet as the visible murmur of their vaporising breath" (*Absalom, Absalom!* 143). Instead, the reporter is himself "the nebulous and quiet ragtag and bobend of touching and breath and experience"—the subject itself is yet another representational field and there is no author, anywhere, to tell him or us or even itself that all this is probably true enough. The reporter realizes the provisionality of his own subject position, the tenuous assemblage of his self as well as his imagination. He is no more reliable as entity in the world at large than would be a projection of a shadow on a magic lantern screen; the same capacity he possesses to "see" the steam train and the departure allows him also to "see" himself as himself, to occupy not only in time and space but language, the ragtag and the bobend of old tales and talking, and of new tales and flying.

As the reporter sits in the newsroom attempting to envision Shumann's family back home in Ohio, he resembles Quentin in Rosa's office trying to envision what she remembers, until "Quentin seemed to see" the Sutpen family arranged in a photograph (9). As Quentin learns more, his vision sharpens and becomes distinct, intimate, and painfully truthful; in the language of high modernism, his creation is well-wrought, a thing of beauty. "I see so little of it," the reporter says (309). Then he nearly vomits, "again it tasted, felt, like so much dead icy water, that cold and heavy and lifeless in his stomach; when he moved he could both hear and feel it sluggish and dead within him as he removed his coat and hung it on the chairback and sat down" (310). This statement is followed by thirteen pages of Jack Shumann's abandonment scene. But there is no author to tell us "what" the scene is: Is it narrated by the author? Is it imagined by the reporter? Did it "really" happen? With postmodern sensibilities, one may see how absurd such questions become when we are discussing a work of art.

Michael Zeitlin refers to the ending of the text as "the beginning of literature," specifically, "the literature that was *Pylon* and that will be *Absalom, Absalom!*"[33] This nicely dodges the absurd question that the novel itself begs by its final scene, and sets us back to thinking instead about *Absalom, Absalom!*, where creative insight is celebrated, not expelled. Gary Harrington incorporates the idea of *Pylon* as a creative recharge into the thesis of his book about all the non-Yoknapatawpha novels. "The reporter's aspiration to be a writer of fiction," Harrington argues, "combined with his attempt to 'read' the situation of the fliers affirms his function as both an artist-figure and a reader; hence, *Pylon*, like the other non-Yoknapatawpha novels, may be read as a fable of creativity."[34] In the organic metaphor I have employed, this makes *Pylon* less vomit and more like a burp, easing the digestion of more important matters. Reynolds Price will have none of this, and sees the ending of *Pylon* as the prelude to more vomiting. The ending, Price argues, makes the self-condemnatory admission "that the years and energy which he had spent among pilots and planes (seduced by *something*) had yielded only turgid bafflement, ashes-in-the-mouth."[35] Hugh M. Ruppersburg implicitly concurs, and locates a major theme in the novel, "that communication's failure isolates the individual intellectually, emotionally, and socially" and also, that "language proves ineffective, purposeless" in the novel.[36]

Well, either it's art or it's ashes-in-the-mouth—or else it's neither, just as postmodernism is not really an era but an age turned wrongsideout, a meta-era during which all that has enabled us is undercut by profound second thoughts. Postvomiting, the reporter either creates literature or he does not; there's no need for us to make the choice, simply to recognize the situation. Postvomiting, that which is flown from the mouth is either food or it is not; well, of course it is not food, and neither is it not notfood, like that "long silence of notpeople in notlanguage" (5) to whom Quentin must listen in order to digest and produce the narrative of his own self-creation. Not the Quentin who goes to Harvard, but the other Quentin, the one "who was still too young to deserve yet to be a ghost but nevertheless having to be one . . . since he was born and bred in the deep South" (4). In *The Sound and the Fury* Faulkner explained Quentin's death; in *Absalom, Absalom!* we learn of his creation, the reason he lived and why he lived at all. Nineteen-ten was to be Quentin's butterfly summer and he doesn't make it that far, but he leaves behind him something of beauty which he has extricated from and then attached to the memory of that other doomed family, the Sutpens. Can we believe it? We cling to that statement, "probably true enough" like a supplicant clinging to a petition or a pilgrim with his crucifix, because it marks our faith—our faith in the authority of what human beings create, our faith in what we do when we engage our social stomachs. We really must "try to keep the vomit swallowed," as does the reporter, in his (and our) "profound and detached desolation and amazement" (106) at what we can manage, in this world, to do.

Pylon records the creation of something more tangible than a good story about incest and miscegenation, even more impressive than a woman with two husbands who accept the assignment of paternity on chance. In *Pylon* Faulkner thinks about creating tangible things, like airplanes and airports, newspapers and loudspeakers. Feinman Airport, according to the novel, was built on land reclaimed from the natural environment and from human waste. The airport is a massive public works project, a supreme reification of the collaborative intellectual project undertaken by Quentin and Shreve at Harvard (maybe something more suited to MIT), and not too far from the private building project undertaken by Sutpen and his slaves. A plaque reads: FEINMAN AIRPORT / NEW VALOIS, FRANCIANA / DEDICATED TO / THE AVIATORS OF AMERICA / AND / COLONEL H. I. FIENMAN, CHAIRMAN, SEWAGE / BOARD. (Sewage Board? And so the Airport is also Postvomit)[37] THROUGH WHOSE UNDEVIATING VISION AND UNFLAGGING EFFORT THIS AIRPORT WAS RAISED UP AND CREATED OUT OF THE WASTE LAND AT THE BOTTOM OF LAKE RAMBAUD AT A COST OF ONE MILLION DOLLARS (10–11). Sutpen's "design" raised Sutpen's Hundred from the Northern Mississippi swampland. Quentin's undeviating vision raised the ghosts of Thomas and Ellen Sutpen, of Henry and Judith, and Charles Bon. The reporter's vision (if he had one) may have accomplished something (if it did). But Feinman's vision built an airport out of a lake: like the *Be Sutpen's Hundred* which Sutpen created "out of the soundless Nothing" (4), Feinman's *Be Feinman Airport*, with help from public administration, brought from the wasteland of modernism the postvomit spew: destinationless travel, ubiquitous mediation, and the absence of narrative or authorial focal point. "This Feinman," Jiggs said, "He must be a big son of a bitch" (11); bigger than Thomas Sutpen? His social stomach was large, for out of it a topography was reclaimed from its modernist wasteland.

There is tremendous faith in *Absalom, Absalom!*, faith in human creativity and intellectual power, faith in the capacity of human beings to negotiate some kind of peaceful coexistence with their time, their place, and their conditions. But the line between that faith and despair is thin, and the ability to maintain faith under modern conditions is easily broken. Faulkner wrote *Absalom, Absalom!* while confronted with this century's most challenging affronts to that faith: massive commercialization in Hollywood, the forging of fascism in Europe, the depths of economic despair in the United States. *Pylon* represents a fissure in the faith we know Faulkner, throughout his career, maintained—it represents a kind of intellectual paroxysm, a vomiting of all that *Absalom, Absalom!* asserts with such ferocious certainty. In the vomit of *Pylon* we see so many uncollected fragments of postmodernism: the flight from clarity, the insistence upon the unprecedented in language, the assumption that a breakthrough is imminent. When all else fails, build something, invent something, name something—call this era postmodern. In the digestion of *Absalom, Absalom!*, however, we find human beings struggling, as they have always struggled, with the place and the purpose of their bodies and their minds, largely in the absence of certainty from god, history, or their communities. We know Quentin's anguish as well as we know our own: *I dont hate it; I dont hate it!* Well, Yair.

NOTES

1. Gregory Forter, "Faulkner's Black Holes: Visions and Vomit in *Sanctuary*," *Mississippi Quarterly* 49:3 (1996): 539, 553. André Bleikasten comments generally on vomiting as "a gesture of refusal and protest" in *Sanctuary*; see *The Ink of Melancholy: Faulkner's Novels from "The Sound and the Fury" to "Light in August"* (Bloomington: Indiana University Press, 1990), 248.

2. William Faulkner, *As I Lay Dying* (1930), *The Corrected Text* (New York: Vintage International, 1990), 261.

3. William Faulkner, *Absalom, Absalom!* (1936), *The Corrected Text* (New York: Vintage International, 1990), 288. Subsequent textual references are to this edition.

4. William Faulkner, *Pylon* (1935), *The Corrected Text* (New York: Vintage Books, 1985), 39. Subsequent textual references are to this edition.

5. Hans Bertens, *The Idea of the Postmodern: A History* (New York: Routledge, 1995), 11.

6. Ibid., 247.

7. Michael Zeitlin sees the vomiting as Faulkner's "own violent purging of a narrative language into which the commodified stamp of 'the age of mechanical reproduction' has sunk deeply." See "Faulkner's *Pylon*: The City in the Age of Mechanical Reproduction," *Canadian Review of American Studies* 22:2 (Fall 1991): 237.

8. Donald T. Torchiana, "Faulkner's 'Pylon' and the Structure of Modernity," *Modern Fiction Studies* 3 (Winter 1957–1958): 299.

9. John T. Matthews, "The Autograph of Violence in Faulkner's *Pylon*," *Southern Literary Theory*, ed. Jefferson Humphries (Athens: University of Georgia Press, 1990), 258.

10. T. S. Eliot, "The Lovesong of J. Alfred Prufrock," in *Selected Poems* (New York: Harcourt Brace Jovanovich, 1964), 16.

11. Edward O. Wilson, *In Search of Nature* (Washington, D.C.: Island Press, 1996), 67–8.

12. George Monteiro, "Bankruptcy in Time: A Reading of William Faulkner's *Pylon*," *Twentieth-Century Literature* 4 (April-July 1958): 12.

13. Richard Pearce, "*Pylon*, 'Awake and Sing!' and the Apocalyptic Imagination of the 30s," *Criticism* 13 (1971): 137.

14. John Duvall, *Faulkner's Marginal Couple: Invisible, Outlaw, and Unspeakable Communities* (Austin: University of Texas Press, 1990), 12.

15. Ann Goodwyn Jones suggested, following the presentation of this paper, that birthing (or lying-in) may be seen as uterine vomiting, linked to Faulkner's sense of creation in this text.

16. Judith Bryant Wittenberg, *Faulkner: The Transfiguration of Biography* (Lincoln: University of Nebraska Press, 1979), 137.

17. Joseph Blotner, *Faulkner: A Biography*, 1-vol. ed. (New York: Random House, 1984), 364.

18. Frederick L. Gwynn and Joseph L. Blotner, eds., *Faulkner in the University: Class Conferences at the University of Virginia, 1957–1958* (New York: Vintage Books, 1969), 75–6.

19. Richard C. Moreland, *Faulkner and Modernism: Rereading and Rewriting* (Madison: University of Wisconsin Press, 1990), 27.

20. Jean-François Lyotard, *Postmodern Fables* (Minneapolis: University of Minnesota Press, 1997), 95–6.

21. Ibid., 236.

22. Perry Anderson, *The Origins of Postmodernity* (New York: Verso, 1998), 14.

23. Ibid.

24. Terry Eagleton, *Literary Theory: An Introduction*, 2nd edition (Minneapolis: University of Minnesota Press, 1996), 201.

25. Ibid.

26. Olga Vickery, *The Novels of William Faulkner: A Critical Interpretation*, revised edition (Baton Rouge: Louisiana State University Press, 1964), 243.

27. Irving Howe, *William Faulkner: A Critical Study*, 2nd edition (New York: Vintage, 1952), 219.

28. William Faulkner, *Selected Letters of William Faulkner*, ed. Joseph Blotner (New York: Vintage Books, 1978), 79.

29. John Duvall, "Faulkner's Crying Game: Male Homosexual Panic," *Faulkner and Gender: Faulkner and Yoknapatawpha, 1994* (Jackson: University Press of Mississippi, 1996), 65. Duvall also suggests that "*Pylon*, as a novel literally framed by the writing of *Absalom, Absalom!*, can be read against the more famous novel in ways [similar to] the contrapuntal relation between 'The Wild Palms' and 'Old Man.' "

30. *Selected Letters*, 79.

31. Ibid., 83–4, 85.

32. Joseph R. McElrath, Jr., "*Pylon*: The Portrait of a Lady," *Mississippi Quarterly* 27 (Summer 1974), 283.

33. Michael Zeitlin, "*Pylon*, Joyce, and Faulkner's Imagination," *Faulkner and the Artist: Faulkner and Yoknapatawpha, 1993* (Jackson: University Press of Mississippi, 1996), 204.

34. Gary Harrington, *Faulkner's Fables of Creativity: The Non-Yoknapatawpha Novels* (Athens: University of Georgia Press, 1990), 48.

35. Reynolds Price, "*Pylon*: The Posture of Worship," *Shenandoah* 19:3 (1968): 60.

36. Hugh M. Ruppersburg, "Image as Structure in Faulkner's *Pylon*," *South Atlantic Review* 47:1 (January 1982): 84.

37. In the question and answer session following this paper's presentation, Jay Watson suggested that excrement may contend with vomit for metaphoric strength in the novel, given the fact that the airport is piled on shit.

Make Room for Elvis

Cheryl Lester

"He who denies his heritage has no heritage."
MISSION STATEMENT IN ST. JUDE CHILDREN'S
RESEARCH HOSPITAL

Alluding to Danny Thomas's 1950s TV show *Make Room for Daddy*, with its quirky suggestion that Daddy doesn't quite fit in, my title is aimed at challenging the commonsensical belief that Elvis Presley and William Faulkner have little or nothing in common. It is strange how commonalities appear, even when you are not looking for them. When I struck upon the title of this paper, for example, I did not realize that Elvis actually had an association with Danny Thomas. At the very least, Elvis Presley appeared with Danny Thomas in order to raise funds for St. Jude Children's Research Hospital, which Thomas founded in Memphis. Two days after I delivered this paper, I was in Holly Springs at Graceland Too, where I saw an elegant black and white photo of Elvis with Danny Thomas. Calligraphically inscribed in the dome of the Danny Thomas/ALSAC (American Lebanese Syrian Associated Charities) Pavillion of the Hospital are three maxims, one of which I have taken as an epigraph to this paper: "He who denies his heritage has no heritage." In spite of their strikingly different cultural significance, Elvis and Faulkner share the problematic heritage of the American South.

The idea of pairing Faulkner and Elvis was not mine; rather, I fell upon it the last time I was in Oxford, in the summer of 1995. I like to review the memorabilia I collected that summer, which has already begun to yellow. I spread it out across my bed and am reminded by my own motley collection of printed matter of the unprocessed contents of the boxes or "time capsules" stored in the archives of the Andy Warhol Museum in Pittsburgh. From time to time, Warhol just swept the stuff that he had accumulated into a cardboard box, labeling it with a date, and recognizing it as a kind of raw material history, similar to the capsules sent down during the Kennedy era into the recesses of the earth, for posterity. My collection of ephemera from the summer of Faulkner and Elvis begs for order and meaning—whether through some orderly scrapbook process of selection and classification or through some wilder aesthetic effort at historical arrangement and interpretation.

I just fell into this. I was in Oxford to present a paper at the Faulkner Conference, but the Elvis Conference, scheduled for the following week, began to seem more and more important to me. It was as if I had never before realized that Elvis was a Southerner, born and raised no more than a hundred miles from Faulkner. As if I had never stopped to think that, when Elvis was born on January 8, 1935, Faulkner was only thirty-seven years old, or that when Faulkner passed away on July 6, 1962, Elvis was already twenty-seven. Simply processing the fact that these two figures had occupied the same world for twenty-seven of the same years was an imaginative challenge. Their purchase on that world had been so different, and they have come to stand for ways of feeling and being that seem impossibly distant from one another. It startled me with the reminder that time and place and culture are processes that people take part in, not fixed elements they inhabit together. I imagine Faulkner and Elvis as a Janus-faced couple, tied to one another yet each ineluctably facing the opposite direction.

My cats scratch and sniff at the detritus that constitutes my hasty record of that provocative time and place, sensually rubbing themselves or entirely flopping down upon Chamber of Commerce booster literature, newspaper clippings, lecture and conference announcements, posters, merchandise order forms, and crumpled receipts. Plaster, our eleven-pound white male, settles heavily on "Faulkner in Cultural Context," the poster and conference program cover whose predictable format announced the twenty-second annual Faulkner and Yoknapatawpha Conference, while his sister Paris, our eight-pound black female, paws at the cover of the ample yet elegant Elvis Conference program.

Capaciously entitled "In Search of Elvis: Music, Race, Religion, Art, Performance," Ole Miss's First International Conference on Elvis Presley was stylishly presented; the artwork for the Elvis poster also appeared on the glossy cover of the forty-page program. Yet for all the classy swag, Oxford seemed less hospitable to the Elvis Conference than it was to the Faulkner Conference, which it had hosted for the twenty-second consecutive year. More comfortable with its affiliation with William Faulkner and his fictional town of Jefferson, Oxford felt awkward being asked to adopt Elvis, who—as if his distance from Faulkner could be measured in miles—was born a good fifty miles east of Oxford and grew up even further away, after the Presleys moved from East Tupelo to Memphis in 1948.

Natural as it was to present itself as the home of William Faulkner, it was apparently unsettling for some residents of Oxford to be called upon to accommodate the glitzy and widely noted Elvis Conference. Oxford had of course been disturbed before. It suffered a Yankee invasion during the Civil War, entertained the lynching of Nelse Patton right on the Square in 1908, and furnished principals and extras for the on-location shooting of Faulkner's *Intruder in the Dust* in 1948. During the making of that film, embarrassing as it may be to recall, special arrangements had to be made in order to lodge the cast and crew's people of color. Faulkner himself, when he hosted a party at Rowan Oak, deemed it necessary to exclude the film's main character, who might have otherwise shown up with his nonwhite local hosts. Ten years later, Oxford was even more disturbed when the efforts of James Meredith to attend Ole Miss provoked riots, National Guardsmen, and a curfew. Recollections of this period, which commenced a few months after Faulkner's death, are not frequently volunteered and, as far as I know, are little explored by Faulkner scholars. Quiet as it's kept, the erasure of this violently conflicted history from Oxford's self-presentation might be linked in a subtle way to the ambivalence with which Oxford and Ole Miss greeted the Elvis Conference.

After its second summer, the conference was dispatched from Oxford and relocated in Memphis by conference founder and former Ole Miss faculty member Vernon Chadwick. Signs of ambivalence surfaced about a month before the conference, when Oxford's Mayor John Leslie vetoed the decision of the town board, which perennially supports the Faulkner Conference, to appropriate $7,000 to the Elvis Conference. Described as a "cultural war," the conflict was featured in a pun-ridden article published in the *Boston Globe* on 4 July 1995. In the article, Oxford's back-to-back conferences were presented as though they were contestants in a poetry slam. Below a headline that read "Sound and Fury arising over Elvis at Ole Miss," two short columns of copy were topped by identically sized head shots of Faulkner and Elvis. Below the photo of Faulkner—haloed by books, gazing studiously downcast, and sporting a neat shirt and tie, the caption read: "Challenged in hometown." Above the caption " 'King' goes academic" was a late and cheesy photo of Elvis, his face as poofy as his hair and open shirtcollar, the background vacant, like his gaze and once impudent lip.

Interviewed for the *Boston Globe* article, Bill Ferris, director of the Center for the Study of Southern Culture, which sponsored the Elvis Conference, and later chairman of the National Endowment for the Humanities, described the controversy over the conference as "a feud between the landed gentry and the redneck arrivistes, the Compsons and the Snopeses," as silly as "a skit on 'Saturday Night Live.' " However, underneath the antics and bluster, this prominent native Mississippian perceived a more serious conflict rooted in longstanding structures of privilege connected with class and race.

> "Here you had a poor kid whose dream was to come to Ole Miss and play football," he said, referring to Presley's boyhood days in nearby Tupelo. "But he was from the working class and couldn't get in. Blacks were not allowed here back then, either. Faulkner came from the privileged, educated elite, and this was his school. There is a deep and enduring division between the powerful elite, whose literary canon is represented by Faulkner, and the working class and blacks whose values are represented by Elvis."

The *Boston Globe* did not pursue the history and life of this deep and enduring social divide, nor did it interrogate Ferris's arguable claim that Elvis represented both white working-class and black values. Instead, the article focused on the provocative yet previously unthought similarities between Faulkner and Elvis. Like the majority of other articles covering the Elvis Conference, this newspaper article recognized that, unlikely as it seemed, Faulkner and Elvis *were* related. The *Globe* piece noted that both Faulkner and Elvis wore outlandish clothing, had nicknames associated with royalty, went to Hollywood yet maintained a residence in the South, and inhabited large homes that became shrines after their deaths. More extended interrogations of this conceit have also been offered by academics such as Charles Reagan Wilson, Karal Ann Marling, and Joel Williamson.[1] Elvis's biographer Peter Guralnick opens the first volume of his two-volume biography with an imaginary depiction of the famous 1950 meeting between Sam Phillips and Dewey Phillips at the Peabody Drugstore. Guralnick suggests—who knows?—that Faulkner, who always stayed at the Peabody when he visited Memphis, might have witnessed the very scene.[2]

The questions and challenges that arose from the powerful yet failed effort to bring Faulkner and Elvis together at an institutional level raises an impressively broad range of questions concerning cultural values and the social interests they serve. Linked, as Bill Ferris noted, to structures of privilege associated with class and race, the issues surrounding the poor local reception of the Elvis Conference are thoughtfully explored by Vernon Chadwick in his lively and theoretically sophisticated introduction to the published proceedings of the conference.[3] Chadwick's exploration of these issues may explain why many people respond with baffled amusement or disdain to any attempt to relate the lives and careers of Faulkner and Elvis. It is not, as my big brother inquired, that Elvis wrote anything that I could compare to Faulkner's writing, or that Faulkner sang or moved his body in any way I might compare to the inimitable style of Elvis. Rather, I would like to explore the Southern heritage that Faulkner and Elvis share, as well as the points of difference that lead most people to see them as light years apart.

2

Interested for a long time in the indirect methods Faulkner employed to weave undeveloped topics into those that emerge in his work as prominent themes, I ultimately began to link Faulkner's methods of indirection to his ever present yet superficial examination of African American history and life, a testimony, as I read it, to the profound impact that twentieth-century black migration had on relationships, identities, and culture in the South.[4] Given my efforts to flesh out this underdeveloped thematic in Faulkner's writing, and to place it in historical and cultural context, it is a surprisingly short leap to Elvis, who was born into and shaped by the same historical environment. Rather than simply opposing the elite Faulkner to the working-class Elvis, or claiming that either figure in any way stands for African American experience in the South, I would like to explore the ways in which each related to and deployed the racialized markers of Southern identity, particularly as the meaning and value of these markers was renegotiated during the fifty-odd-year-period (1915–1960s) of mass black migration. Racialized markers of deportment, for example, included the way a person dressed, held his or her body, walked, directed or averted his or her gaze, used terms of address, and so forth. Both Faulkner and Elvis revealed that what was black and what white in Southern culture, fixed as Jim Crow sought to make it, was particularly hard to delineate, and although both drew expectations, behaviors, practices, and styles from a shared fund of racialized signifiers, neither drew freely from this fund. Family history, as I will suggest, led them to adopt and relate to racialized markers of identity with different degrees of freedom and constraint. Faulkner frequently appeared in public wearing old raggedy jackets and trousers, for example, although such clothing was a marker of poverty and rural blackness, yet he would never have dressed in the flashy brightly colored clothing Elvis bought on Beale Street, racial markers of Afro-urban identity.

Within the context of the broad period from the settlement of the Southwest frontier to the development of newly discovered electronic frontiers, the recording and broadcasting industries, I want to briefly sketch out the history and life of two families, William Faulkner's and Elvis Presley's. Both families trace their ancestry to Scotch-Irish immigrants and to a pioneering male descendant who joined the nineteenth-century mass migration from the coastal South to the Southwest frontier. Renowned and colorful, Faulkner's paternal great-grandfather William

C. Falkner, known as the Old Colonel, bequeathed to his great-grandson and namesake a contradictory and inexhaustible legacy of entrepreneurship, authorship, soldiering, landholding, empire building, railroad owning, office holding, lawyering, slaveholding, murdering, bastarding, horsing, drinking, and hunting. (See figure 1.) First and foremost, however, he bequeathed his financial and cultural capital to an eldest son J. W. T. Falkner (Faulkner's grandfather), who was able to keep it. Lawyer, statesman, inheritor of a railroad (which he sold), and founder of a bank, this man was successful as a lawyer, solid citizen, and financial conservative and succeeded in maintaining the elite status that was bequeathed to William Faulkner, despite the perception in Oxford that he was an outsider, drank too much, and couldn't trace his family back farther than the Old Colonel.[5]

The closest comparable forefather in Elvis's ancestry is his maternal great-great-great-grandfather William Mansell (d. 1842). (See figure 2.) After fighting in Andrew Jackson's campaigns against the Creeks and the Seminoles, Mansell ironically married the full-blood Cherokee Morning Dove White (1800–35), with whom he migrated from Tennessee to Alabama, bought farmland, and built a substantial home. Morning Dove died giving birth to their third child. Of these children, the most prosperous was the middle child, Morning Dizenie Mansell (b. 1832), who married the town doctor, a large landowner. Of their twelve children, the males included three farmers, one minister, a merchant, and two doctors. William and Morning Dove's eldest son, John, from whom Elvis is descended, also had at least a dozen children, but his children did not fare so well.

Seven years old when he lost his Cherokee mother, perhaps John Mansell was unable to reconcile the conflicting legacy that descended to him as the eldest son of a white Indian fighter and a Cherokee mother. Appetitive and profligate, John fathered children by several women before squandering the family farm and abandoning his wife, her sister, his mistress, and his numerous offspring. According to Elaine Dundy, who conducted the research on Elvis's maternal ancestry, he ran off with another woman and relocated in Oxford, Mississippi, in 1880, under the name of Colonel Lee Mansell.[6] If so, then Faulkner's great-grandfather, William C. Falkner, who was murdered in the fall of 1889, and his son J. W. T. (1848–1922), are likely to have known the man who squandered Elvis's birthright.

Faulkner derived from his family a materially fading yet culturally vital legacy of wealth and achievement, whereas Elvis inherited from his a legacy of false starts, abandonments, and dispossessions. Whereas four generations of Falkners moved from one large house to another, with

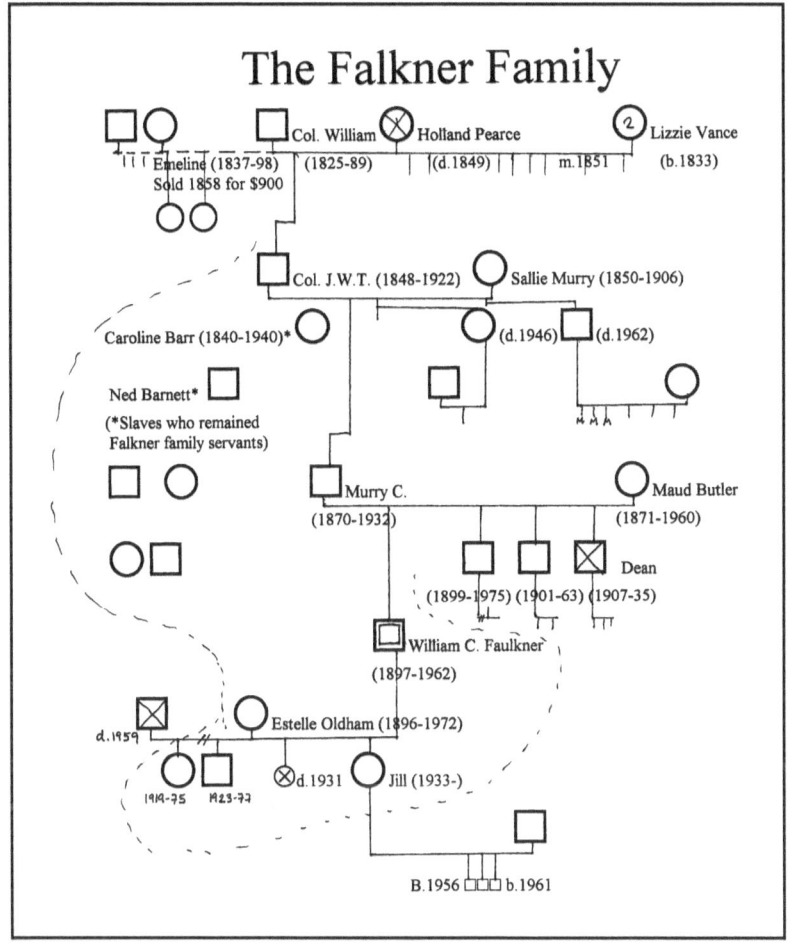

The Falkner Family

Figure 1

roots and property in Oxford, Mississippi, Elvis's maternal and paternal descendants were ever and always on the move, sharecroppers for more than four generations. (See figures 2 and 3.) With the family moving as often as once every two years, it is dizzying to count the number of residences Elvis's mother, Gladys, occupied during her childhood and adolescence before settling, after the untimely death of her father and at the age of nineteen, in East Tupelo, Mississippi, where she met and married Elvis's father, Vernon. In short, whereas the property and social status acquired by one pioneering ancestor did devolve to William Faulkner, in the case of Elvis, the legacy followed a different course. Thus, although

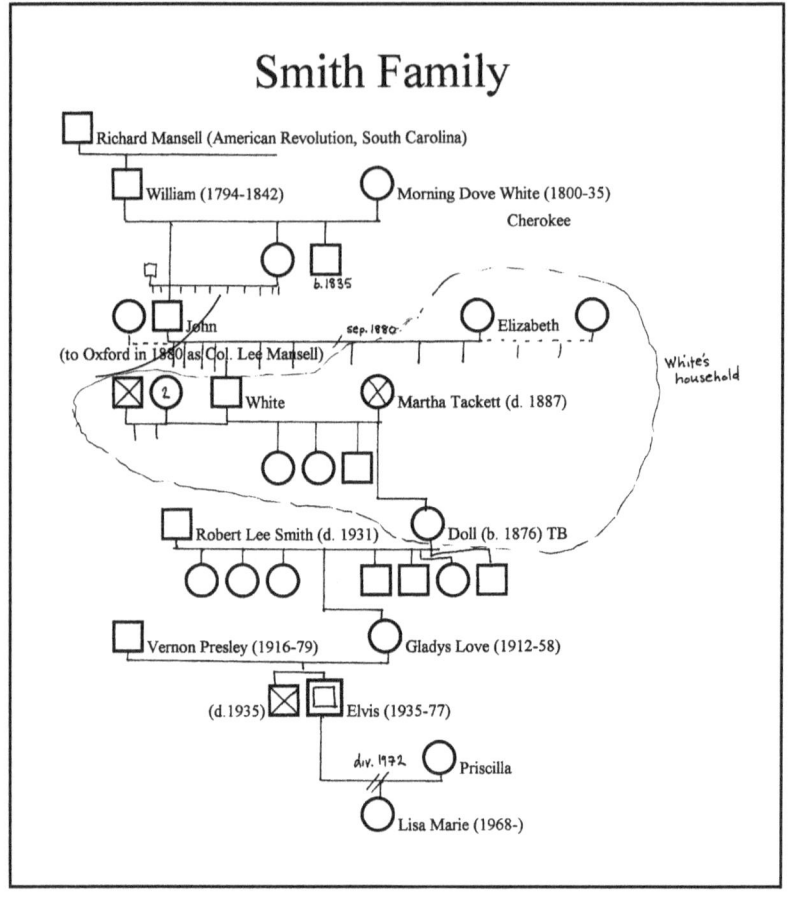

Smith Family

Richard Mansell (American Revolution, South Carolina)

William (1794-1842)

Morning Dove White (1800-35)
Cherokee

b.1835

John
(to Oxford in 1880 as Col. Lee Mansell)

sep. 1880

Elizabeth

White's household

White

Martha Tackett (d. 1887)

Robert Lee Smith (d. 1931)

Doll (b. 1876) TB

Vernon Presley (1916-79)

Gladys Love (1912-58)

(d.1935)

Elvis (1935-77)

div. 1972

Priscilla

Lisa Marie (1968-)

Figure 2

Elvis's family shared a history of immigration, pioneering, military service, and professional distinction with white Southern families like the Falkners, a history that depended on the "forced removal" of Native Americans and the enslavement of African Americans, their history of landlessness, dispossession, and itinerancy intersected with that of white Southern families like Faulkner's Snopeses and with those of the Native American, African American, and mixed-race Southern families that Faulkner left largely underrepresented and nameless.

In order to emphasize here the intersection of Elvis Presley's family history with that of millions of Afro-Southerners, I must mention briefly the development of the so-called New South, a name that signified the relatively belated post-World War I arrival to the Southern states of the

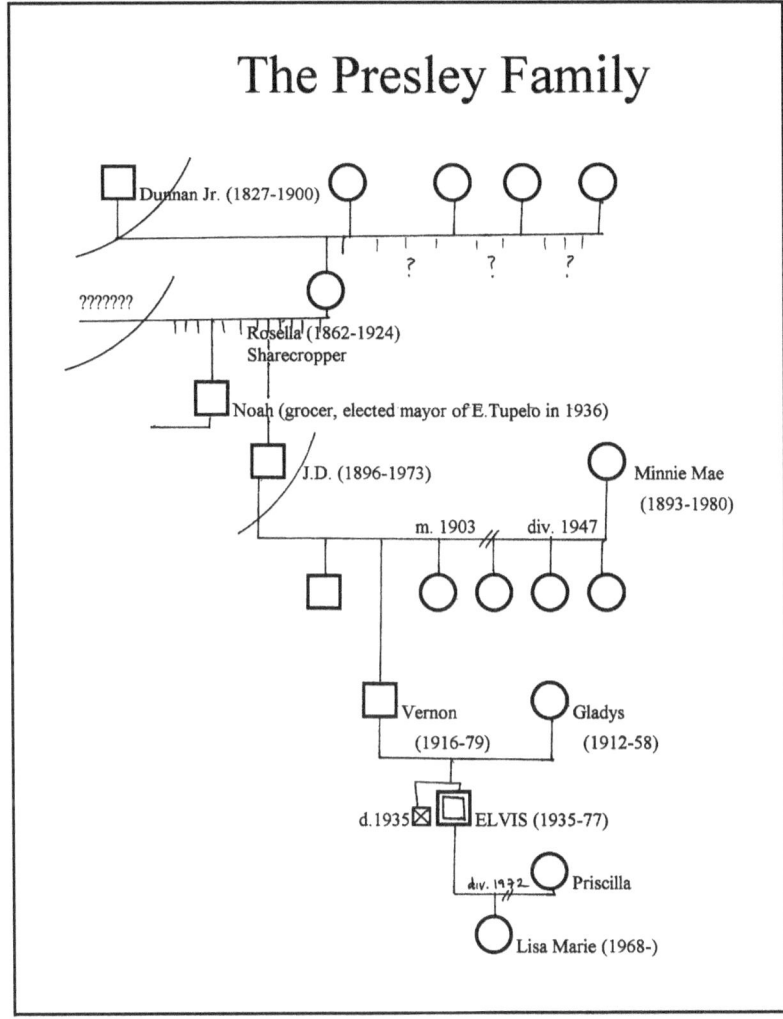

The Presley Family

Figure 3

changing political economy associated with modernization, rural-to-urban migration, industrialization, and proletarianization. With World War I also came the first peak of black mass migration from the South, a phenomenon that resulted by the 1960s in a net migration of around six million Afro-Southerners. Already associated with Afro-Southerners because of their poverty and landlessness, Southern families like the Presleys were coded blacker still when, beginning in 1915, hundreds of thousands of black Southerners managed for the first time in history to leave the South or to move from the rural South to the city. For hundreds of years, Southern culture had depended on the immobilization of Afro-Southerners, so it was radically destabilized by the newfound mobility and sudden departure of hundreds of thousands of African Americans.

Yet this destabilization and recirculation of racial markers served to profit Elvis Presley, who in the forties and fifties drew upon previously taboo signifiers of blackness to capitalize on and introduce into the repertoire of whiteness a new and unheard of identity and style. William Faulkner, on the other hand, confronted this destabilization of racial identity from a different vantage point. For Faulkner, the unsettling impact of black migration on the racialized signifiers of Southern identities threatened to erode his privileges and opportunities. His sensitivity to this environment as a threat made him particularly attentive to the sudden motility of Southern identities, and he used his writing to construct portraits of characters in various states of self-making and undoing, with varying capacities for resistance or adaptation to change. (What suddenly comes to mind, perhaps because of my dozen years in the state of Kansas, is the scene in *The Wizard of Oz* when Dorothy conquers the Wicked Witch of the West by dousing her with a bucket of water. I hear the Witch screaming as she melts, dissolving as she cedes her former domain.) Faulkner's sensitivity to this destabilized context informs such dissolving and reconstituting racialized characters as the Compsons (and their servants) in *The Sound and the Fury*, Temple Drake and Popeye in *Sanctuary*, the Reverend Hightower and Joe Christmas in *Light in August*, and the Sutpens, legitimate and illegitimate, in *Absalom, Absalom!* As both Faulkner and Elvis demonstrate, each in his own way, this period of destabilization was felt not only as a shortage of labor in the fields and in some people's homes but also as a crisis or turning point at the core of personal identities, an upheaval of the long and elaborate chains of signifiers that once served to maintain the interconnected and assymetrically empowered distinctions that separated black from white. Thus, the specific experience of change in the post-World War I South, although it intersected with the disillusionment of an entire "lost generation," was uniquely enmeshed with the newfound mobility of Afro-Southerners and the destabilization of racialized identities that it brought about.

Among the Southern identities destabilized by increasing black mobility was that of the ancestral pioneer, whose descendants looked to that ancestor to legitimate the proprietary privileges and rights they claimed in the South. The legitimacy of this figure was destabilized when blacks became as mobile and potentially pioneering as the founders were said to have been. The clash of the various meanings associated, on the one hand, with the heroic white pioneers of the Southwest frontier and, on the other, with the ignoble black Southerners venturing to leave the South with similar hopes for bettering their fortunes, produced insoluble contradictions. This once resilient image of the pioneering Southwestern settler, which had not been tarnished by the forced migration of African slaves or by the wars of extermination and forced dislocation of indigenous peoples, was suddenly collapsing. Black migration seems to have opened a festering wound that was perhaps already brought to a head by the turn-of-the-century influx of millions of "swarthy" eastern and southern European immigrants, eroding the heroic signification of mobility in American culture.

Twentieth-century mobility, associated with sharecropping in the South and with factory jobs within and beyond the region, was not a strictly Afro-Southern phenomenon. As sociologist John Shelton Reed pointed out at the 1995 Elvis Conference, "[b]y the beginning of the twentieth century, many of the South's white yeomen had lost their land and had joined the great majority of Southern blacks as sharecroppers and tenant farmers. Half the South's farmers—two-thirds of all cotton farmers—didn't own the land they farmed, and half of the South's tenants and sharecroppers were white." Reed also emphasized that many of these white Southerners migrated, as the Presleys did, to Southern cities, and thus participated in one of the largest mass migrations in history, ten million people by 1960, of whom Reed counts two-thirds white.[7] Yet the unprecedented inclusion of masses of African Americans in this migration, however one calculates the racial percentages, fundamentally altered the cultural significance of mobility.

For reasons I have tried to suggest, Faulkner's writings register this change. Published by Random House in an edition of 6,000 copies just a few months before Elvis's birth, Faulkner's 1936 *Absalom, Absalom!*, for example, depicts the eroding impact of racial markings in the life of the wannabe ancestral pioneer Thomas Sutpen. Moving as a child from the coastal South to the Southwest frontier, Sutpen in his migration narrative reveals, behind his determined effort to achieve higher status, his anxious desire to distinguish himself from blacks. According to this allegorical narrative, the racialized displacement and disorientation of his surviving descendants, who are all isolated, deranged, lost, or incompetent, can be blamed on Sutpen's single-minded design. Notably, Faulkner confines his attribution of cause for what he recognizes as a crisis in the values of racialized markers of identity to the overreaching of white men, failing to mention the impact caused when millions of black men and women began to succeed in migrating from the South. For me, Faulkner and Elvis come together in this narrative, in which I would cast Colonel Lee Mansell as the ferociously determined Thomas Sutpen, whose belatedness and outrageous extremity ennobles those slightly better established families like the Compsons who, if read as stand-ins for later fictional families like Faulkner's McCaslins or for actual families like the Falkners, had also left behind and repudiated "shadow" families.[8]

In Faulkner, migration in the lives of post-Reconstruction white tenant farmers or sharecroppers like the Bundrens or the Snopeses no longer has any connection to empire building but is embedded in the degradations of modernization, urbanization, industrialization, and Northernization in the South. In *As I Lay Dying*, "Barn Burning," *If I Forget Thee, Jerusalem*, and the Snopes trilogy, Faulkner emphasizes the outrage of poor white folks, moving ceaselessly within rural environments as tenant farmers or seasonal migrant laborers, or even worse from the country to the factories in the city. At times, the racialized encoding of these figures is so fluid that it becomes difficult for readers to be certain about which characters in Faulkner are white and which black, an uncertainty Faulkner thematized in *Light in August*. As much to assuage his own guilty part as to reflect first-hand knowledge of the ubiquity (call it universality) of bitter feelings and dashed hopes, Faulkner's writings not only reveal the intensified crossing of racialized markers of identity but also the anxiety that attends this crossing on all sides of the divide. Outraged folks—aggressive, self-destructive, desperate, stubborn, shortsighted—increasingly cross gender, class, and racial lines in Faulkner, expressing the underlying anxiety that drove all the deeply divided people who had a share, however unequal, in the past. Bayard Sartoris, Jason Compson, Anse Bundren, Rosa Coldfield, the tall convict, Lucas Beauchamp, Mink Snopes, William Faulkner, Elvis Presley—something of the same anxiety drove them all as they sought to hold on to or acquire a viable position in life or, failing that, to find a way to even the score for their disappointments.

For all their differences, both Faulkner and Elvis, an eldest son and an only son (whose twin brother was stillborn), were sensitive to the disappointments of their parents. Faulkner's father, Murry, like his son William, was not a motivated student at the University of Mississippi. He was more interested in, even passionate about, the family concern, the Gulf & Ship Island Railroad, and, after two years at the University, he quit school to work on the line. Shoveling coal in 1888, when he first began, Murry had been an engineer for six years when he eloped with Maud Butler, against the wishes of her mother, Lelia, in 1896. Two years later he had two sons and a promotion, and by 1901, when his third son was born, Murry owned a farm, where he raised horses and bird dogs, and a share in the Ripley pharmacy. His father, J. W. T., was also prospering (a state senator and University trustee, he owned a farm, other real estate, and was involved in a developing telephone company), and, for reasons no one has fathomed, he decided to sell the profitable railroad, his eldest son's passion. Murry, who lived another thirty years, never seems to have recovered from this unexpected dislocation and, according to Blotner, never forgave his wife, Maud, for having refused at this point to leave Mississippi and move to the West on the uncertain hope that he would find a way to become a cattle rancher.

Faulkner's mother, Maud, had reasons of her own for refusing to leave home and family in pursuit of her husband's fantasy. Little was known about Maud's family until historian Joel Williamson, who also disclosed the African American "shadow family" of William C. Falkner, discovered more about the marital indiscretion and hot-tempered feud that led Maud's father, Charles E. Butler, the turn-of-the-century town sheriff, to leave Oxford, where his father had been the town surveyor and a large property owner, and abandon his family. (See figs. 1 and 4.) Left penniless and forced to turn for support to extended family members, it was Maud and not her elder brother, Sherwin, who assumed responsibility for their mother, Lelia. Maud was unwilling to relinquish the financial security and social respectability her marriage to Murry had promised. When her husband's fortunes changed and he lost his will to renew them, Maud must have turned redoubled expectations upon her sons, particularly her eldest William, to recuperate the fragile family legacy.

Notoriously spoiled, Elvis's maternal grandmother Doll grew up in the unstable, crowded, tumultuous environment her father, White, devoted his life to overcoming. Having resettled in Lee County, Mississippi, with two of his brothers, White had already married and had four children, including Doll, by the time his father ran off to Oxford ten years later. Tenant farming afforded him a large enough home to accommodate his mother, her sister, and their offspring, and his home was also large enough to take in his sister Ann and her children when Ann left her husband. White remarried after his wife died in 1887 but lost his house in the panic of 1890, leaving his extended family to shift as best they could as sharecroppers, forced to reside in an endless string of tiny, crowded, run-down houses. Doll's life changed little when, at the ripe age of twenty-seven, she married her first cousin, Robert Lee Smith, a poor sharecropper but a renowned moonshiner. Neglected by her neurasthenic mother, Elvis's mother, Gladys, one of eight children and lazy like her mother, was cared for by her elder sisters. Gladys's often-remarked nervousness, a byproduct of the constant movement to which she was compelled to adjust, became temporarily debilitating when she lost her father; for some time, she suffered uncontrollable shakes whenever she tried to leave the house.

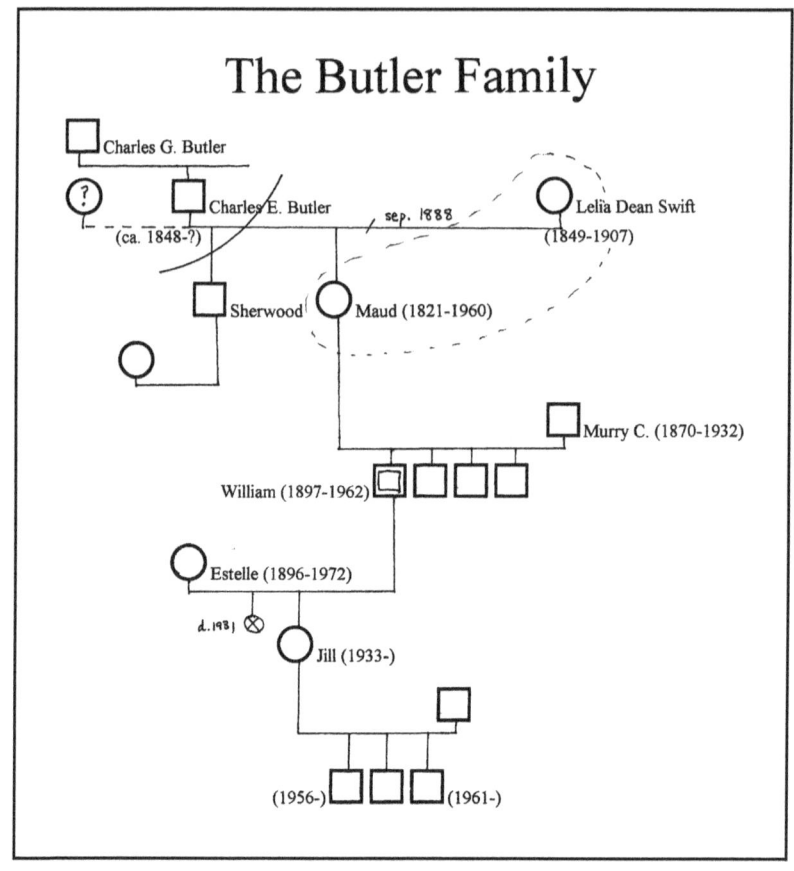

Figure 4

Elvis's father, Vernon, however, was descended from a different sort
of woman. (See figure 3.) When Elvis's paternal great-great-grandfather
abandoned his multiple wives and their children, his daughter Rosella
(Elvis's great-grandmother) became a sharecropper herself and, although
she had ten children, including Elvis's grandfather, J. D., she never told
any of them the identity or identities of their father(s). While one of her
sons, Noah, became a generous, public-minded grocer in East Tupelo,
who was elected mayor in 1936, Elvis's grandfather J. D. was known as
a good-looking but bitter n'er do well. Repeating the pattern, J. D. also
had a "good" and a "bad" son, and the latter was Elvis's good-looking
father, Vernon. As good as his forefathers, J. D. in time abandoned his
wife and children, who fell predictably into the care of his "bad" son
Vernon and thus ultimately to his grandson Elvis.

One anecdote can serve to illustrate the disappointment and despera-
tion of Vernon Presley, who resembles various characters in Faulkner.
First, some necessary background. Seventeen-year-old Vernon married
Gladys Love Smith shortly after she lost her father, secured a factory job,
and for a very short time assumed responsibility for some members of
her scattered family, whom she briefly reunited in a single residence in
East Tupelo. At the time, Vernon lived nearby with his father, J. D., a
sharecropper for Orville Bean. Perhaps owing to repeated displacement,
poverty, and desertion, as well as their Scottish and Scots-Irish ancestry,
the Smiths and the Presley's faced adversity with the expectation that
some extended family member would offer them shelter and support
whenever necessary. They were accustomed to frequent moves, sometimes to live with relatives and sometimes on their own, but never far
from family. Gladys and Vernon slept on the floor of a friend's house until
Vernon borrowed enough money from landowner Orville Bean to build
a house on Old Saltillo Road, next door to his family's house. This home,
where the Presleys lived for only a brief time, is the well-known birthplace of Elvis.

A short while after baby Elvis was born, Vernon was arrested and jailed
for forgery. Apparently, he had disagreed with landowner Orville Bean
over the price of a hog Vernon was selling. When Bean gave Vernon a
check for $4.00, Vernon and two others, including his brother-in-law
Travis Smith, in an impotent expression of anger, resentment, and defeat,
changed the amount shown on the check. They soon found themselves
in Tupelo jail, where Vernon remained until they were tried and sentenced to three years at the Parchman Farm State Penitentiary. Vernon's
father, J. D., posted bail for Gladys's younger brother, Travis, but he
refused to post bail for his son. Faulkner's Mink Snopes, sentenced to
Parchman Farm in 1908, the year Nelse Patton was lynched in Oxford,
would still have been there during the eight months Vernon spent at
Parchman in 1938 and '39. Although Vernon was repudiated by his
father, Gladys remained loyal to her husband and succeeded in winning
his pardon.

Faulkner's Mink Snopes, who murdered Jack Houston after a quarrel
over the boarding of a cow, offers insight into the desperate and stubborn
mental processes that must have led Vernon Presley to forge that check.
Perhaps, like the tall convict in "Old Man," Vernon was inspired to commit such a preposterous, self-destructive act by some fantasy derived
from popular culture. Or perhaps, like *The Sound and the Fury*'s Jason
Compson, he forged that check in an effort to even a familial score in
which he always came out last. Or again, like the Lucas Beauchamp of
Go Down, Moses, who threatened to kill Zack Edmonds for presuming

too much of Lucas's wife, Molly, perhaps Vernon's blatant forgery was motivated by outraged pride and wounded manhood. Beyond differences in class, race, and even gender (think, for example, of *Absalom, Absalom!*'s Rosa Coldfield), Faulkner points us to a shared legacy in the post-Confederate South of outraged dispossession, which I associate with the shifting terms of racialized identity and with the privileges that accrued from these identities.

Faulkner and Elvis explored and expressed an anxiety characteristic of the South yet did so by way of different cultural expectations, opportunities, sensibilities, tastes, behaviors, and practices. Faulkner's entrenchment in a cultural landscape that was losing dominance made him reluctant to embrace new dimensions of the cultural milieu, specifically those involving electronic transmission, like the phonograph and the radio, through which Elvis achieved success, fame, and wealth. Conversely, the mobility of the Presleys made Elvis anxious to find a foothold in what had remained for his family a stubbornly inhospitable environment. For Elvis, the virtual frontier opened up by electronic media provided the homestead that his sharecropping farming family had never managed to secure in the South.

Linked to the rearticulation of class, race, and gender identities, the emergence of new cultural forms in response to changing political economies affects individuals according to their present status.[9] Thus, for instance, the process of modernization, urbanization, industrialization, migration, and proletarianization in the South offered new opportunities to great numbers of people, including many who were formerly disenfranchised in the dissolution of former ways of racializing Southern life. In the 1920s, the recording industry, which recognized in black migration new opportunities for commodification, began a special line of so-called race records.[10] A small but visible segment of Afro-Southerners who were eking out their livelihoods as sharecroppers or domestic servants in the South took advantage of new opportunities in the emergent music business that developed as a consequence of black migration. Faulkner was disturbed by phonographs and radios, which had the capacity to introduce black and lower-class cultural forms and practices into private and public spaces that were formerly out of their reach and to render once-dominant cultural practices and forms obsolete. Conversely, the dominance these new cultural forms were achieving represented an opportunity for Elvis.[11]

The recording and broadcasting industries had been developing and transforming with unequaled rapidity throughout Faulkner's lifetime, and included the evolution from photography to motion pictures and from recording technology to broadcast radio, talking movies, and television. The wire telegraph, whose transcontinental cables were laid in the late nineteenth century, introduced a modern transmission system that would shrink the globe. Radio, the wireless telegraph, continued a process whose rapid and continuous transformation we are still experiencing today. From where we sit, President Woodrow Wilson's depiction of the world created by the burgeoning technology of transmission systems as "one single whispering gallery" was as astonishingly sanguine as it was misguided about our future capacity to interpret anything as either singular or quiet.[12]

From one pioneering station in Pittsburgh (KDKA) in 1920, commercial broadcasting was originating from 508 radio stations by the year 1922. Within the next seventeen years, the number of families owning radios went from 60,000 to almost 14 million.[13] In addition to the fact that rapid internal migration, and especially black migration, was occurring simultaneously with the rise of these new modes of transmission were the facts that both phenomena were developing rapidly, transforming space and time and in consequence giving rise to new cultural practices. Even the relationship between the president and the public was affected; Roosevelt's "fireside chats," which began in 1933, broadcast his voice to 60 million listeners dispersed across the country. On the ground, the development of radio shows began to provide gathering places for local musicians and to attract others who were passing through. Attracted to these shows as a listener and hopeful participant, the young Elvis Presley frequented Tupelo's WELO, which began broadcasting in 1941. There, a poor boy with working parents and no cash could listen to and learn from Mississippi Slim's live Saturday afternoon show entitled *Singin' and Pickin' Hillbilly*.[14]

In the 1920s, so-called race records had already begun to transform the production, distribution, and consumption of black musical forms, just at the moment when black mass migration had reached its first peak. At the same time as hundreds of thousands of rural Afro-Southerners were finding opportunities to change their lives by relocating to Southern and Northern cities, Afro-Southern musical forms were becoming commodity forms, transforming material life and upsetting and rearticulating the very meaning of location and culture. Even as Alan Lomax was making his way to "the land where blues began" to record the music of African Americans (music we can now hear without even traveling to Smithsonian Museum in Washington, D.C., but simply by visiting a web site anytime night or day), the relationship of the music to the Southern field as the location of its production and consumption was undergoing radical upheaval. As the German Jewish cultural theorist Walter Benjamin observed in his famous essay entitled "The Work of Art in the Age of Mechanical Reproduction," cultural objects were losing what he called their "aura," or in other words, their necessary link to a given time, place, or cultural context. As popular as the so-called race records of the twenties were, there was no race radio station established in the South until 1949—almost thirty years into the history of radio—when Memphis station WDIA began to broadcast all-black programs, dubbing itself "The Mother Station of the Negroes."[15] Increasingly, race music was making its way into places forbidden to the musicians who produced it, crossing boundaries in a manner neither Jim Crow nor any other privileged place or social order was prepared to prevent.[16]

When Elvis's mother, Gladys Love Smith, was born in 1912, Faulkner was fifteen years old, and by the time she was fifteen, she was interested in recorded music. Too poor to own a Victrola, Gladys—like the young Billie Holiday, who worked in a house of prostitution—first discovered the Victrola when she got a job working as a domestic. With ample opportunity to listen to musical recordings, Gladys distinguished herself during this period as a remarkable dancer, especially when she danced to Jimmie Rodgers's "Corinna, Corinna." "When one says she was dancing," wrote Elaine Dundy,

> one is not talking about tap, toe, or ballet: or ballroom or square-dancing, or "round dancing," which is what they call it in Mississippi when two people dance together; one is talking about "buck" dancing which is one person dancing alone. . . . Buck dancing—really good buck dancing—is done only by switching off your mind and allowing your body to take over; and stepping into the rhythm, rejoicing and jubiliating in the surrounding shower of notes and obeying the words of the song.[17]

The sort of physical excess represented by her dancing is frequently connected to Gladys's much remarked nervousness and to its legacy in the signature moves of Elvis. I mentioned earlier that after Gladys's father died and the family had to disperse, Gladys, reputedly a habitual worrier, was overcome by her worries and fears. Whenever she tried to leave the house, her legs shook uncontrollably. Slowly, she managed to dissipate this nervous energy by participating in the emotionally expressive Holy Roller church meetings and by securing a job at a garment factory in Tupelo.[18] Remaining active in the church after she married and started a family, Gladys retained her foothold in this expressive culture, performing with Vernon and Elvis as a gospel trio. Yet when Vernon returned from Parchman Farm, Gladys's heightened nervousness spilled over, and all three members of the Presley family experienced "action" nightmares and sleepwalking. Elvis inherited this nervous physical exuberance which, in adolescence, emerged in periodic involuntary shakes as well as in the habitual expression of emotional energy in movement and song.

By 1947, when Vernon took a factory job in Memphis, the Presleys managed to buy a radio, and by the time Elvis appeared on *The Milton Berle Show* in 1956, his parents owned a television as well, and his mother and paternal grandmother, Minnie Mae, were already fans of Uncle Miltie.[19] By that time, Elvis had already been transmogrified, as Faulkner might have said, to another world, living on the road, onstage, and in recording studios. Although Elvis weathered the transition to Hollywood, his celebrity seems to have literally worried his mother to death. Elvis and Vernon (and even J. D.) lived into the 1970s, yet I suspect that they all suffered from what Vernon expressed as a "constant fear that something . . . would befall them, and that one day [they] would find themselves back in Tupelo."[20]

The flood of mass cultural modes of production and transmission represented an opportunity for the Presleys to get out of "Tupelo," yet it was greeted by many, including Faulkner, with discomfort, resistance, and even outrage. Whether it was the production of ready-made clothing or the construction of urban and suburban environments, Faulkner expressed his opposition to new forms and sung the praises of the old. Ready-made clothing, for example, like the new modes of mass electronic transmission, especially radio, erased markers that formerly indicated class and racial status. In the past, ill-fitting garments were distinctions of lower-class and often racial status, while properly fit clothing had been a clear sign of upper-class status. To reinforce a distinction that mass production was threatening to erase in the arena of clothing, by making everyone poorly fit, Faulkner began ordering tailor-made clothing and fitted footwear. Descriptions in Faulkner's writings aimed at marking the lower-class status of whites often emphasize the visible folds that revealed a garment as mass-produced and recently store-bought. In the case of black characters, as the laborious description of Dilsey's body in *The Sound and the Fury* illustrates, the marker of race is not yet mass-produced clothing but rather the adaptively reused garments and shoes of white folks.

While Faulkner spent much of his energy laboring to maintain racialized distinctions that established his whiteness, people like Dewey Phillips and Elvis Presley deliberately adopted signifiers of racial identity that suggested blackness. Dewey Phillips, whose WHBQ radio show, broadcast from the Gayoso Hotel, played exclusively black music for an almost exclusively black audience, was frequently described as "transracial." [21] According to Sam Phillips, producer of Sun Records, who first met Elvis in 1953, when he was looking for a white man who sounded black, even Elvis's bearing was cross-racially marked: "He tried not to show it, but he felt so *inferior*. He reminded me of a black man in that way; his insecurity was so *markedly* like that of a black person."[22]

Although the number of households owning televisions went from 8,000 in 1946 to 3.9 million in 1950 and over 47 million in 1960, Faulkner remained a vocal opponent of these emergent forms, demonstrating a stubborn and perhaps characteristic refusal, for a white Southern man of his generation and station, to listen, to absorb or deal with material conditions emerging in the present. As late as 1950

> there was still no radio [at Rowan Oak], and [Faulkner's daughter] Jill could hear programs only at Miss Maud's house or the homes of friends. One day Bill Fielden [Faulkner's stepdaughter Victoria Franklin's husband] said, "Pappy, if you don't let Jill have her fun at home, she'll go outside her home for it." And so Faulkner consented to Bill's giving her a phonograph, though she could not play it when her father was at home.[23]

As little as is published about Faulkner's relationship with his daughter Jill, who presently resides in Virginia and rarely returns to Oxford, it seems that Faulkner imposed his cultural values and practices, or at least those that were gender appropriate, on her. While he shared literary favorites, horseback riding, and sailing with her, and even asked his daughter to type his manuscripts, he was unwilling to tolerate her interest in a changing cultural environment that included the pervasive sounds of radio and popular music.

Around the time Elvis was born, Faulkner's music- and dance-loving wife, Estelle, expressed her unhappiness with her husband's strictly regulated cultural habits and tastes in a parodic poem she sent to her sister:

> While *he* in dignity sits alone,
> Aghast at the sound of e'en a trombone.
> And whiles his joyless hours away
> Reading a book—or maybe a play
> That very few people save he—understand—
> *This* breathing soul is my own hus-band![24]

Expressing himself with equal mean-spiritedness, Faulkner took out the well-known 1936 ad in the Oxford *Eagle* refusing to pay any debts incurred by Estelle. In a letter he wrote to his lover Meta Carpenter, he complained that among Estelle's unreasonable purchases on credit had been a radio, which he "had expressly forbidden to be brought into the house."[25] Outside his own house, Faulkner also objected to radios. Blotner notes that Faulkner's "irascibility [in 1946] extended to all kinds of sensory intrusion." In particular, Faulkner was disturbed by the entry of popular music into public space. Aubrey Seay, owner of Oxford's Mansion restaurant, "had [in the late 1940s] already begun the practice of unplugging the gaudy jukebox whenever Faulkner entered." After having asked Aston Holley, pharmacist of the Gathright-Reed drugstore, to turn off the radio, Faulkner complained that "it just looks like all the people of this world must have a lot of noise around them to keep them from thinking about things they should remember."[26] Disapproving of radio as mere noise that distracted people from more important thinking, Faulkner expressed his position in the continual struggle involved in the establishment of cultural values and in the uses of cultural space, the determination of what belongs in public and what does not, of what is worthy of attention, concern, and even study, and what is decidedly not. In the segregated South, this vigilant protection of the racialized dimension of public space would have to have been troubled by a new cultural form that evaded the old rules and regulations for maintaining, among others, racial and class distinctions.

Faulkner's allergy to the media in which Elvis worked, not only radio but also television and film, emphasizes the limits of his insights into the material conditions of his own time and place. Perhaps anyone intent on elaborating his thoughts and deeds and achieving individual goals must reject a great deal of life as distracting and extraneous. Yet as a twentieth-century reader, I feel obliged to struggle against the powerful undertow of Faulkner's boundaries, particularly after World War II, to gain a broader view of the range of material from which he carved his work. To see his work accurately requires that we consider not only what he saw, felt, and articulated, but also what he rejected and left out. However distracting the ubiquity of electronic sounds (and sights) that Faulkner wished to obliterate, it is clear that these dimensions of experience, as much as black migration and the racialization of American life, needed to be reckoned with and were intricately woven into the fabric of people's lives.

Although it can be argued that the Presleys were early sacrifices to postmodernity, I would argue that their particular family history contributed to the manner in which they faced the opportunities and challenges of their lives. Like the Falkners and William Faulkner, Elvis brought a reservoir of nervous energy to particular cultural practices associated with particular cultural values. In spite of the gulf that separated them and their publics, each expressed the exhilirating yet desperate experience of change during the breathtakingly rapid shifts of twentieth-century life. If Elvis and his kin can be recognized, as I have suggested, in the variety of Faulkner's characters seeking to rectify generations of frustration, upheaval, disappointment, and loss, Faulkner and his kin can also be recognized in the nervous and uncontrollable vocalizations of

Elvis Presley. *All Shook Up*, to take just one example, registers the nervous delight and hysteria of political economic shifts that divest people suddenly of themselves and that leave them grasping at emergent culture, out of defiantly vicious refusal or desperately needy attachment. The opening phrase, "Well my hands are shaking and my knees are weak," celebrates the delirious abandon of a subject all charged up with nowhere to go but in the direction of death or somebody else: "There's only one cure for this body of mine, I'm in love, huh, I'm all shook up." It is a stretch, I admit, yet it is somehow entirely possible to imagine more than a few of Faulkner's male characters gyrating with conviction to this jittery classic. Byron Bunch? Harry Wilbourne?

That feeling of disequilibrium, transmitted as nervous energy and channeled into cultural expectations, practices, and milieux appropriate to the multiple positions occupied by particular subjects is what, in the end, I found most similar in Faulkner and Elvis. White Southern sons, an eldest and only, powerfully attached to their families of origin and to the generations of struggle bequeathed to them, these two men were compelled to enter their family legacies as redeemers. However desperate the task of redemption, each man was propelled by the withdrawal of his father and the insistence of his mother. Race and racial markers could never have meant the same thing to them, for Faulkner's family owned slaves, and kept them in the family for generations, like heirlooms. Faulkner's famous great-grandfather had children with his black slave woman Emmeline, fathering a family that did not stand as equals beside his white offspring as his heirs. After slavery, Faulkner's family retained black servants to work in their households and on their farms, to drive their buggies and their cars. From his family, Faulkner inherited the necessity of constantly establishing, maintaining, and enforcing the distinction between himself and his white family from the blacks who served them. To imitate the signs of black identity, as Elvis did, required distance from any legacy that demanded, as did Faulkner's, the daily performance of whiteness. For Elvis, however, a legacy of dispossession bequeathed to him the need to constantly perform, to assert himself as something rather than nothing, to exhaust himself in the performance of an inexhaustible repertoire of musical material. A "little mixed up," as the song lyrics understatedly suggest, by the burdens of these legacies—and all shook up by social, cultural, familial, and geographic upheaval—Faulkner and Elvis testified to the nervous economies, more fundamental than the racialized channels through which they were published or broadcast, that moved each to his own inimitable beat.

NOTES

1. See Karal Ann Marling, *Graceland: Going Home with Elvis* (Cambridge: Harvard University Press, 1996), Charles Reagan Wilson, *Judgment and Grace in Dixie: Southern Faiths from Faulkner to Elvis* (Athens: University of Georgia Press, 1995), and Joel Williamson, "Elvis, Faulkner, and Feminine Spirituality," unpublished paper delivered at the second Elvis Conference, "Elvis and the Sacred South," in August 1996.

2. Peter Guralnick, *Last Train to Memphis: The Rise of Elvis Presley* (Boston: Little, Brown, 1994), 3–4. The second volume of the biography is *Careless Love: The Unmaking of Elvis Presley* (Boston: Little, Brown, 1999).

3. Vernon Chadwick, ed., *In Search of Elvis: Music, Race, Art, Religion* (Boulder, Colo.: Westview Press, 1997).

4. On Faulkner's indirect methods of exposition see my "From Place to Place in *The Sound and the Fury*: The Syntax of Interrogation," *Modern Fiction Studies* 34.2 (1988): 141–56. On the indirect treatment of black migration in Faulkner's writings, see my article "Migration (African American)," in *A William Faulkner Encyclopedia*, ed. Robert W. Hamblin and Charles A. Peek (Westport, Connecticut: Greenwood Press, 1999), 158–61; "Racial Awareness and Arrested Development: *The Sound and the Fury* and the First Great Migration (1915–28)," *The Cambridge Companion to William Faulkner*, ed. Philip Weinstein (Cambridge: Cambridge University Press, 1994), 123–45; and "*If I Forget Thee, Jerusalem* and the Great Migration: History in Black and White," in *Faulkner in Cultural Context*, ed. Donald Kartiganer and Ann J. Abadie (Jackson: University Press of Mississippi, 1997), 191–227.

5. See Joseph Blotner, *Faulkner: A Biography*, 2 vols. (New York: Random House, 1974) and Joseph Blotner, *Faulkner: A Biography*, 1-vol. ed. (1984: New York, Random House, 1991), 8.

6. Elaine Dundy, *Elvis and Gladys* (New York: Macmillan, 1985).

7. "Elvis as Southerner," in Chadwick, 90.

8. See Joel Williamson, *William Faulkner and Southern History* (New York: Oxford University Press, 1993), especially 22–9 and 64–72.

9. George Lipsitz has analyzed this in reference to the post-World War II era. See *Class and Culture in Cold War America: A Rainbow at Midnight* (South Hadley, Mass.: Bergin and Garvey, 1982) and *Time Passages: Collective Memory and American Popular Culture* (Minneapolis: University of Minnesota Press, 1990), 99–132.

10. See William Barlow, "Cashing In (1900–1939)" and "Commercial and Noncommercial Radio," in Jannette L. Dates and William Barlow, *Split Image. African Americans in the Mass Media* (Washington: Howard University Press, 1990), 25–56 and 175–252. See also William Howland Kenney, *Recorded Music in American Life: The Phonograph and Popular Memory, 1890–1945* (Oxford University Press, 1999), 109–34.

11. To read further on this notion of culture not as a uniform environment or milieu but as a living process involving the struggle—inequitable because of the assymmetrical distribution of power—of past, present, and future (residual, dominant, and emergent) institutions, traditions, formations, etc., see Raymond Williams, *Marxism and Literature* (Oxford University Press, 1977), 121–7.

12. Mary Beth Norton et al., *A People and a Nation: A History of the United States*, 5th ed. (Boston: Houghton Mifflin, 1998), 639.

13. Ibid., 698. See also Barlow, "Commercial and Noncommercial Radio," in *Split Image*, 175–252.

14. Guralnick, *Last Train to Memphis*, 20–1.

15. Ibid., 39. On the establishment of black radio stations in the North, see Barlow.

16. Guralnick, *Last Train to Memphis*, 6.

17. Dundy, 39.

18. Ibid., 45.

19. Guralnick, *Last Train to Memphis*, 264.

20. Guralnick, *Careless Love*, 191.
21. Guralnick, *Last Train to Memphis*, 4, 6.
22. Ibid., 43.
23. Blotner, *Faulkner: A Biography*, 1-vol. ed., 506.
24. Ibid., 359.
25. Ibid., 372.
26. Ibid., 476.

Faulkner by the Light of a Pale Fire: Postmodern Textual Scholarship and Faulkner Studies at the End of the Twentieth Century

PHILIP COHEN

I begin not with *The Sound and the Fury* or *Absalom, Absalom!* or some other Faulkner work but with *Pale Fire*, that difficult and delightful triumph of postmodernist fiction by quite a different sort of author, Vladimir Nabokov. Published in 1962, this dazzlingly original collection of puzzles and parodies masquerading as a novel is both a side-splittingly funny and painfully moving meditation on the parallels and differences between art and lunacy, artists and madmen, and artistic creation and schizophrenic projection. Conceiving of both art and delusion as apparently similar but ultimately quite different forms of thievery and transformation, *Pale Fire* is a tour-de-force self-reflexive entertainment about the necessities and dangers that attend our compulsive need to create fictions to live by.

A narrative disguised as a scholarly edition of the last poem by John Shade, a recently murdered American poet, with notes and commentary by his self-proclaimed intimate friend and literary adviser Charles Kinbote, a professor of Zemblan language and literature at Wordsmith University, *Pale Fire* is also a savage parody of academic literary criticism. Through a series of increasingly comic dramatic ironies, the reader gradually learns that Kinbote is a loveless and unloved paranoid schizophrenic, a failure constantly ridiculed by those around him. To keep his demons at bay, moreover, he has manufactured a wildly romantic fantasy world in which he is actually Charles the Beloved, the adored, dispossessed king of a Central European kingdom named Zembla. Kinbote's mad ramblings are ultimately delusions of grandeur designed to minister to the insecurities and fears generated by his miserable existence. And his edition of Shade's poem, also entitled "Pale Fire," is less a celebration of his alleged friend and his art than his revenge on the man who spurned his friendship, his homosexual advances, and his hope that his own "story" and not that of Shade's much-loved wife and dead daughter would be the subject of Shade's last poem. This revenge seeps into every line of Kinbote's annotations, transforming Shade's "Pale Fire" into the poem that Kinbote so wanted him to write.

Nabokov's novel thus posits a parasitical relationship between authors and critics, proposing that the latter consciously or unconsciously hijack the former's creative efforts by disguising as an act of interpretation their importation of their own obsessions into the literary work at hand. And its parody of editorial work may hit a little too close to home for those academic critics, like myself, who are interested in textual scholarship, the discipline of literary study traditionally concerned with the genesis, transmission, and editing of texts and the physical documents that contain them. After all, Kinbote is a comic disaster as Shade's utterly obtuse and misguided editor. His annotations, usually more about himself than Shade, are almost always grandly irrelevant, betraying a thoroughly sweeping ignorance of Shade's aesthetic program, his poetry, and this particular poem. Every editorial comment exhibits a powerful self-aggrandizement at the expense of Shade and his poetry. Under the guise of equanimity and disinterested analysis, Kinbote maintains a proprietorial attitude toward Shade, defending his own reputation and settling old scores with rivals. Just as importantly, he often presents as fact speculations that lack any supporting evidence whatsoever. He rarely remembers the exact literary or critical passage he wishes to cite or where it may be found. As a scholarly editor, however, Kinbote's worst crime is that he writes variant readings in broken meter and then palms them off as Shade's. At every turn then, Kinbote drives out Shade and his poem, even rewriting it at certain points to fit his mad fantasies. Yet he insists that "Pale Fire" is incomprehensible without his commentary: "Let me state that without my notes Shade's text simply has no human reality" and "for better or worse, it is the commentator who has the last word."[1]

What, one may ask, does Nabokov's deluded editor have to do with Faulkner and his fiction? Because I am interested in the relevance of contemporary textual scholarship and editorial theory to literary study in general and Faulkner studies in particular, I want to inoculate readers against the charge that contemporary textual scholars like myself have anything in common with Kinbote's appropriation of Shade's poetic labors. Simply put, my thesis is that the entire textual process of a literary work is an important if often neglected body of evidence for critics regardless of their theoretical orientation and the arguments they wish to make about that work because literary works often manifest themselves in different versions that contain significantly different and differently ordered stanzas, passages, and chapters. The interpretive significance of such substantive variation goes well beyond earlier editorial stress on the

importance of the numerous but essentially minor variants in the different published texts of literary works.[2]

Relevant also to academic criticism is the involvement of different
agents, authors, and others in creating, shaping, and altering the evolving
textual process of a work as it moves towards publication and beyond.
When his publisher insisted that his first novel *The Floating Opera* "conclude on a less 'nihilist' note," for example, John Barth made a number
of major changes to get a book into print that several publishers had
already rejected.[3] Specifically, he substituted a more upbeat conclusion
for "the original, apocalyptically shrug-shouldered ending" in which
Todd Andrews's plan to blow up Captain Osborn's showboat and all
aboard it including himself is inexplicably averted.[4] Thus the 1956 Apple-
ton-Century-Crofts first edition features an ending in which a crew-
member foils Todd's plan for mass destruction and Todd then decides not
to commit suicide after hearing little Jeannine go into convulsions. After
he made his reputation, Barth then restored the original ending along
with some other excised material in a 1967 Doubleday Anchor revised
edition of the novel. As one would expect with a writer, however, Barth
did not restrict himself to restoring deleted passages. Instead he made
numerous other changes as well, thus creating a third version of *The
Floating Opera* rather than simply restoring the original version.[5]

That publishers often require authorial revision of a novel, including
alternative endings, as a condition of publication just as Hollywood pro-
ducers and executives dictate changes that lead to a final cut should not
surprise us. What should surprise us is the lack of critical interest in the
question of whether or not one can fundamentally change the ending of
a novel without producing a slew of unforeseen problems and complica-
tions. Such a question rests not so much on the presupposition of a formalist aesthetic that values the criteria of unity and harmony as on the
rather practical assumption that endings of novels frequently build upon
what came before in the preceding chapters. Now John Barth may feel
that the existential aesthetic that underpins his first novel may well support either ending. But it is not far-fetched to argue that writers compose
material based on what they had previously written and that even the
most well thought out of revisions can jar with previously inscribed material, thus creating unintended problems in a text.[6] Indeed, Sherry Zivley
has persuasively argued that Barth's initial revision of the novel's ending
resulted in a characterization of Todd that is inconsistent with his various
philosophical ruminations throughout the rest of the book. This brief history of how different hands produced *The Floating Opera* illustrates my
contention that even the most postmodernist critical and theoretical
moves might benefit from an awareness of the entire textual process of a

work, of the temporal as well as spatial dimension of texts and textuality, and of authorial and nonauthorial intertextuality.

Over the last two decades, textual scholarship has increasingly focused on the reality of textual instability. Whereas earlier Anglo-American textual scholars and editors sought to constitute texts and editions according to single-text and authorial intentionalist premises, recent textual scholars as diverse as George Bornstein, Jerome McGann, Peter Shillingsburg, D. C. Greetham, and Hans Walter Gabler have argued that competing theoretical assumptions lead editors to constitute different texts for the same literary work.[7] Contemporary textual scholarship now seeks less to stabilize texts than to draw our attention to textual instability, to the fact that most writers collaborate, delegate, and cooperate with friends, lovers, colleagues, editors, and publishers and that they continue to rewrite the texts of literary works for different reasons, for different audiences, and under different circumstances.[8] But one does not have to be an editor to observe that our modern critical emphasis on a single authorial textual manifestation of a much more complex textual process derives from the Romantic-Modernist notion of the literary work as a physical object best represented by a single stabilized text. And this textual conception has its origins in both the development of print technology from Gutenberg on with its ability to produce a series of texts that closely resemble each other and in the Romantic emphasis on authorial consciousness as the ultimate source and ground of the constitution and unity of a text.

Although a complex dialectical relationship exists between literary theory, with its current emphasis on reception, and textual scholarship, with its emphasis on production, many contemporary critics continue to overlook the contribution that textual scholarship can make to the study of texts and textuality.[9] Thus we have the paradox in American literary studies of massive authorial, single-text editions, produced by substantial investments of time, money, and labor, being used, if at all, by poststructuralists quoting Foucault, Derrida, Barthes, Kristeva, and Fish who seem to have accepted without cavil that an authoritative text has been produced. This is still the case in Faulkner studies where many critics have a postmodern critical orientation but a traditional if unacknowledged and unexamined Romantic-Modernist textual orientation.[10] This lack of interest in the relevance of contemporary textual scholarship to critical work on Faulkner may be seen, for example, in Stephen Hahn and Arthur F. Kinney's excellent collection *Approaches to Teaching Faulkner's "The Sound and the Fury"* that features a number of essays by scholars representing diverse critical approaches and interpretations of the novel, from traditional to poststructuralist.[11] Regardless of their theoretical orientation, however, the various contributors share a common tendency: in a collection devoted, among other things, to ways of teaching Faulkner's brilliant modernist poeticizing of prose in the novel through a variety of linguistic, stylistic, and typographical innovations, almost none of them comment on the difficulty of establishing which of the book's many variants were introduced by Faulkner and which were introduced by his editors during the publication process.[12]

New twentieth-century formalist critics typically focused on a single authorial textual manifestation of a Faulkner work rather than its entire textual process because their textual ontology was primarily spatial rather than temporal in nature. Their emphasis on a solitary textual manifestation of a work frequently led them to ignore the much larger textual process that often lies behind a published Faulkner text. Thus Cleanth Brooks's influential 1963 New Critical study *William Faulkner: The Yoknapatawpha Country* rarely draws on the composition, revision, and publication of Faulkner's fiction to support its critical judgments. For example, his description of *Sanctuary* as "Faulkner's bitterest novel" in which Horace Benbow realizes "that women have a secret rapport with evil which men do not have, that they are able to adjust to evil without being shattered by it" applies questionable gender assumptions only to the 1931 published version of the novel and not to the earlier version that Faulkner tried to publish in 1929.[13]

But formalist premises alone cannot explain the widespread critical refusal to consider the entire textual situation of a work.[14] When mythic and psychoanalytic critic Leslie Fiedler discusses Faulkner's commercial manipulation of popular literary genres in *Sanctuary*, for example, he examines only the published version of the novel as well. Fiedler merely refers to the earlier version as "inchoate" because "Faulkner had not disentangled the Popeye-Temple story from the Sartoris saga."[15] And earlier critics who paid close attention to Faulkner's manuscripts, typescripts, galleys, and proofs, critics such as Michael Millgate in his seminal *The Achievement of William Faulkner*, frequently did so in order to explicate better the published version of the work.[16] Unlike Millgate, however, the work of some of these scholars was often vitiated by a formalist New Critical conception of Faulkner as an ahistorical abstract entity, whose revisions allegedly brought texts closer to the unified ideal work he originally intended regardless of the passage of time. Indeed, most Faulkner critics have shared a common albeit unrealistic view of how and why a professional author writes and revises his or her work and assumed that the best text of a work is usually the published one or the last one that an author revised.[17]

But why should contemporary Faulkner scholars focus on a single stable textual product when their own poststructuralist theories often de-center and disperse interpretation by means of multiple contexts rather than delimit it? Why should they accept without cavil stabilized Faulkner texts that reflect a textual ontology ratified by capitalism, individualism, and Romantic-Modernist ideology, critical dispensations now so out of favor in the academy? Why should they bring postmodern critical practice to bear on such texts while ignoring the available evidence about the genesis and transmission of these texts, especially when contemporary scholars have often severed the act of interpreting Faulkner's texts from his intentions? True, assembling a work's entire textual history through collation can often be a tedious, time-consuming, and labor-intensive process. But numerous scholarly resources that contain such collations and facsimiles of many of the texts of Faulkner's works are available. The academy's emphasis on reception and its general ignorance about the relevance of contemporary textual scholarship to English studies, along with the authorial orientation and positivistic tendencies of earlier textual scholars, may be to blame for this current state of affairs.

In arguing that scholars need not confine themselves uncritically to a single text or version of a work (whether produced by a commercial publisher or a scholarly editor), I am not trying to argue that scholarly editors ought to produce only certain sorts of editions or edited texts. Although novels are indeed written for readers, different sorts of general and academic readers may wish to read different parts of a work's textual process or as much of that process as possible for different reasons. Thus text constitution and selection ought to be a function of the various needs that different readers have. I am simply proposing that scholars may be able to answer some sorts of critical questions better by looking at a work's entire textual process. Indeed, consulting only published versions of a work may be entirely appropriate for some kinds of critical activity. Nevertheless, poststructuralist scholars often seem unconcerned with the origins of the physical documents and the texts contained therein, and they frequently underestimate how relevant the entire textual process of a work may be to their projects.

If individual Faulkner works often cannot be adequately represented by a single text, his lifelong habit of retelling earlier stories in later works further complicates the nature of Faulknerian textuality by blurring the borders between what are sometimes only nominally discreet textual processes. One thinks immediately of the episodes that are retold in varying ways throughout the Snopes stories, *The Hamlet* (1940), *The Town* (1957), and *The Mansion* (1959). But Faulkner also routinely imported characters from previous works into later narratives. Thus Quentin Compson from *The Sound and the Fury* (1929) reappears in *Absalom, Absalom!* (1936); Horace Benbow from *Sartoris* and *Flags in the Dust* is a central character in *Sanctuary* (1931); and *Sanctuary's* Temple Drake appears again in *Requiem for a Nun* (1951). Indeed, a venerable if often controversial tradition in Faulkner criticism has been to discuss such characters in terms of their previous incarnations in earlier works.[18] Such a critical practice generally has the merit of emphasizing qualification, development, and conflict in Faulknerian textuality. Yet all too frequently, traditional and poststructuralist critics have assumed nonproblematic relationships between recurring characters and narratives in different works. They have also tended to attribute such continuity to authorial intention even though a glance at *Faulkner in the University* suggests that Faulkner's memory of the specifics of his earlier novels was often hazy. Exemplary though they may be other ways, such readings may seem ahistorical when they treat Faulkner's retellings as conscious and deliberate revisions of earlier work.[19]

Even one of the most sophisticated postmodern discussions of Faulknerian authorial intertextuality I have yet encountered, Martin Kreiswirth's " 'Paradoxical and Outrageous Discrepancy': Transgression, Auto-Intertextuality, and Faulkner's Yoknapatawpha," limits the textual embodiment of Faulkner's works to their published versions, ruling out any consideration of the larger textual processes behind those texts. Kreiswirth takes as his subject both the "transformations, absorptions, and 'operative repetitions' " of elements from one Faulkner text to another.[20] He quite rightly observes that many previous studies of Yoknapatawphan intertextuality have stressed comprehensiveness, totality, unity, and monologism, thus marginalizing those other equally important "semiotic, rhetorical, and narrative maneuvers that leave fissures, gaps, and discrepancies, and point toward instability, indeterminacy, and otherness" (165). Uninterested in questions of intentionality, Kreiswirth deliberately avoids any discussion of "Faulkner's exchanges with his editors and the minutia of textual revisions, balks, reversals, [and] rerevisions" (171). But attending to the complete textual process of a Faulkner work in no way entails an allegiance to the authorial orientation. Indeed, such a commitment can easily have the opposite effect of rejecting authorial and editorial claims to limit that textual process to one of several texts.

Poststructuralist critics like Kreiswirth who resist attempts to stabilize textual boundaries and meanings and delight in "irresolvable base-level contradictions" and "textual instabilities" are unnecessarily limiting the number of these contradictions and instabilities by restricting their critical attention to a single manifestation of an entire textual process (177). But why should scholars uninterested in questions of intentionality limit themselves to a single text constituted by an author and his various commercial and scholarly editors? Attending to a work's entire authorial and

nonauthorial textual process instead frequently adds even more contradictions and instabilities to those already present in Faulknerian auto-
intertextuality of the sort that Kreiswirth explores so ably.[21]

If meaning is indeed the product of the dialectical relationship between textual production and textual reception, moreover, postmodern
criticism of Faulkner might be better served by relating the process by
which different hands constructed different stages of an entire textual
situation to the process by which its individual products have been received. This actual web of inextricably interconnected documents, texts,
and textual processes, both published and unpublished, suggests a notion
of collaborative intertextuality that is the material counterpart of postmodernist notions of intertextuality that focus on the discursive relationships between works by different authors.[22] Instead of the stable, fixed
texts produced by modern Anglo-American editors for formalist critics,
this notion of collaborative intertextuality assumes that it is only in the
context of particular theoretical frameworks or of particular commercial
and scholarly publishing arrangements that we can think of published
works as discrete entities.

The advantages that can accrue to applying postmodernist interpretive
strategies to an entire Faulknerian textual process rather than to a single
textual manifestation of that process may be seen, for example, in Minrose Gwin's deft application of gender and queer theory in "Did Ernest
Like Gordon?" to the cuts that Faulkner's editors at Boni & Liveright
made in his second published novel *Mosquitoes* (1927).[23] In exploring
uneasy "disruptive performances of the 'queer' abject" in several textual
spaces in the novel, Gwin makes a persuasive case that male homoeroti-
cism in the text works with masturbatory, incestuous, and lesbian sexual
activity in cut and uncut material to reveal the compulsory nature of
normative heterosexuality.[24] Her nuanced attention to how the homo-
erotic material in the cut passages originally worked in tandem thematically and structurally with similar passages in uncut material to
destabilize heterosexual activity and bodies ultimately persuades one that
the excisions reduced the amount of gender trouble in the novel. With
the recent publication of the facsimile edition of the holograph manuscript draft of about a third of *Mosquitoes*, Gwin and other scholars may
be able to test her argument about gender trouble in the novel against
this newly available portion of the novel's textual process.[25]

Compared to the composition and publication processes of the work of
other modern authors, Faulkner's textual situations are representatively
rather than exceptionally unstable, and much of the documentary evidence for this instability survives in various library special collections
such as those at Austin, Charlottesville, and here in Oxford. Multiple

versions of his works abound with substantive differences between manuscripts, typescripts, galleys, and proofs, and published versions that reflect the conflicts, agreements, and compromises that Faulkner struck with others and with himself. For example, he was not personally involved in cutting 15 percent from his third novel, *Flags in the Dust*, which Harcourt, Brace then published as *Sartoris* in 1929.[26] An earlier allegiance to individual authorship and to single authorial texts once led me to privilege *Flags* in an intermediate version of the novel that appeared posthumously in 1973 over *Sartoris*.[27] But it is the entire textual process of *Flags/Sartoris*, a process that is not limited either to the text validated by the act of publication or to the text that Faulkner preferred, that enables us to understand better his exploration of the early twentieth-century crisis of traditional masculinity at the beginning of a crucial period in his artistic development.[28] Much of what was cut in *Flags* was material dealing with failed Prufrockian lawyer Horace Benbow and sexually frustrated Sartoris bank teller and eventual bank robber Byron Snopes, characters that were originally juxtaposed with the more aggressive but equally frustrated and doomed young Bayard Sartoris. This crisis of masculinity connects Faulkner to other early twentieth-century American male writers like Hemingway and Fitzgerald for whom the destabilization of traditional gender roles as much as World War I had turned the world upside down.

Faulkner, however, was the primary agent in the peculiar revision process during the fall of 1930 that transformed the galleys of the original version of *Sanctuary* into a best-seller: in order to save money, he reordered chapters, cut whole chapters and beginnings and endings of chapters, and did very little rewriting or new writing.[29] The extant evidence suggests that Faulkner did not, as he claimed in his notorious introduction to the Modern Library edition of the novel, originally write a potboiler and then revise it with an eye toward improving it aesthetically so that it would not shame *The Sound and the Fury* and *As I Lay Dying*.[30] Rather he may have deliberately abandoned his initial attempt at a serious, experimental successor to *The Sound and the Fury* in order to create a more commercial work. Thus his revisions were not improvements on his original plan for *Sanctuary* but rather efforts to subvert it. Moreover, the published novel bears the stamp of Faulkner's attempt to alter the original version drastically with a minimum of rewriting or writing of new material in order to keep his share of the costs of publishing *Sanctuary* down.

As with *Flags* and *Sartoris*, the complete textual process of *Sanctuary* rather than either the 1929 or the 1931 version alone may help feminist scholars better understand how central the failure of traditional masculinity actually was to the young Faulkner and his work. Much of what Faulkner cut in *Sanctuary* was again material dealing with Horace Benbow, whose passivity and idealism were originally juxtaposed with Popeye's aggressive misogyny. Feminists and new historicists might be interested in how the complex editorial processes that produced both of these print novels were, in part, ideologically inflected collaborative acts involving Faulkner and other agents such as friends and publishers that resulted in downplaying and obscuring his earlier depictions of this crisis. Rather than argue for the superiority of one version over another, Faulkner critics might do better to attend to the work's entire textual history.[31]

Nevertheless, contemporary scholars frequently discuss Faulkner's most controversial novel by appealing only to the originally published version of *Sanctuary*. In a densely argued Freudian essay, for example, Gregory Forter interprets the novel's pervasive incidents of vomiting, spitting, oozing, and bleeding as signaling "the novel's tendency to 'say' things that it also does not say."[32] Although he does cite one alteration to the original version that supports his thesis (545, n13), Forter seems unaware of the extensive nature of Faulkner's rewriting and reordering of the novel and of any relevance to his argument that this process might have. Believing that the novel's deliberate confusion between subjectivity and objectivity creates "insoluble interpretive difficulties" that can result in "proportionally impoverished" readings, he neither inquires whether Faulkner's revisions provide evidentiary support for this claim nor asks if one version is more confused than the other (543). Similarly, James Polchin maintains that Faulkner courted commercial success with *Sanctuary* by drawing on popular interest in Freudian psychology with its emphasis on "psychosexual behavior and the importance of proper childhood mental development."[33] But he fails to recognize that Faulkner's numerous alterations in the novel's galleys, especially his late addition of Popeye's childhood biography, could help him confirm or qualify his arguments. And Michael Lahey's insightful discussion of Faulkner's corpus as a provocative critique of the law's complicity in constructing terrible social norms and realities focuses on Horace's utter failure before the district attorney during the novel's climactic trial scene but seems unaware that Faulkner cut lengthy passages dealing with Horace's relations with women from the original version of *Sanctuary*, wrote some new material, and rearranged large chunks of already composed material.[34] Thus Lahey can neither say whether any part of this process confirms, revises, or refutes his arguments nor explore how the trial, which remained relatively unaltered, functions differently in each version of the novel because different and differently ordered material led up to it.[35]

Faulkner also occasionally wrote introductory pieces for his novels not only to make some money but also to shape his readers' expectations and responses. For example, he insisted on placing the influential Compson Appendix, initially written for Malcolm Cowley's *Portable Faulkner* sixteen years after the publication of *The Sound and the Fury*, at the front of what became the most important reissue of any of his works: Random House's Modern Library double edition of *The Sound and the Fury* and *As I Lay Dying* (1946). As a result of Faulkner's steadily increasing popularity, this edition was reprinted and reissued frequently from 1954 to 1961 under the inexpensive paperback Modern Library and Vintage imprints.[36] During the 1960s, the Appendix appeared at the back of several reissues of the novel and some omitted it entirely.[37] The wheel came full circle when Noel Polk omitted the Appendix from his Random House corrected text of *The Sound and the Fury* in 1984, his Vintage paperback of the same text in 1987, and a facsimile reprint of the 1984 text in a different format in a 1990 Vintage International volume. To be sure, he did include it along with a brief explanatory note at the rear of another facsimile reprint, the 1992 Modern Library volume.[38]

In attempting to explain his favorite novel once again to readers who had rejected it earlier, Faulkner, by framing rather than rewriting it, created a kind of authorially sanctioned fifth section of *The Sound and the Fury* that shaped the readings of a generation of critics in the 1950s and the 1960s.[39] If earlier critics tended to view the Appendix ahistorically as a faithful guide to the 1929 novel, more recent commentaries have instead stressed the many conflicts between the 1929 novel and the Appendix.[40] Indeed, Faulkner's inclusion of the piece in later editions of *The Sound and the Fury* recontextualizes the work and thus may be said to reontologize it as well. Regardless of the many clashes between the novel and the Appendix, its addition arguably creates either a new version of the work or a new and separate work.[41] Skeptical scrutiny of the Appendix constitutes a marked improvement over earlier critical practice, which often read it as a gospel guide to the novel rather than to the fiction Faulkner had written in the years since the publication of *The Sound and the Fury*. Still, contemporary discussion over whether the Appendix is or is not part of *The Sound and the Fury* becomes a false choice if one accepts the reality of textual instability and the existence of multiple versions of a work. The Appendix *is* part of the 1946 version of the work known as *The Sound and the Fury* and a number of subsequent versions as well, even though it is not part of the 1929 version of that same work.

Yet another feature of Faulknerian textual instability is that he substantially reworked in varying degrees a number of published and unpublished short stories and sketches into novels such as *The Unvanquished*

(1938) and *Go Down, Moses* (1942).[42] In doing so, Faulkner made changes that reflect the different purposes, needs, and audiences of the longer works.[43] He produced *The Unvanquished* by making substantive additions to the five Civil War and Reconstruction stories that the *Saturday Evening Post* had published earlier and by writing the concluding story, "An Odor of Verbena," three years after the publication of those stories. Noel Polk notes that Faulkner's revision of these five stories in 1937 for book publication reflects "the same sort of commercial haste that had gone into their writing," and other readers have also found them too romantic, uncomplicated, and superficial.[44] While scholars have often neglected the entire textual process of *The Unvanquished*, Susan Donaldson's "Dismantling the *Saturday Evening Post* Reader" demonstrates the value of combining textual scholarship with a postmodern interest in disruption and contradiction.[45] Employing Jaussian reception aesthetic, she shows how Faulkner's "An Odor of Verbena" and his revisions of the earlier pieces first arouse and then undermine the expectations of conservative white middle-class readers of the sort who read the formulaic Civil War stories the *Post* ran in the 1930s. Attentive to the book's larger textual process, Donaldson concludes that Faulkner's additions support "An Odor of Verbena" in cautioning readers that "expectations attuned to tales of adventure and glory can be misleading and even dangerously blind to the rigid codification of storybook legends."[46]

The unusual structure of *Go Down, Moses* may have resulted, in part, from Faulkner's creation of the novel by combining new material with rewritten unpublished pieces and six previously published short stories.[47] As with *The Unvanquished*, Faulknerians have often produced readings of *Go Down, Moses* that stress the narrative, imagistic, or thematic unity and coherence of its very different constituent stories or that comment on the difficulty of doing so.[48] In fact, the novel's complicated but frequently overlooked textual history provides a wealth of evidence that would seem relevant to any discussion of whether *Go Down, Moses* is a novel, a collection of stories, or some sort of hybrid genre. Even Susan Donaldson's ambitious "Contending Narratives: *Go Down, Moses* and the Short Story Cycle" could have benefited, as did her piece on *The Unvanquished*, from yoking the available textual evidence to her poststructuralist interpretive moves. Reading the book as a postmodern short story cycle within which "individual stories of resistance and discontinuity" contend with the McCaslins's patriarchal narrative of brutal appropriation, domination, and exploitation of blacks, women, and Native Americans, Donaldson emphasizes how these stories formally and thematically counteract this inflexible system of power and authority.[49] It is a deft and instructive performance. Nevertheless, she might have ascertained whether the substantive textual variations among versions of individual stories reflect an increase in either unity or disruption.[50]

With its overlapping interests in subject formation, subjectivity, and the complexity of Faulkner's textual situations, Philip Weinstein's " 'He Come and Spoke for Me': Scripting Lucas Beauchamp's Three Lives," on the other hand, demonstrates how postmodernist scholarship can effectively draw upon textual scholarship. Weinstein's argument that the character of Lucas Beauchamp's identity depends on the signifying economy and textual situation within which he is situated rests on the fact that Faulkner produced Lucas three different times: first, in the group of short stories that appeared in 1940; then in the revised stories for *Go Down, Moses*; and finally in *Intruder in the Dust* (1948). The differences behind these several versions of Lucas chart, for Weinstein, shifts in Faulkner's own racial identity as he repeatedly tried and failed to imagine a black consciousness. If Lucas is first a racial stereotype of the wily Negro, he becomes in *Go Down, Moses* a character whose "heroic status is conditional upon his being figuratively removed from his own black heritage" and finally more a "congealed icon" than an "imagined subjectivity" in *Intruder*.[51] True, Weinstein does not try to corroborate this shift in representations of Lucas by comparing passages dealing with him in the magazine stories with their revised counterparts in *Go Down, Moses*. Nor is he much concerned with exploring conflicts in Lucas's character that may result from Faulkner's side-by-side placement of new and old material and of revised and unrevised material in *Go Down, Moses*. In place of the racist aspects of Lucas's depiction in the magazine stories, for example, Faulkner occasionally presents the readers of his novel with a more complex character that may appear somewhat inconsistent with the comic Uncle Remus figure Lucas cuts in earlier-inscribed but unrevised material. Moreover, the omniscient narrator of *Go Down, Moses* occasionally seems ambivalent on the issue of race perhaps because he is the product of different periods of composition and revision. Nevertheless, Weinstein's discussion of the linguistic entity known as Lucas Beauchamp as it manifests itself in several compositionally related Faulkner texts demonstrates that poststructuralist analysis and textual scholarship need not be at odds with each other.

Of course, determining the boundaries between the textual process of one work and that of another is a notoriously difficult, perhaps impossible interpretive task. Most writers, professional and amateur, repeatedly employ the same material in more than one context, often developing new material out of old material. As James McLaverty notes, these issues of textual identity and ontology recall the often-debated philosophical problem of Theseus's ship: "Theseus sets sail with a new ship, but before long it has got to go in for repair: old planks, nails, and sails are taken out and replaced by new ones. Over a long period of time, through numerous repairs, all the old material is replaced by new, and the problem is raised: Is this the same ship that Theseus started out with?"[52] Like his beloved twilight, that time when day merges indistinguishably but inevitably into night, Faulkner's texts and textual processes, seemingly so distinct, often blend into one another because he frequently used the same characters and events in different works and mined different works from the same quarry of imaginative materials.[53] A daunting number of novels, stories, film treatments, screenplays, and speeches, some worthy, some less worthy but all related to each other, were constantly overlapping and jostling each other for his attention. Thus Faulkner wrote the original text of *Sanctuary*, wrote *As I Lay Dying*, and then reordered and rewrote the *Sanctuary* galleys. Or consider how the writing of *Pylon* (1935) interrupted the composition of *Absalom, Absalom!* (1936) and how eleven years passed between the initial conception of *A Fable* in 1943 and its eventual publication in 1954. Or consider how Faulkner wrote *Father Abraham* in the mid-1920s, used some of this material in the Snopes stories of the 1930s, but did not complete the Snopes trilogy until the publication of *The Mansion* in 1959. Because his texts often elaborate on, influence, and argue with each other, the study of what he was working on at a given time may help elucidate another work from the same period.

Faulkner scholars can only benefit from mining the rich vein of authorial and nonauthorial intertextuality constituted by the entire textual process of his works.[54] Although such revisions are a key piece of evidence for those critics interested in authorial intention, attending to the entire textual process of a work, to the changes made by various hands over time in its texts, does not presuppose a critical practice founded on authorial intention. As we have seen, the entire textual process of a work can be an important if neglected body of evidence for confirming, revising, or refuting arguments that nonauthorial critics wish to make about a particular Faulkner text or work. Moreover, postmodern textual scholarship encourages us to see that both the complete textual process of a work and even a single textual embodiment of that work are frequently the site of conflicts rather than resolutions, conflicts between authors and publishers and editors and collaborators. Such conflicts in textual production are often the norm rather than the exception and make formalist assumptions about unity and coherence as *a priori* aesthetic criteria seem mistaken. Indeed, many textual scholars have become as suspicious as any poststructuralist hermeneut about the formal unity of literary works. Recognizing that Faulkner, like most writers, routinely revised and recycled his work for various reasons and that many other agents routinely joined him in altering these texts can only help postmodernist scholars explore textual contradiction, disruption, and discontinuity in his novels rather than search for hitherto unrecognized unifying figures in the carpet.

Up to this point, I have concentrated on the linguistic dimension of Faulkner's texts. Postmodern textual scholars such as Jerome McGann and George Bornstein, however, have also expanded our notion of what constitutes a text or a work by attending carefully to the interpretive significance of the "bibliographical" codes governing the physical documents that contain linguistic texts.[55] That the physical features of a document containing a linguistic text may also be constitutive of meaning is itself, of course, a postmodern social conception of text construction and textuality.[56] Now Faulkner scholars have often commented on those features of his visual codes that are clearly authorial in origin, such as the image of an eye in *The Sound and the Fury*, the image of the coffin in *As I Lay Dying*, and the map of Yoknapatawpha County in *Absalom*. But the nonauthorial bibliographical features of his books such as layout, typeface, ornamentation, and dust jacket art and copy may also be important insofar as they helped shape the responses of readers to his work. Thus scholars interested in Faulkner's critical and commercial reception ought to examine the physical documents that contain the linguistic texts of his works.[57]

Attempting to factor such features into considerations of Faulkner's critical reception seems an important if difficult critical task. Indeed, aspects of his reception may have been shaped by whether or not readers were holding in their hands a first edition of a particular novel, a New American Library or Signet paperback from the late 1940s and the 1950s with its lurid cover art and breathless, suggestive blurbs, or one of the glossy, upscale Library of America trade editions of the late 1980s and the 1990s. Such comparisons suggest that a work's different physical texts may indeed help regulate the expectations and responses of different audiences. Of course, gauging whether these bibliographical differences are actually substantive enough to have had an impact on readers is no easy task. A sociology of Faulkner's readers might enable us to measure, if even roughly, the efficacy of the cultural and ideological work, such as constructing and supervising subjects, that poststructuralist critics often see the writing, publishing, and reading of his novels performing. A major obstacle to developing such a sociology, however, is that detailed responses to fiction—other than the published record of reviews and academic criticism—are notoriously difficult to document. Moreover, a causal connection would have to be established between the responses of Faulkner's readers to his fiction and their actual choices and actions.

Such considerations may also lead us to attend more to how the linguistic and bibliographical codes of a particular work may conflict as well as work in tandem with each other.

Textual and documentary instability and intertextuality in Faulkner's fiction are fundamental realities of his and indeed any writer's corpus, but an awareness of such instability has no necessary connection with a biographical orientation that stresses authorial intention. Poststructuralist practices that value social discursive formations over individual consciousness, collaboration and circulation over self-sufficiency and autonomy also stand to benefit from thinking of Faulkner's fictions as textual processes that involve negotiations among an author and other individuals and that produce a variety of textual products. Charles Kinbote's lesser light may pale, like that of the moon to the sun, in comparison with John Shade's poetic genius. But attending to the entire textual process of Faulkner's work is no mad attempt to supplant the man from Mississippi. A postmodern theorist of historiography told me recently that when faced with several variants in a text, he is increasingly prone to say that they are all valid. Precisely. And much contemporary Faulkner scholarship has yet to make use of this recognition.

NOTES

1. Vladimir Nabokov, *Pale Fire* (1962; New York: Vintage International, 1989), 28, 29.

2. Bruce Harkness's "Bibliography and the Novelistic Fallacy" (*Studies in Bibliography* 12 [1959]: 59–73) reflects this earlier emphasis.

3. John Barth, "Foreword," *"The Floating Opera" and "The End of the Road"* (New York: Doubleday, Anchor Books, 1988), vii.

4. Barth, "Foreword," vii.

5. In his "Prefatory Note" to the 1967 Doubleday Anchor revised edition of the novel (reprinted in the 1988 Doubleday reissue), Barth tells his readers only that he has restored excised material. Sherry Lutz Zivley's "A Collation of John Barth's *Floating Opera*" (*Publications of the Bibliographical Society of America* 72 [1978]: 201–12) admirably describes and expounds the critical significance of the substantive differences between the several textual versions of the novel.

6. Hershel Parker has argued at length in *Flawed Texts and Verbal Icons: Literary Authority in American Fiction* (Evanston: Northwestern University Press, 1984) that revisions made after an author's creative process has ended often create more problems than they solve by undermining the textual coherence produced by a determinate psychological and compositional process.

7. Readers may consult essays by these scholars in my collection *Devils and Angels: Textual Editing and Literary Theory* (Charlottesville: University Press of Virginia, 1991). D. C. Greetham's "Editorial and Critical Theory: From Modernism to Postmodernism," in *Palimpsest: Editorial Theory in the Humanities*, ed. George Bornstein (Ann Arbor: University of Michigan Press, 1993), 9–28 and "Literary and Textual Theory: Redrawing the Matrix" in *Studies in Bibliography* 42 (1989): 1–24; and Michael Groden's "Contemporary Textual and Literary Theory," in *Palimpsest*, 259–86), are also helpful. Contributors to my collection *Texts and Textuality: Textual Instability, Theory, and Interpretation* (New York: Garland, 1997) attempt to bring different theoretical orientations to bear upon different

textual situations or histories in order to explore how different textual situations and their material means of production help generate different theories of textuality and how different conceptions of textuality help generate an understanding of different textual situations and their material means of production. Thus the contributors take as their collective subject the dialectical relationship between texts and textuality.

8. For a useful critique of the myth of individual authorship, see Jack Stillinger's *Multiple Authorship and the Myth of Solitary Genius* (Oxford: Oxford University Press, 1991).

9. Despite their various cutting-edge critical methodologies with their stress on multiple, overlapping interpretive contexts, for example, many of the contributors to David Mc-Whirter's recent collection *Henry James's New York Edition: The Construction of Authorship* (Palo Alto: Stanford University Press, 1995) display little interest in employing textual scholarship for interpretive and theoretical purposes. While they scrutinize various aspects of the Edition's physical format, photographs, order and omission of selections, many of the contributors frequently treat the Edition as a fixed, stable textual product even when discussing James's theories of writing and revision. For example, few of the essays bring James's composition of the prefaces, his substantive revision of earlier work, and his authorial intertextuality—that is, the other works he wrote while he worked on the Edition—to bear on their arguments. Indeed, most of the contributors expatiate at length on James's published and unpublished comments on composition and revision but curiously avoid exploring in any substantive way what he actually did to his earlier fiction as he prepared the Edition. For an extended review of this collection, see my "The Lesson of the Master" in *Studies in the Novel* 31 (Spring 1999): 98–115.

George Bornstein's excellent collection *Representing Modernist Texts: Editing as Interpretation* (Ann Arbor: University of Michigan Press, 1991), on the other hand, seeks to remedy this neglect by exploring in a series of pieces on modernist writers by different hands "the implications for literary critics and theorists of the recent revolution in editorial theory" (5). Readers interested in how critics may make use of a work's entire textual process may also consult James West's collection *Dreiser's "Jennie Gerhardt": New Essays on the Restored Text* (Philadelphia: University of Pennsylvania Press, 1995), with its essays on West's 1992 University of Pennsylvania edition of an earlier version of the novel that Dreiser sought to publish before the editorial staff at Harpers cut and revised the work for its 1911 publication. In placing the novel in a host of autobiographical, biographical, literary, and historical contexts, many of the volume's contributors refer not only to the restored text but also to the numerous substantive differences between the two versions.

10. Postmodernist Faulkner scholars, for example, have generally drawn on Noel Polk's 1980s corrected Random House editions of the novels for their quotations with little or no comment on the eclectic editorial assumptions and policies used to constitute them. Even more telling, they have often simply replaced some novel titles that may have been imposed on Faulkner with titles that evidence shows he preferred. In "The Guns of *Light in August*: War and Peace in the Second Thirty Years War," for example, Warwick Wadlington thoughtfully examines Faulkner's fiction produced during the period bounded by World War I and World War II as a "peculiarly intense hybrid of war and peace" (*Faulkner in Cultural Context*, ed. Donald M. Kartiganer and Ann J. Abadie [Jackson: University Press of Mississippi, 1997], 131) but frequently refers to Douglas Day's edition of *Flags in the Dust* (New York: Random House, 1973) without ever alluding to Harcourt, Brace's initial 1929 publication of the novel in a truncated form as *Sartoris* (see also 128, 129, 139, 143). Similarly, Neil Schmitz's "Faulkner and the Post-Confederate" explores the historical, social, and literary contexts of *Intruder in the Dust*'s reworking of the narrative and linguistic practices of postbellum Southern writing, cites Faulkner's treatment of race in passages from *Flags*, but never mentions its earlier incarnation as *Sartoris* (*Faulkner in Cultural Context*, 248). And Pamela Rhodes's discussion in "Who Killed Simon Strother, and Why?" (*Faulkner and Race*, ed. Doreen Fowler and Ann J. Abadie [Jackson: University Press of Mississippi, 1987], 93–110) of Faulkner's abrupt racist termination of his development of a realistic African American character in *Flags* makes no mention of *Sartoris* either. The actual novel and title that Faulkner originally published, which has just as much historical and social and literary significance as the novel and title he preferred, has simply disap-

peared. For a delightful discussion of the relevance of the entire textual histories of Faulkner's works to criticism and scholarship and of the principles behind his new Random House editions, see Polk's "Where the Comma Goes: Editing William Faulkner" in Bornstein, *Representing Modernist Texts*, 241–58.

11. New York: Modern Language Association, 1996.

12. Although the manuscript and carbon typescript for the first edition of *The Sound and the Fury* (New York: Cape & Smith, 1929) survive, the setting copy and galleys that would help document the extensive copy-editing of the novel do not. Noel Polk discusses the various issues involved in editing the novel and Faulkner's repudiation of some of the editorial changes in the Introduction to his *Editorial Handbook for William Faulkner's "The Sound and the Fury"* (New York: Garland, 1985), 1–22.

13. Cleanth Brooks, *William Faulkner: The Yoknapatawpha Country* (New Haven: Yale University Press, 1963), 127, 128. Brooks is aware of *Sanctuary*'s unusual composition history, but he accepts Faulkner's assertion in his notorious Introduction to the Modern Library edition of the novel that he originally conceived of the novel as a "cheap idea" but then "thoroughly . . . reworked the original galleys" in order to improve the book (396, 397). He never attempts to support his arguments by looking at the original version of the novel that Faulkner sought to publish.

14. And formalism in no way provides an *a priori* guarantee that its adherents will emphasize only the published version of a textual process. For an example, David Madden's entertaining, semi-autobiographical, but ultimately formalist discussion of "Photographs in the 1929 Version of *Sanctuary*" (*Faulkner and Popular Culture*, ed. Doreen Fowler and Ann J. Abadie [Jackson: University Press of Mississippi, 1990], 93–109) contends that his excision of many of these images for the 1931 version of the novel radically disrupted and altered a good deal of its meaning. Madden is particularly concerned with how Faulkner's revisions made certain portions of the earlier version that survive in the published version problematic to the point of incomprehensibility. Thus Horace's repeated contemplation of the increasingly ambiguous appearance of Little Belle's photograph, a sequence in the original version that was radically truncated in the revised version, was clearly intended to prepare for and to help explain his climactic shattering bout of hallucinatory nausea in his bathroom after his interview with Temple at Miss Reba's brothel.

15. Leslie Fiedler, "Pop Goes the Faulkner: In Quest of *Sanctuary*" (*Faulkner and Popular Culture*, 83).

16. See Michael Millgate's *The Achievement of William Faulkner* (1966; Lincoln: University of Nebraska Press, Bison Books, 1978). Regina Fadiman's excellent *"Light in August": A Description and Interpretation of the Revisions* (Charlottesville: University Press of Virginia, 1975) uses bibliographical and linguistic evidence derived from a close examination of the methods and stages of Faulkner's revision of the novel to support her interpretation of the published work. Similarly, James Early's *The Making of "Go Down, Moses"* concerns itself with "the gradual development of [Faulkner's] themes, his verbal and narrative techniques, and his conception of his characters" from the hunting stories of 1934 and 1935 to the published novel in order to better understand *Go Down, Moses* (Dallas: Southern Methodist University Press, 1972, ix).

17. Wordsworth editor Stephen Parrish has dissented from this approach which he humorously but accurately refers to as "Whig interpretations of a literary text, with their notions of an inner logic of inexorable growth toward what could have been foreseen from the start as the author's final intention" ("The Whig Interpretation of Literature," *TEXT* 4 [1988]: 349). He notes that for such critics "Rejected drafts, discarded variants, abandoned versions, while sometimes dutifully catalogued, are looked upon as false starts, misjudgments, or lapses of taste on the part of the poet, all happily rectified as the work, by obedience to some inner logic, reaches final form" (344–5).

18. One of the most influential attempts at this approach, John T. Irwin's *Doubling and Incest / Repetition and Revenge* (1975; Expanded Ed., Baltimore: Johns Hopkins University Press, 1996), psychoanalytically reads *The Sound and the Fury* and *Absalom* as a sort of meta-text in which Quentin Compson's tortured relations in the earlier novel with his parents and siblings, especially his father and Caddy, are crucial for understanding his

situation in the later one. Similarly, Estella Schoenberg's *Old Tales and Talking: Quentin Compson in William Faulkner's "Absalom, Absalom!" and Related Works* (Jackson: University Press of Mississippi, 1977), argues that *Absalom* is "Faulkner's means of retelling Quentin's story and explaining Quentin's suicide," drawing on published fiction and unpublished stories and fragments by Faulkner to make the case that Quentin's "dejection and psychic withdrawal throughout the last half of [*Absalom*]" is inexplicable to readers unless they are aware of his suicide in *The Sound and the Fury* (4).

19. See *Faulkner in the University: Class Conferences at the University of Virginia 1957–1958*, ed. Frederick L. Gwynn and Joseph L. Blotner (1959; New York: Random House, Vintage, 1965). For example, Judith Bryant Wittenberg's penetrating "Temple Drake and *La parole pleine*" (*Mississippi Quarterly* 48 [1995]: 421–41), an intertextual, dialectical reading of *Requiem* and an important paper by Lacan from the early 1950s, argues that Temple undergoes a Faulknerian "talking cure," moving toward self-understanding, subjectivity, and a fully individualized speech. This movement is constrained by the linguistic codes and conventions available to her, however, and by the patriarchal inadequacies of Gavin Stevens, which take their toll on Temple's rhetorical versatility and ability to narrate lucidly. Citing *Requiem*'s numerous explicit references to *Sanctuary*, Wittenberg then examines how the failures of Horace Benbow, Temple's failed interlocutor-analyst in the earlier novel, compound her "relative lack of individualized speech" and her inability "to arrive at a state of integrated psycho-linguistic selfhood" (428). As insightful as it is, the essay's assumption that *Sanctuary* played such a key role in the genesis of *Requiem* has perhaps a whiff of the totalizing impulse behind it. We know that Faulkner rarely reread earlier work and frequently remembered it incorrectly in details both small and large. Moreover, he had also written a great deal of fiction in the intervening years, and his current projects may have had more relevance to the writing of *Requiem* than *Sanctuary*. If Wittenberg had pointed out and accounted for the many differences between the two novels, one might object less to her so intimately connecting aesthetically, intellectually, and biographically works separated by over twenty years.

In the same vein, Michael E. Lahey's "Narcissa's Love Letters: Illicit Space and the Writing of Female Identity in 'There Was a Queen'" discusses how the negotiations between Narcissa Benbow and an FBI agent over Byron Snopes's love letters play "with available notions of feminine identity, as they are privately and publicly imagined" to demonstrate how "female identity in the world of the story is imagined and written by men, with women serving as screens onto which identity is projected" (*Faulkner and the Artist*, ed. Donald M. Kartiganer and Ann J. Abadie [Jackson: University Press of Mississippi, 1996], 161). Much more so than Wittenberg, Lahey assumes a nonproblematic seamless intertextual relationship between Narcissa's character and actions in "There Was a Queen" and the earlier *Flags in the Dust* (see especially 164–5, 172–3).

20. "'Paradoxical and Outrageous Discrepancy': Transgression, Auto-Intertextuality, and Faulkner's Yoknapatawpha" (*Faulkner and the Artist*, 162).

21. Thus Barbara L. Pittman argues persuasively in "Faulkner's Big Woods and the Historical Necessity of Revision" that when Faulkner transformed parts of *Go Down, Moses* into *Big Woods* (1955), he excised, perhaps for commercial reasons, from the material he would use in *Big Woods* much of the earlier work's insistent emphasis on racial injustice, miscegenation, and incest. Unlike the obsessive historical investigation of these issues in *Go Down, Moses*, the truncated *Big Woods* becomes a dehistoricized allegory that "preserve[s] the past in a static myth" and its elegiac tone "a lament for the loss of white domination" and "the sense of the white man's increasing insignificance in the face of the newly decreed sharing of his power" (*Mississippi Quarterly* 49 (1996): 478, 477, 492).

22. Noel Polk's interpretive work often demonstrates both an interest in the relation between authorial intertextuality and biography and an awareness of the limits involved in making such connections, especially through psychoanalysis. His essays routinely make intriguing connections between the primary work under discussion and whatever else Faulkner was writing at the time, whether published or unpublished. See, for example, his "'The Dungeon Was Mother Herself': William Faulkner: 1927–1931" (*New Directions in Faulkner Studies*, ed. Doreen Fowler and Ann J. Abadie [Jackson: University Press of

Mississippi, 1984], 61–93); "The Space Between *Sanctuary*" (*Intertextuality in Faulkner*, ed. Michel Gresset and Noel Polk [Jackson: University Press of Mississippi, 1985], 16–35); and " 'Polysyllabic and Verbless Patriotic Nonsense': Faulkner at Midcentury—His and Ours" (*Faulkner and Ideology*, ed. Donald M. Kartiganer and Ann J. Abadie [Jackson: University Press of Mississippi], 297–328).

23. Gwin's "*Mosquitoes*' Missing Bite: The Four Deletions" (*Faulkner Journal* 9 [Fall 1993/Spring 1994]: 31–41) helpfully prints for the first time the complete text of the four excised passages.

24. "Did Ernest Like Gordon?: Faulkner's *Mosquitoes* and the Bite of 'Gender Trouble' " (*Faulkner and Gender*, ed. Donald M. Kartiganer and Ann J. Abadie [Jackson: University Press of Mississippi, 1996], 121).

25. With the help of David Vander Meulen, Thomas L. McHaney has edited *William Faulkner's "Mosquitoes": A Facsimile and Transcription of the Holograph Manuscript* (Charlottesville: Bibliographical Society of the University of Virginia and the University of Virginia Library, 1997). Another example of how postmodern criticism and textual scholarship may be fruitfully combined in Faulkner studies may be found in Joseph R. Urgo's "Faulkner Unplugged: Abortopoesis and *The Wild Palms*," which maintains that printing "Old Man" and "Wild Palms" separately, as some editions in the 1950s did, destroys Faulkner's poetics and thematics of abortion in the novel's twinned alternating narratives which interrogate "the discordant sexual bases of male and female social and cultural autonomy" (*Faulkner and Gender*, 256).

26. George Hayhoe's "William Faulkner's *Flags in the Dust*" (*Mississippi Quarterly* 28 [1975]: 370–86; rpt. in *Critical Essays on William Faulkner: The Sartoris Family*, ed. Arthur P. Kinney [Boston: G. K. Hall, 1985], 233–45) contains a concise biographical account of the composition of the novel, Ben Wasson's editorial surgery, and its publication as *Sartoris*. See also Joseph L. Blotner's *Faulkner: A Biography*, vol. 1 (New York: Random House, 1974), 527–611. In 1987, Garland published Blotner's edition of the manuscript and typescript of *Flags in the Dust* in two volumes as *William Faulkner Manuscripts 5*.

27. In "The Last Sartoris: Benbow Sartoris' Birth in *Flags in the Dust*" (*Southern Literary Journal* 18 [1985]: 30–9), for example, I argued that the excision of *Flags* material dealing with Horace and Narcissa Benbow for *Sartoris* unintentionally turned an ironic closed ending in which the future holds little promise for the young Sartoris whether paternal or maternal genes come to dominate his character into a more ambiguous open-ended conclusion even though the endings remain substantially the same in both versions.

28. In "William Faulkner, the Crisis of Masculinity, and Textual Instability" (*Textual Studies and the Common Reader: Essays on Editing Novels and Novelists*, ed. Alexander Pettit [University of Georgia Press, 2000], 64–80), I contend that the entire textual process of *Flags/Sartoris* anticipates Faulkner's work to come on the psychological, social, and cultural perils of masculinity.

29. For concise accounts of *Sanctuary*'s composition, revision, and publication, see Noel Polk's introduction to his edition of the 1987 two-volume Garland facsimile of the *Sanctuary* manuscript and typescript (vol. 1, vii–ix) and the afterword to his edition of the original version of the novel that Faulkner sought to publish in 1929 (*Sanctuary: The Original Text* [New York: Random House, 1981], 293–306).

30. See Faulkner's Introduction to the 1932 Modern Library edition of the novel, reprinted in *Sanctuary: The Corrected Text*, ed. Noel Polk (New York: Random House, Vintage, 1987), 339. See also my " 'A Cheap Idea . . . Deliberately Conceived To Make Money': The Biographical Context of William Faulkner's Introduction to *Sanctuary*" (*The Faulkner Journal* 3 [Spring 1988]: 54–66) and Noel Polk's Afterword to *Sanctuary: The Original Text*, 295.

31. Noel Polk makes a similar point when he writes that "taken together, in their inter- and intratextual relationships with each other and with the other novels and stories in the space between, the two versions form a single literary text that is far more significant than either of the versions taken singly" and that we cannot "understand either *Sanctuary* without also coming to terms with the other" ("The Space Between *Sanctuary*," 34).

32. "Faulkner's Black Holes: Visions and Vomit in *Sanctuary*," *Mississippi Quarterly* 49 (1996): 553.

33. "Selling a Novel: Faulkner's *Sanctuary* as a Psychosexual Text" (*Faulkner and Gender*, 145).

34. See Michael Lahey's "The Complex Art of Justice: Lawyers and Lawmakers as Faulkner's Dubious Artist Figures" (*Faulkner and the Artist*, 250–68).

35. In like fashion, Kathryn M Scheel contends in "Incest, Repression, and Repetition Compulsion: The Case of Faulkner's Temple Drake" (*Mosaic* 30 [1997]: 39–55) that the real mystery of *Sanctuary* is not Temple's rape at the Old Frenchman's Place but her very real earlier incestuous rape by her brothers. Scheel's provocative psychoanalytic reading suggests that Temple has repressed any awareness of this previous rape but that the repressed trauma nevertheless manifests itself in her complex and apparently contradictory speech and behavior. Given the controversial nature of her argument and her assignation of agency to Faulkner, Scheel might have consulted the original version of *Sanctuary* to see if Faulkner's drastic revisions provide any confirmation or qualification of her thesis. In marked contrast, Kevin Railey's plea in "The Social Psychology of Paternalism: *Sanctuary*'s Cultural Context" for an ideological, Althusserian rather than humanistic, Freudian interpretation of *Sanctuary* gains from his interest in the novel's entire textual process. Railey explores how "the dynamics of Horace Benbow's world set the conditions for Temple Drake's story" and how the novel's narrative perspective emphasizes the "upper-class, aristocratic paternalist male mentality" that constitutes their world (*Faulkner in Cultural Context*, 75). His treatment of the original and the published versions of *Sanctuary* as a single extended text is a useful strategy because Faulkner excised so much material dealing with Horace, especially his waking and sleeping dreams about the women in his life.

36. The text of the 1946 Modern Library edition was first reprinted as a Modern Library paperback in 1954 and first published as a Vintage paperback in 1961. The 1946 Modern Library text forms the basis for the text in Random House's *Faulkner Reader* (1954) and for the 1959 New American Library Signet edition of the novel. The Appendix appears at the end of the novel in both the 1954 *Reader* and its reprint in the Modern Library but is located at the front of the 1959 New American Library Signet edition. Most of the relevant bibliographical information on *The Sound and the Fury* may be found in James B. Meriwether's "Notes on the Textual History of *The Sound and the Fury*" (*Publications of the Bibliographical Society of America* 56 [Third Quarter, 1962]: 285–316); his "The Books of William Faulkner" (*Mississippi Quarterly* 35 [Summer 1982]: 268–9); and his "The Books of William Faulkner: A Guide for Students and Scholars" (*Mississippi Quarterly* 30 [Summer 1977]: 419).

37. In 1962, Vintage reissued the novel's 1929 text in paper with "Appendix: Compson: 1699–1945" at the back of the volume (Polk, *Editorial Handbook*, 18). In 1966, a Modern Library reissue of the 1946 text also positioned the Appendix at the novel's rear, while Random House reissued the 1929 text of *The Sound and the Fury* without it. The next year saw the 1929 text reissued as a "Modern Library College Edition" in paperback with the Appendix once again at the rear.

38. When David Minter reprinted Polk's text in his 1987 and 1994 Norton Critical Editions of *The Sound and the Fury*, however, he included the Appendix in the "Backgrounds and Contexts" sections.

39. On this subject, see my " 'The Key to the Whole Book': Faulkner's *The Sound and the Fury*, the Compson Appendix, and Textual Instability," in Cohen, *Texts and Textuality*, especially 246–7 and 250–2.

40. For example, Dawn Trouard finds in the "discrepancies and ruptures" in the 1929 novel's representation of Caddy and the other Compson women, a progressive rewriting of the novel in terms of gender, arguing that the Appendix continues to present in the persons of Melissa Meek and Caddy "a [feminist] model of the caring possibilities yet to be realized" ("Faulkner's Text Which Is Not One," *New Essays on "The Sound and the Fury*," ed. Noel Polk [Cambridge: Cambridge University Press, 1993], 25, 57). Similarly, Susan Donaldson has contended that the Compson Appendix is Faulkner's self-reflexive critique of "the [patriarchal] structures of narrative, authority, and gender defining" the 1929 *Sound and*

the Fury ("Reading Faulkner Reading Cowley Reading Faulkner: Authority and Gender in the Compson Appendix," *The Faulkner Journal* 7 [Fall 1991/Spring 1992]: 27–8). Alternatively, Thadious M. Davis describes the piece as a conservative revision that emphasizes the Compson patriarchal line at the expense of women and blacks whose roles are diminished, thus presaging Faulkner's work in the 1950s with its "ridiculing of women . . . the complicated immersions in historical narratives of war, the dismissal of blacks from all but the most visually benign texts" ("Reading Faulkner's Compson Appendix: Writing History From the Margins," *Faulkner and Ideology*, 251).

Several essays in Hahn and Kinney's *Approaches to Teaching Faulkner's "The Sound and the Fury"* recapitulate the historical diversity of critical opinion on the Appendix's relationship to the novel by differing widely over whether the Appendix is part of the novel, is a separate work, or is part of the novel's ongoing textual process. Whereas Walter Taylor writes that "the appendix may create [for first-time readers] as many problems as it solves" ("The Compson Appendix as an Aid to Teaching *The Sound and the Fury*," 64), Charles Peek sees no discrepancies between the 1929 novel and the Appendix which enables readers to "engage issues of race and gender without being so influenced by Dilsey's indomitability or distracted by the by the Compson brothers' obsession with their sister, Caddy" ("Order and Flight: Teaching *The Sound and the Fury* Using the Appendix," 68). If Jun Liu suggests that teachers draw students' attention to Faulkner's comments on Jason in the Appendix as a means of understanding him better ("Nihilists and Their Relations: A Nietzchean Approach to Teaching *The Sound and the Fury*," 93), John T. Matthews advises them to concentrate instead "on what the novel itself looks at (and what it does not)" ("Text and Context: *The Sound and the Fury* after Deconstruction," 123).

For examples of earlier ahistorical readings of *The Sound and the Fury* in terms of the Appendix, see Cohen, " 'The Key to the Whole Book,' " 250–2. In "Jason's Role-Slippage: The Dynamics of Alcoholism in *The Sound and the Fury*," Gary Storhoff continues this tradition of uncritical intertextual readings when he notes that Jason has in the novel amassed a small fortune over the years from stealing Caddy's money and working in Earl's store; "Yet we discover [in the Appendix] that he has accumulated less than $7,000" (*Mississippi Quarterly* 49 [1996]: 530). Storhoff then analyzes how Jason has thrown his money away in the novel, in effect reading the novel through the lens of the Appendix with little awareness that it represents Faulkner's rewriting of the novel many years later. Similarly, Rick Wallach argues in "The Compson Family Finances and the Economics of Tragic Farce" that Jason's ultimate failure in the cotton market proceeds "according to principles of exchange which reflect and elaborate the [novel's] themes of emotional dissolution and loss" but uncritically uses the Compson family's long history of financial decline in the Appendix to interpret Jason's motives in the 1929 novel (*South Atlantic Review* 62 [1997]: 80).

41. For extensive discussion of some of these clashes, see Cohen, " 'The Key to the Whole Book,' " especially 237–8 and 242–9.

42. Hans H. Skei's recent collection *William Faulkner's Short Fiction: An International Symposium* (Oslo: Solum Forlag, 1997) provides a welcome counter to the current critical tendency to ignore the larger textual process behind a particular Faulkner text. Many of the papers by well-known Faulkner scholars at this1995 conference concentrate on the relationship between various published and unpublished stories and sketches and the novels. See especially the volume's fourth section, "From Short Story to Fiction."

43. Faulkner's revisions for *The Unvanquished* of stories that had earlier appeared in the *Saturday Evening Post* are discussed in Joseph L. Blotner's notes in *Uncollected Stories of William Faulkner* (New York: Random House, Vintage Books, 1979), 681–4; James B. Carothers's *William Faulkner's Short Stories* (Ann Arbor: UMI Research Press, 1985), 84–7; and Joanne V. Creighton's *William Faulkner's Craft of Revision: The Snopes Trilogy, "The Unvanquished," and "Go Down, Moses"* (Detroit: Wayne State University Press, 1977), 73–84. For discussions of Faulkner's composition of short stories for various magazines and his subsequent revision of them for *Go Down, Moses*, see Carothers, 88–9, 91, and Blotner, *Faulkner: A Biography*, vol. 2, 1077–8, 1087–8, 1089, and 1093.

44. *Faulkner: Novels 1936–1940* (New York: Library of America, 1990), 1110. In "Diving

into the Wreck: Faulknerian Practice and the Imagination of Slavery," Philip Weinstein calls *The Unvanquished* "for the most part (and despite a good deal of current critical attention), a racially retrograde text," citing the prior publication of much of the novel in the *Post* as "one explanation for its conventional thinking" (*Faulkner Journal* 10 [1995]: 29).

45. Neither Deborah Clarke nor Patricia Yaeger evinces much interest in Faulkner's revision of the stories that constitute the book. Emphasizing the social construction of gender, Clarke claims that Drusilla Hawk presents a radical challenge to the South's race and gender hierarchies by dressing and fighting like a man "in order to preserve the man's world against which she rebels" ("Gender, War, and Cross-Dressing in *The Unvanquished*," *Faulkner and Gender*, 242). When the war ends and she is returned to dresses, marriage, and an antebellum gender position, Drusilla "uncovers the power of the feminine in language" by using her femininity and sexuality with a vengeance to urge men, including Bayard, to violence (246). For Yaeger, Drusilla's white woman's body, especially in "An Odor of Verbena," "becomes a screen or symbol for the text's [and the region's] unresolved political issues," a screen on which Faulkner maps "the grotesque trivialization of African-American's [sic] rights and humanity" ("Faulkner's 'Greek Amphora Priestess': Verbena and Violence in *The Unvanquished*," *Faulkner and Gender*, 207, 219). Although neither Clarke nor Yaeger discusses the genesis of *The Unvanquished*, the textual relationship of the first five stories to the last-written "An Odor of Verbena"—the stories were written at different times for different audiences—seems relevant to arguments about characters like Drusilla that recur throughout the collection.

46. "Dismantling the *Saturday Evening Post* Reader: *The Unvanquished* and Changing 'Horizons of Expectations' " (*Faulkner and Popular Culture*, 180). Likewise, Peter Nicolaisen makes productive use in " 'Because we were forever free': Slavery and Emancipation in *The Unvanquished*" of Faulkner's revisions in a close reading that draws attention to Faulkner's vacillations and contradictory attitudes concerning race, slavery, and freedom by focusing on "the often abrupt transitions from one mode of writing to another," transitions which seem deliberate given the details of Faulkner's revision of the earlier stories (*Faulkner Journal* 10 [1995]: 82).

47. Faulkner also produced a heavily revised and abridged version of "The Bear," a new story he had already written for the novel, and sold it to the *Saturday Evening Post* for publication in early 1942.

48. In one such recent attempt to unify the various stories, Glen Meeter displaces Cass Edmonds's and Isaac McCaslin's competing visions in the novel with the competing visions of Isaac and Molly Beauchamp. Reading the book's biblical allusions typologically, Meeter sees Molly as a prophetic visionary who envisions the South as Canaan, a land promised to the inheritors of both races, while Ike's repudiation of his inheritance reflects the story of the fall and the original sin of "trying to own and tame the land" ("Molly's Vision: Lost Cause Ideology and Genesis in Faulkner's *Go Down, Moses*," *Faulkner and Ideology*, 288). The novel's meaning thus arises from the dialectical relationship between these two visions which ultimately gives primacy to Molly. To counter the objection that Molly does not receive as much time, space, or dialogue as Ike, Meeter might have looked for textual evidence, especially in Faulkner's revision of the magazine stories, that supports his claim.

Those critics who have attended to the entire textual process of *Go Down, Moses* have often viewed Faulkner's revisions of previous published and unpublished work as authorially intended improvements that serve the different purposes of the novel and create a more unified work. Thus Jane Millgate's detailed examination of Faulkner's revision of his *Atlantic Monthly* story "Gold Is not Always" concludes that he "deliberately reworked his material in such a way as to fit it into the framework of an overall thematic pattern" ("Short Story into Novel: Faulkner's Reworking of 'Gold Is not Always,' " *English Studies* 45 [1964]: 315). Millgate is not much interested in the issue of how these revisions may have created new problems at the same time that they solved others. Joanne Creighton's *William Faulkner's Craft of Revision*, one of the earliest studies of Faulkner's incorporation of preexistent short stories into longer works, also exhibits a similar lack of interest in the conflicts or problems created by Faulkner's revisions. Creighton emphasizes Faulkner's "skillful revision" and "the control that [he] exercises over the diffuseness of his Yoknapatawpha material" as he refashioned in *Go Down, Moses* "comparatively simple and one-dimensional stories into an integrated whole" (149, 154). A refreshing if extreme exception to this tendency is Marvin Klotz who contends in "Procrustean Revision in Faulkner's *Go Down, Moses*" that Faulkner jammed "great chunks of unassimilated, mostly expository, prose" into his "tightly structured and lucid magazine stories," material which blurred thematic focus and destroyed established characterization (*American Literature* 37 [March 1965]: 16).

49. "Contending Narratives: *Go Down, Moses* and the Short Story Cycle" (*Faulkner and the Short Story*, ed. Evans Harrington and Ann J. Abadie [Jackson: University Press of Mississippi, 1992], 147).

50. Similarly, John Carlos Rowe has argued in "The African-American Voice in Faulkner's *Go Down, Moses*" that because Faulkner was unable to grant his African American characters the independent voices he knew they deserved, the book contains two narratives contending with each other for dominance: Ike McCaslin's myth and the stories of African Americans seeking freedom (*The Modern Short Story Sequence: Composite Fictions and Fictive Communities*, ed. J. Gerald Kennedy [Cambridge: Cambridge University Press, 1995], 76–97). Rowe's contention that the volume's short story sequence defends the integrity of its threatened cohesion might have profited from an examination of the variants in the work's textual history. On the other hand, Arthur F. Kinney's account of the centrality of the issues of racism and miscegenation to its themes, characters and families, and narrative and metaphoric structures in *"Go Down, Moses": The Miscegenation of Time* (New York: Twayne, 1996) is notable for its frequent attempts to relate what we know about Faulkner's composition and revision of the novel and related texts to his developing plan for the novel and to how we might best collaborate in producing its meanings. Nevertheless, some may disagree with how tightly integrated he feels the individual chapters of *Go Down, Moses* are.

51. Philip Weinstein, " 'He Come and Spoke for Me': Scripting Lucas Beauchamp's Three Lives," *Faulkner and the Short Story*, 237, 244. Weinstein here parallels, in part, Michael Grimwood's argument in *Heart in Conflict: Faulkner's Struggles with Vocation* that as Faulkner revised the short stories, he repudiated the formulaic Anglo-American depictions of comic "darkies" inherited from plantation literature that characterized the stories in their original appearance in national magazines such as *Harper's*, the *Atlantic Monthly*, and *Collier's* (Athens: University of Georgia Press, 1987, 275–7).

52. James McLaverty, "Issues of Identity and Utterance: An Intentionalist Response to 'Textual Instability' " (Cohen, *Devils and Angels*, 136).

53. Faulkner's work in Hollywood is also intimately connected to the textual processes of his fiction. While many of Faulkner's screenplays are far from being first-rate screenplays, they are proof, as Bruce Kawin argues in his edition of Faulkner's MGM screenplays, that his derogatory comments and subsequent disdainful critical comments about his years in Hollywood's salt mines need to be qualified somewhat (*Faulkner's MGM Screenplays* (Knoxville: University of Tennessee Press, 1982), xxxvii–xxxix). True, screenwriting kept Faulkner from Oxford and drained him of time and energy needed for his fiction, but it also exerted some influence, for good or bad, over that fiction. Although fiction would always remain his primary medium, the products of his efforts in Hollywood suggest that Faulkner genuinely cared about some of them. More importantly, his screenplays frequently show him transforming and revising earlier and current work in fiction which then plays into his later fiction even if these screenplays probably reflect Faulkner's already established narrative techniques. Even if Faulkner as screenwriter began by cynically cutting creative corners by recycling his work into script, his imagination frequently kicked in and soon he was rewriting rather than hacking, driven by obsession to revisit issues and themes.

54. For example, contemporary reviewers frequently praised *Sanctuary* at the expense of *The Sound and the Fury* and *As I Lay Dying* in part because Cape & Smith included the following copy on the front inside flap of the first five printings: "This new novel shows the further simplification of an amazing style which, while it could not hide the greatness of Faulkner's work, made both *The Sound and the Fury* and *As I Lay Dying* difficult for many

readers" (*Sanctuary* [New York: Cape and Smith, Fifth Printing, July, 1931], Linton Massey Faulkner Collection, Alderman Library, University of Virginia). Reviews of *Sanctuary* with their slighting of his two earlier novels, both tour-de-forces, may have been one of several factors that inspired Faulkner to write his notorious Introduction for the 1932 Modern Library edition of the novel, in which he contemptuously dismissed both the book and its readers and profoundly shaped criticism of *Sanctuary* for several decades. For an extensive discussion of this issue, see Cohen, " 'A Cheap Idea . . . Deliberately Conceived to Make Money.' "

55. See Jerome J. McGann's "How to Read a Book" in *The Textual Condition* (Princeton: Princeton University Press, 1991) and *Black Riders: The Visible Language of Modernism* (Princeton: Princeton University Press, 1993) and Bornstein's "What Is the Text of a Poem by Yeats?" (*Palimpsest*, 167–93). For instructive examples of criticism that makes use of the bibliographical or material features of a work, see Marta Werner's *Emily Dickinson's Open Folios: Scenes of Reading, Surfaces of Writing* (Ann Arbor: University of Michigan Press, 1995) and Cathy N. Davidson's "The Life and Times of *Charlotte Temple*: The Biography of a Book" in *Reading in America: Literature and Social History* (Baltimore: Johns Hopkins University Press, 1989), 157–79.

56. In *Making the Team: The Cultural Work of Baseball Fiction* (Urbana: University of Illinois Press, 1997), Tim Morris has astutely observed that the journey of Patrick O'Brien's Aubrey/Maturin novels from genre fiction to Literature with a capital "L" is materially manifested in the contrast between the "kitschy cover art and pulpy pages" of Lippincott's editions of his novels in the early 1970s and Norton's repackaging of them in the 1990s as "a uniform set of exquisitely produced trade paperbacks" (150).

57. Panthea Reid's analysis of how Faulkner's nonrepresentational Modernist aesthetic evolved in "The Scene of Writing and the Shape of Language for Faulkner When 'Matisse and Picasso Yet Painted' " (*Faulkner and the Artist*, 82–109) provides a fascinating example of how to make critical use of the materiality or physicality of textual production. Reid observes that extant manuscript evidence reveals that Faulkner's composition process for prose, unlike that of his poetry, involved interlineations, marginal insertions, and the reordering of passages and blocks of fictional material. Faulkner's "spatial sense of arrangement" led him to create the literary equivalent of a Post-Impressionist collage and involve the reader in making connections and thus in constructing meaning by juxtaposing materials with disparate characters, events, linguistic styles, and narrative techniques (100). Reid thus provides textual evidence to support arguments about Faulkner and Post-Impressionist painting that she earlier advanced in "The Cubist Novel: Toward Defining the Genre" ("*A Cosmos of My Own*," ed. Doreen Fowler and Ann J. Abadie [Jackson: University Press of Mississippi, 1981], 36–58); "Faulkner's Cubist Novels" ("*A Cosmos of My Own*," 59–94); and "The Economy of Desire: Faulkner's Poetics from Eroticism to Post-Impressionism" (*Faulkner Journal* 4 [1988–89]: 159–77).

My Faulkner

JOHN BARTH

It's understood, I trust, that I'm with you today not in my capacity as a Faulkner specialist, for I have no such capacity, but merely and purely as a writer of fiction, who will presently read a short passage from a not markedly Faulknerian work in progress. But the great American writer celebrated by this annual conference happens to have been among my first-magnitude navigation stars during my literary apprenticeship, and I'd like to speak a bit to that subject before I change voices.

In 1947, virtually innocent of literature, I matriculated as a freshman at Johns Hopkins University. I can scarcely remember now what I had been taught before that in the English courses of our semi-rural, semi-redneck, eleven-year county public school system on Maryland's lower Eastern Shore; I certainly don't recall having been much touched by any of it, or inspired by any of it, or inspired by any of my pleasant, well-meaning teachers. I borrowed books busily from the available libraries—Tom Swift, Edgar Rice Burroughs—and indiscriminately from my father's small-town soda fountain/lunchroom, whose stock in trade included magazines, piano sheet music, and the newfangled paperbound pocket books: Ellery Queen, Agatha Christie, Raymond Chandler, and my favorite of all, the Avon Fantasy Reader series (Abe Merritt, John Collier, and H. P. Lovecraft, *inter alia*). I remember being baffled but intrigued by an item called *Manhattan Transfer*, by one John Dos Passos, and by another called *Sanctuary*, by somebody named William Faulkner, when they turned up randomly in my borrowings. Those were, I came to understand later, my accidental first exposures to modern lit; I sensed their difference from my regular diet, and even found and read some other items by that Faulkner fellow in the pile: *The Wild Palms, Soldiers' Pay*, and *Pylon*. On the whole, however, I was more intrigued by another anthology series just then appearing on Dad's shelves, called *The Ribald Reader*: pretty spicy stuff by my then standards, and illustrated with titillative line drawings. What I only dimly registered at the time was that those naughty anthologies were of considerable literary quality and admirable eclecticism: Their ribaldry was culled from the *Decameron, Pentameron*, and *Heptameron*, from *Thousand and One Nights* and the *Gesta Romanorum* and the *Panchatantra*, among other exotic sources—all news to me, and not be found in either the Dorchester County Public or the Cambridge High School libraries (where *The Arabian Nights* was a much-abridged and expurgated edition illustrated by N. C. Wyeth). But all this was by the way, for my then ambition was to be a jazzman—a professional "arranger," as they were called in those big band days. From high school I went up to Julliard's summer program to try my hand at that vocation, soon enough realized that my talent was insufficient, and *faute de mieux* enrolled at Hopkins on scholarship in the fall as a journalism major. One was obliged to choose *something*, and I had done a humor column for our school newspaper in my senior year.

Never mind how I stumbled from journalism into fiction-writing. What's relevant here in retrospect is that the literature most provocative to my adolescent curiosity, apart from the mystery novels and Tom Swifties, was not the canonical classics, but Modernism on the one hand (as represented in its American grain by the Dos Passos and those early, mostly minor Faulkners) and on the other hand the venerable tale-cycle tradition, as represented ribaldly in those Avon Readers. At Hopkins I had professors both excellent and inspiring and was at last baptized, though not totally immersed, in the canonical mainstream—but two circumstances, fortunate for me, reinforced those earlier, fugitive, extracurricular samplings.

The first, as I've written elsewhere, was my very good luck in having to help pay my way by playing in dance bands on weekends and by filing books on weekdays in the university library. "My" stacks happened to be the voluminous ones of the Classics Department and of William Foxwell Albright's Oriental Seminary, as it was then called; the books on my cart therefore included not only Homer and Virgil and other such standard curricular items, but also Petronius and Apuleius and the unabridged Scheherazade and the *Panchatantra* and *The Ocean of Story* and the *Vetalapanchavimsata* as well as, by some alcove-gerrymandering, Boccaccio and Rabelais and Marguerite of Angouleme and Giovanni Basile and Poggion Bracciolini and Pietro Aretino—hot stuff, which I sampled eagerly as I filed, and often borrowed from the book cart to take home and read right through: what I think of as my *à la carte* education.

The second lucky circumstance is that in Hopkins's literature departments at that time, one did not generally study still-living or even recently dead authors; but our brand-new and somewhat frowned-upon Department of Writing, Speech, and Drama (later renamed the Writing Seminars) broke ranks and energetically held forth on Proust, Joyce, Kafka, Mann, Eliot, Pound, Hemingway, and Faulkner—this last via my very first fiction-writing coach, a Marine-combat-veteran teaching assistant from the Deep South at work on the university's first-ever doctoral dissertation on the sage of Oxford, Mississippi.

Let's cut to the chase: For the next three years I imitated everybody, badly—*reorchestrated* them badly, let's say (failed arranger that I was)—in search of my writerly self, while downloading my innumerable predecessors as only an insatiable green apprentice can. Owing to some tension between our writing operation and the English Department, my curricular reading in literature was freighted with the Greek and Roman classics, with Dante and Cervantes and Flaubert, and with the big Modernists aforementioned, while my library cart supplied me with extracurricular exotica. What I never got, for better or worse, was the standard fare of English majors: good basic training in Chaucer and Shakespeare and the big eighteenth- and nineteenth-century English novelists, though there had been some naughty *Canterbury Tales* in those *Ribald Readers*, and I reveled in Fielding and Dickens on my own. So many voices; so many eloquent and wildly various voices—none more mesmerizing to me (thanks to that ex-Marine T.A. writing coach, the late Robert Durene Jacobs of Georgia State University) than Faulkner's. I read all of him, I believe—all of him as of that mid-century date—and I saw that the Faulkners I'd stumbled upon in high school days were mostly warmups for such *chef d'oeuvres* as *The Sound and the Fury*, *As I Lay Dying*, *Light in August*, and *Absalom, Absalom!* It was Faulkner at his most involuted and incantatory who most enchanted me, and while I had and have never thought of myself as a capital-S Southerner (nor a Northerner either, having grown up virtually astride Mason's and Dixon's Line), I felt a strong affinity between Faulkner's Mississippi and the Chesapeake marsh country that I was born and raised in. My apprentice fiction grew increasingly Faulknerish, and when I stayed on at Johns Hopkins as a graduate student, my M.A. thesis and maiden attempt at a novel was a heavily Faulknerian marsh opera about sinisterly inbred Chesapeake crabbers and muskrat trappers. The young William Styron, visiting our seminar fresh from winning his National Book Award for *Lie Down in Darkness*, listened patiently to one particularly purple chapter, a mishmash of middle Faulkner and late Joyce, and charitably praised it; but the finished opus didn't fly—for one thing, because Faulkner intimately *knew* his Snopeses and Compsons and Sartorises, as I did not know my made-up denizens of the Maryland marsh. A copy of the manuscript made the rounds of Manhattan in vain until my agent gave up on it; I later destroyed it as an embarrassment. The original languished in the dissertation stacks of the Hopkins library for a couple of decades until, to my indignant half-relief, some unprincipled rascal stole it. Thanks anyhow, Bill Faulkner and Bill Styron.

And where were Scheherazade and company all this time? Singing in my other ear and inspiring my second and final major apprentice effort: A Faulknerian/Boccaccian hybrid this time, called *The Dorchester Tales:* 100 tales of my Eastern Shore Yoknapatawpha at all periods of its human history. This, too, failed, at round about Tale 50, and this manuscript too I later destroyed lest it come back to haunt me, except for a few nuggets that later worked their way, reorchestrated, into *The Sot-Weed Factor*. But I like to think that it was a step in the right direction: an attempt to combine the two principal strains of my literary DNA. In hindsight, as I've declared elsewhere, it's clear to me that what I needed to do was find some way to book Faulkner, Joyce, and Scheherazade on the same tidewater showboat with myself at both the helm and the steam calliope. Another way to put it is that I needed to discover, or to be discovered by, what later came to be called Postmodernism. With the help of yet another fortuitous and highly unlikely input—the turn-of-the-century Brazilian novelist Joaquim Machado de Assis, whose works I stumbled upon in the mid-1950s, this came to pass.

In the decades since, I am obliged to report, although the figure of Ms. Scheherazade has remained so central to my imagination that merely to hear one of the themes from Rimsky-Korsakov's suite is enough to deliquesce me yet, Mr. Faulkner's currency in my shop has had its ups and downs. My wife, Shelly, used to teach *Light in August* to her high school seniors, and while rereading it periodically for that purpose she would recite memorable passages to me, and a time came when the rhetoric that had once so appealed to me now seemed . . . overpumped. I would tease her (and Faulkner, and myself) by wondering for example whether it was the Immemorial Wagonwheels going down the Outraged Path or the Outraged Wheels on the Immemorial Path, and what final difference there was between those sonorous propositions. But this oedipal chafing passed, and while it has been long now since I've actually reread my Faulkner, his luster as a navigation star was considerably brightened for me some years ago by Gabriel Garcia Marquez's remark in an interview, after acknowledging Hemingway and Faulkner as his masters, that Faulkner is "actually, you know, a *Caribbean* writer." He didn't elaborate that *aperçu*, as I recall, but I found it charming to imagine that by transposing the greatest of our Southern writers just a few degrees of latitude farther south, he becomes one of the wellsprings of Magic Realism.

In any case, the fact that there's not much Faulkner to be found in my published fiction does not diminish his original and even his ongoing importance to me. One's navigation stars are not to be confused with one's destination.

Contributors

John Barth is the author of twelve works of fiction and two collections of nonfiction. Among his books are *The Floating Opera, End of the Road, The Sot-Weed Factor, Giles Goat-Boy, Lost in the Funhouse, Chimera, Letters, Sabbatical, The Tidewater Tales, The Last Voyage of Somebody the Sailor*, and, most recently, *Once Upon a Time*. Two of his books have been nominated for the National Book Award, and *Chimera* won that award in 1973. He is professor emeritus at Johns Hopkins University.

Philip Cohen is the editor of two volumes, *Texts and Textuality: Textual Instability, Theory, and Interpretation* and *Devils and Angels: Textual Editing and Literary Theory*. He has also published twenty-five essays and reviews on Faulkner. He is presently dean of the Graduate School and professor of English at the University of Texas at Arlington.

John N. Duvall is professor of English and editor of *Modern Fiction Studies* at Purdue University. He is the author of *Faulkner's Marginal Couple: Invisible, Outlaw, and Unspeakable Communities, The Identifying Fictions of Toni Morrison: Modernist Authenticity and Postmodern Blackness*, and *Don DeLillo's "Underworld."* He also has edited the collection *Productive Postmodernism: Consuming Histories and Cultural Studies*.

Doreen Fowler, professor of English at the University of Kansas, is the author of *Faulkner's Changing Vision: From Outrage to Affirmation* and *Faulkner: The Return of the Repressed*. She has also coedited, with Ann J. Abadie, twelve volumes of proceedings of the annual Faulkner and Yoknapatawpha Conference.

Ihab Hassan, Vilas Research Professor of English and Comparative Literature at the University of Wisconsin-Milwaukee, is the author of twelve books, including *The Dismemberment of Orpheus: Toward a Postmodern Literature, Paracriticisms: Seven Speculations of the Times, The Right Promethean Fire: Imagination, Science, and Cultural Change, The Postmodern Turn: Essays in Postmodern Theory and Culture*, and *Rumors of Change: Essays of Five Decades*. He has received two Guggenheim

Fellowships, held visiting professorships at sixteen universities, and has lectured in thirty different countries.

Molly Hite is professor of English at Cornell University. She has written two critical studies, *Ideas of Order in the Novels of Thomas Pynchon* and *The Other Side of the Story: Structures and Strategies of Contemporary Feminist Narrative*, and two novels, *Class Porn* and *Breach of Immunity*. She is currently at work on a book-length study, "Virginia Woolf and Her Others."

Martin Kreiswirth, University of Western Ontario, is the author of *Faulkner: The Making of a Novelist* and coeditor of *The Johns Hopkins Guide to Literary Theory and Criticism*. He was founding director of the Centre for the Study of Theory and Criticism, University of Western Ontario, and has recently been a fellow at the Porter Institute at the University of Tel Aviv in Israel.

Cheryl Lester is associate professor of English and graduate coordinator of American Studies at the University of Kansas. She has written essays and reviews on Faulkner, with particular attention to his Mississippian historical and cultural content. One of her current projects is a book-length study, "Faulkner and the Great Migration."

Terrell L. Tebbetts, W. C. Brown Jr. Professor of English at Lyon College, received the Arkansas Professor of the Year Award from the Council for Advancement and Support of Education and the Carnegie Foundation in 1992. His areas of expertise are Faulkner's fiction and Shakespeare's plays. Among his publications is "Giving Jung a Crack at the Compsons."

Joseph R. Urgo is professor and chair of the Department of English at the University of Mississippi. He is the author of *Faulkner's Apocrypha: "A Fable," Snopes, and the Spirit of Human Rebellion, Willa Cather and the Myth of American Migration, Novel Frames: Literature as Guide to Race, Sex, and History in American Culture*, and, most recently, *In the Age of Distraction*.

Philip Weinstein is Alexander Griswold Cummins Professor of English Literature at Swarthmore College. He is the author of four volumes, including *Faulkner's Subject: A Cosmos No One Owns* and *What Else But Love? The Ordeal of Race in Faulkner and Morrison*, and editor of *The Cambridge Companion to William Faulkner*. He is currently at work on a book-length study, "Out of Time: The Moment of Modern Fiction."

Index